Even Angels Ask

Even Angels Ask

A Journey to Islam in America

Jeffery Lang

amana publications

Beltsville, Maryland, USA

First Edition
(1418AH/1997AC)

Second Printing
(1419AH/1998AC)

Third Printing
(1421AH/2000AC)

Fourth Printing
(1423AH/2002AC)

Fifth Printing
(1427AH/2007AC)

amana publications
10710 Tucker Street
Beltsville, Maryland 20705-2223 USA
Tel: (301) 595-5999 / Fax: (301) 595-5888
E-mail: amana@igprinting.com
Website: www.amana-publications.com

Library of Congress Cataloging-in-Publications Data

Lang, Jeffrey 1954 (1373)–
Even angels ask : a journey to Islam in America /
by Jeffrey Lang
    p. 244 cm 23
    Includes bibliographical references
    ISBN 0-915957-67-1
    1. Lang, Jeffrey.
    2. Muslim converts–United States.
    I. Title.
    BP170.5.L35 1997
    297'.0973–dc21   97-26843
                                                           CIP

Printed in the United States of America by International Graphics
10710 Tucker Street, Beltsville, Maryland 20705-2223
Tel: (301) 595-5999 Fax: (301) 595-5888

Website: igprinting.com
E-mail: ig@igprinting.com

CONTENTS

Foreword

When, in 1996, I attended the annual convention of the Islamic Society of North America in Columbus, Ohio, I ran into Dr. Jeffrey Lang's book *Struggling to Surrender* at the **amana** bookstand. At first I thought that it was just another "confession"—popular since St. Augustine and Abu Hamid al Ghazali—in which converts (or reconverts) enthusiastically explain their very special way to their very special religion.

How astonished I was when I realized that this book was of major general import, very well written (as one might not expect from a math teacher) and well researched. Yes, it *was* a vivid description of how Jeffrey Lang, almost torn apart in the process, felt irresistibly drawn to Islam. But the book also offered a solid, well reasoned platform for all other Americans who, like him, require considerable depth of rational inquiry before surrendering to Allah's call.

Even Angels Ask, Dr. Lang's second book—not without significance, written after a year's stay in Saudi Arabia—shows the very same virtues: Total honesty, common sense, a rigorous level of theological investigation, and a thrilling oscillation between gifted story telling and exposition of doctrine. Again, the author demonstrates that (if only as a mathematician) he can only believe in a religion that he finds compelling—rationally, intellectually and spiritually—and that the religion is Islam: A thinking man's faith.

When the author alleges that (Christian) religious dogmas in modern times are only deepening the crisis of faith and religion, he echoes a prediction made by Muhammad Asad (author of *Islam at the Crossroads* and a leading Muslim intellect of the 20th century) in 1934 when he foresaw that the doubts raised by the Nicene Creed, especially the notions of incarnation and trinity, would not only alienate thinking people from their churches but from the belief in God as such. Dr. Lang is also in line with an observation made by Karen Armstrong (author of *On God*) according to which Judaism suffered from closing itself off (by considering itself as the "Chosen People") while Christianity suffered from the opposite, its universality (by absorbing a multitude of traditions into itself). Islam, according to Dr. Lang, is positioned to avoid both pitfalls, and I agree with him.

In Saudi Arabia, the author came to realize that for him "there was no escape from being an American," i.e., an "investigative Muslim," whose way of inquiry into the basis of Islam was considered dangerous, even suspected of leading to "innovation" and even heresy. (To be sure, there is not a single instance in which the author's approach leads to even the slightest deviation from the tenets of Islam.) The conservative attitude that Dr. Lang encountered overseas, had years earlier also affected Muhammad Asad (alias Leopold Weiss). From my association with him I am certain that he would have endorsed both of the author's books wholeheartedly.

Given this background, the book's title is not just an opening gambit but a program: According to the Qur'an, *surat al Baqarah ayah* 30, even the angels (who are never rebellious) were moved to question God's wisdom of creating man (who is rebellious and mischievous). Thus, Muslims too must never stop asking pertinent questions about God, the world and themselves. Nevertheless, in view of the opposite orthodox view, it takes some courage for Dr. Lang to propose that every generation of Muslims is obliged to reinvestigate the foundations of its faith "since knowledge grows with time." As a matter of fact, he holds that it would be a grave error, indeed, to rely blindly on past judgments and to "dogmatize opinion," unless one is willing to accept "atrophy and decay."

This, of course, the author certainly does not accept. On the contrary, he tackles head-on many rather delicate issues, like questions about predestination and theodicy. He offers no solutions to these problems but points out, like Immanuel Kant (*Critique of Pure Reason*) before him, that they cannot be solved because of man's captivity in his mind's categories of time and space, proper to him alone. Thus the author lifts unsoluble problems to a higher level of awareness. More cannot be asked.

Even more important is, however, his substantiated critique of Muslim shortcomings, both inside the United States and aboard. In particular, he denounces
- subculture trends within the American Muslim community;
- the lack of tolerance between Muslim schools of thought;
- the dominance of Middle Eastern and Arabic features of merely cultural, not religious significance;
- traditional Muslim attitudes toward women that violate Qur'anic norms often causing Muslim women to feel unwelcome in mosques;

- over-focusing on nonessential, marginal aspects of the Islamic way of life, instead of looking for the general ethical and spiritual lessons of the Prophet's Sunnah; and
- the systematic distrust shown by "native" Muslims toward contributions by Western converts.

Jeffrey Lang wrote this book first and foremost for his children—leading them through the Qur'an in an eye-opening way and introducing them to the five pillars of Islamic worship in a manner which stresses spirituality rather than legalistic routine. In that, he has done a tremendous service once more to *all* Muslim parents in the United States who are often wondering, worrying and fretting whether in a permissive, consumer and drug-oriented society it is possible to transmit their faith to the next generation. In this respect, the author seems to be somewhat pessimistic. I, however, am inclined to see things in a more optimistic light—if only for one reason: There are two good books that just might move the scales in favor of Islam—*Struggling to Surrender* and *Even Angels Ask* by Jeffrey Lang.

Murad Hofmann
Istanbul, April 1997

Preface

Summer has become my favorite season, with its sunshine, warmth, long days and long walks in the late afternoon; but when I was twelve, it was definitely winter, with its blizzards and snowball fights, ice-football, sled riding and ice hockey! It was also the time of year in which I could steal a few hours alone with my father every once and a while, because the rest of the year he had to work twelve hours a day, seven days a week, at his one-man refrigeration and air-conditioning business. On certain Sundays we would take our German shepherd for a walk along the beach. My father always picked the most bitter days: stormy ones, bleak and gray and frigid, that remind me now of the prize-winning photographs and paintings he had made when he was younger. On one of these walks, we had almost reached the point where we would usually turn back, when I looked up at him and asked, "Dad, do you believe in heaven?"

I knew that I could depend on a straight answer with no punches pulled. My mom would carefully estimate the possible effects of her answers to such questions before she finally framed one, while my father's response would be the same irrespective of the questioner. But he would not answer thoughtlessly, nor for that matter dispassionately; he would personalize and internalize the issue.

He showed no reaction and kept on walking. We continued on into the cold, damp, pounding gales that were blowing back his thick, graying hair and stinging my face. I began to wonder if he had heard me, for it must have been a half mile ago when I had asked him, then he slowed to a stop and turned towards the shoreline. He was looking out past Long Island when he said, almost to himself, "I could believe in Hell easily enough, because there's plenty of that here on earth, but heaven"—he paused for a few seconds and then shook his head—"I can't conceive of it."

I was not entirely surprised, even at that young an age. My father was extremely sensitive and already I understood that life had robbed him of his goals and dreams. Every night after work he would try to numb his anger, but more often than not it would lead to violent eruptions of his frustrated passions. Anguish is contagious, and his angry, dark and cynical view of life infected all of us—after all, we were only children and we were emotionally defenseless. When others of my generation felt cheated by the Kennedy assassinations or Vietnam or Watergate, I was hardly moved; they were only confirmations of what I had already learned.

Religious types will criticize my father for opening a door, but it had been unlocked for some time or I would not have asked the question. If anything my father's answer slowed my inevitable progress towards atheism, for he was not an irreligious man. The fact that he had doubts seemed entirely natural—how can any sane and rational mind not have them?—but he was nonetheless a believer and he must have had some reason to believe. Whatever it was, I never found out.

I continued to have problems with heaven, because every time I imagined that it was within God's power to create such a world, I had to wonder why He created this one. Why, in other words, did He not place us permanently in heaven from the start, with us free of the weaknesses for which He would punish us with earthly suffering? Why not simply make us into angels or something better? Of course, I heard all the talk of God's infinite sense of justice; but *I* did not choose my nature; *I* did not create temptation; *I* did not ask to be born; and *I* did not eat from the tree! Did it occur to no one that the punishment far exceeded the crime?! Even if only an allegory, it does tell us something of the divine nature, something that is extremely difficult to reconcile with "love" and "mercy."

How I came to despise these words! They made me sick with revulsion. Not only were we here for no good reason, but an infinitely innocent sacrifice and acceptance of a blatant contradiction were required before admitting us into paradise. The rest of us, not lucky enough to be born into the right creed or unable to suspend our reason, were destined to be consigned to eternal damnation. Would it not, for goodness sake, have been better to simply leave us as a bad idea never realized?

It was all the sugar-coating that made belief for me so unpalatable. I used to conceal my disregard behind an emotionless exterior as I listened to assurances of divine love; like when you halfheartedly humor someone you feel has lost his mind. When it was clear that I was hopeless, we would invariably revert to the real issue: The Divine Threat! "But what if you are wrong?" I was told; as if you should believe on a hunch, in order to hedge your bets in case this brutal, monstrous vision is a reality.

'Then if I am wrong, I will still be right: for refusing to surrender to the irrational demands of an infinite tyranny, for refusing to indulge an unquenchable narcissism that feeds on helpless suffering, and for refusing to accept responsibility and repent for a grand blunder which I did not commit. In the end, I will be an eternal victim of the greatest injustice and in this way, I will forever represent a higher sense of righteousness than the One that brought us into being. It may not ease my suffering in the everlasting torture chamber, but at least it will give it meaning."

"So how in God's name did you become a Muslim?"

This book is not meant to be an explanation, but the reader should be able to piece together a rational one, perhaps something of an emotional, psychological and spiritual one as well. Frankly, I am not entirely sure exactly how it happened. So much of it seems to have been outside my control, manipulated according to certain key decisions I made along the way. For the curious, they should know that to become a Muslim requires simultaneous commitment to three interrelated principles: the first, *there is no god*; the second; *but God*; the third, *Muhammad is the messenger of God*. What I have written so far outlines how I came to the first of these.[1]

This book, however, has other motivations. It, like my first one, is written first and foremost to my children, with the hope that my struggle may somehow help them in their search for meaning. I want them to understand where I am coming from: that this subject was never for me an academic curiosity—an exercise in rational thought; that I have much more than an interest in it; that it is part of my past, present, and future, part of my seeking, suffering, and desire. The question I asked my father burned inside me, as does what I have learned from it, and I cannot but share that with them. Yet I would hate to see that their search end with mine. My greatest hope is that they begin where I leave off, because no human has a complete and final answer. To rely on someone's past insights is the gravest error, for our knowledge grows with time, and to dogmatize an opinion is to stop our progress towards the truth and to make way for atrophy and decay.

I take no credit for whatever is good in the pages that follow—I did not find it, but it finds me—and for that which is not, I rely on the forgiving kindness of one whose wisdom illuminates our deeds according to our intentions.

---

[1] I explain—or perhaps I should say interpret—my conversion to Islam in greater detail in my first book: Jeffrey Lang, *Struggling to Surrender* (Beltsville, MD: **amana publications**, 1994).

REMARK: I am concerned that the nature of this book may lead the non-Muslim reader to an erroneous and one-sided image of Muslims. Perhaps the western media's continued demonization of Muslims and their religion has caused me to be oversensitive about this matter.

The reader should keep in mind that this book is written primarily for Muslims by one who was once outside their community, who tried, especially in chapters three, five and six, to discuss those behaviors and conceptions of modern believers that he has had difficulty understanding, adjusting to, or accepting. It therefore contains a fair amount of criticism of Muslims. I also have shared with the reader many of the setbacks I have suffered in my own struggle to achieve surrender to God, and I fear that my example may be more discouraging than most.

Let me take this opportunity then to assert that in the past twenty years I have met a multitude of virtuous, warm, noble, magnanimous, deeply religious Muslims, from whom I have gained so much in knowledge and friendship. If I wrote a book about the inspiring examples of Muslims I have known, and someday I may, it would be of greater length than this one. Similarly, if I wrote a critique of other communities to which I belong—for example, the American, the white Anglo-Saxon, or the academic—I am sure it would include far more numerous and more severe criticisms than this book contains.

REMARK: It is a long established and cherished tradition among Muslims to follow the mention of a prophet's name by the benediction "may peace be upon him." In time, this practice was adopted in writing, although the most ancient extant manuscripts show that this custom was not adhered to rigidly by Muslim writers in the first two Islamic centuries. To avoid interrupting the flow of ideas, I have not followed the customary practice. I will simply take this occasion to remind the Muslim reader of this tradition.

REMARK: The transliterations of Arabic words in this book are my own approximations. Each introduction of a transliterated term in the text is followed by an English translation in parenthesis. Experts should be able to discern the corresponding Arabic terms and the transliterations should pose no disadvantage to non-experts.

CHAPTER 1

Introduction

"Brothers, I Lost Him"

The most recollected image from William Somerset Maugham's novel *Of Human Bondage* has to be the Persian rug,[2] the one that Philip, the main character, repeatedly contemplates, following the advice of a friend, in an effort to discover the meaning of life. Upon reaching an especially low point in a young existence filled with terrible and senseless tragedies, lived and observed, he wanders the streets of London. And, once again, the oriental rug possesses his mind. As Philip contemplates its intricate designs, he is suddenly seized by a wondrous insight: the carpet does indeed contain the answer to the riddle that has vexed him. He finally sees that life, like the interwoven patterns of the rug, is always complex, sometimes beautiful and sometimes bewildering—but, in the end, utterly without meaning or purpose.

It was difficult for many critics to empathize with Philip's subsequent contentment at his discovery, and this, I believe, contributed to the book's mostly ambivalent initial reviews. However, those who reached the same conclusion as Philip after their own conservative religious upbringing could surely understand.

Of Human Bondage is a very western novel, part of a genre of literary works that explored the same difficult issues and often arrived at similar conclusions. Not that other cultures entirely bypassed conflicts of faith and reason, but western civilization seems to have been at the front the longest, battling such problems for well over two thousand years. While the declarations of victory for science and rationalism some twenty-five years ago were probably premature, it does appear that religion has had the worse of it and may lose even more of what little ground it still possesses. The ways

---

[2] William S. Maugham, *Of Human Bondage* (New York: Vintage Books, 1961).

we live our lives are shaped by the meanings we read into them, and the course of this battle has greatly informed our society's viewpoint. The question of the purpose of life is fundamental, and we can hardly know a person or a society until we understand how this question is treated.

It is common these days to hear psychologist discuss the modern crisis of meaning. C. G. Jung, one of the first to recognize and publicize it, remarked that most of his patients over the age of forty were suffering from it in one form or another.[3] Where the answers supplied by religion once satisfied a largely illiterate western Europe, in modern times religious dogmas are only deepening the crisis and alienating many from spiritual considerations. Some reject religion entirely, and many who preserve some ties to a faith may find it in conflict with their rational thinking. The result is that religion is pushed ever farther towards the back of the shelf and substitutes must be found for the answers and services that belief once provided. Jung, and many others after him, claimed that this trend will continue unless faith can be made to conform with current knowledge and experience. This is seldom seen as a positive trend, because it appears that human nature includes spirituality and that this can not be ignored in what seems to be our instinctive need to see our lives as meaningful. Victor Frankl frequently states that if one can provide man with a positive "why" to live, he or she will inevitably find a positive and productive "how" to live. But it cannot be just any "why"; it must be one that he or she finds compelling rationally, intellectually, and spiritually.[4]

Enter the Muslim. The last three decades have witnessed a sudden growth in the American Muslim community, spurred mostly by immigration and African American conversion since the civil rights era. The Muslim also finds himself being drawn into the same conflict. With full confidence he critiques, "I don't think that the two major religions in America make much sense."

He receives the reply, "I don't think that any religion makes much sense. For example, from your religion's viewpoint, what is the purpose of life? Why did God create us to suffer here on earth?"

The Muslim thinks back on what he was taught as a child. "I believe He created us to test us."

---

[3] C. G. Jung, *An Answer to Job*, trans. by R. F. C. Hull (New York: Meridian Books, 1960).

[4] Victor Frankl, *Man's Search for Meaning*, trans. by I. Lasch (Boston: Beacon Press, 1992).

Of course he is then asked, "So your religion rejects the omniscience of God, for otherwise, what could He possibly learn from testing us that He does not already know?"

The Muslim feels cornered and searches his past for the universally accepted answers he was forced to memorize. "No, that is not quite it. Ah! Yes!! We are created to worship Him!"

With a sly smile his opponent inquires, "Then you must believe that God has needs and weaknesses, for why else would He demand our worship? When a human demands our devotion, we label him a tyrant or psychopath. Do you hold that God has character flaws?"

The Muslim's head is now spinning in ill-defined questions and doubts. He gropes for a clue from his childhood. It comes to him! "Adam sinned and his punishment was this earthly life!"

His adversary has the cool, calculated look of one about to say "Checkmate! Putting aside scientific difficulties, it appears that you believe that God is unjust; for why punish all of Adam's descendants for *Adam's* sin? Why not give each his own chance? Do you Muslims also believe in original sin?"

"No! No! Of course not!"

The game is over.

A Muslim living in America may have to confront these questions many times; for they are part of the intellectual basis of western civilization. Sometimes the result may be a loss, even an abandonment, of faith. Salmon Rushdie is, for many Muslims, the archetypal case. He confessed in an interview that he had been a very religious child. However, during his education in England, his faith was shaken severely by western attitudes toward religion and Islam in particular. His case is not unique. I have met many university professors in America with Muslim names who disavow any belief in Islam and quite a few who go out of their way to make a point of it.

Most often, however, the faith of a Muslim immigrant will remain intact. He may feel a bit rattled or he might retreat slightly from his belief that "Islam makes sense" to the position that "Islam makes more sense," but the fervor of his commitment, for the most part, will abide, because it is grounded in the life-long experience of being a Muslim. Born into an environment where Islam is practically universally accepted—where it is to one's disadvantage to be a non-Muslim—his faith has had the opportunity to take root and grow unimpeded. Through many years of steady participation and practice there came security, pride, meaning, community, and perhaps, awe inspiring, spiritual encounters—maybe even perceived miracles— that together made the sweetness of faith more real and powerful than any challenge some logical sleight of hand could provide.

The convert's state is more precarious, and there has been a somewhat high rate of apostasy among them in recent years. Whether a convert will remain a Muslim for long usually depends on what originally brought him to the decision and whether that initial need continued to be met long enough to root him in the religion. Frequently, if the initial motivating factor fades and the convert finds that certain negative aspects of being a Muslim outweigh the perceived benefits, the option to leave the community is taken. *Like the immigrant, the convert's commitment to the religion will depend on his or her personal, emotional, and spiritual faith experiences; the same could be said of any religion in the West.* As the convert is fully part of the surrounding society and subjected to its intellectual challenges and criticisms from the very start of his entry into Islam, questions of faith and reason may have greater influence on his religious choices than they do for immigrant Muslims.

Yet the future of Islam in the West, and America in particular, is not primarily about immigrants and converts; it is about children, and the "success" of Islam in Europe and America will be measured by the religiosity of their descendants. The grandchildren of today's Muslims in the West will undoubtedly be western in their attitudes and thinking—their survival depends on it—but to what degree they will claim allegiance to Islam or the worldwide Muslim community is far from certain.

At the 1993 ISNA meeting in Tulsa, Oklahoma, Dr. Jamal Badawi recalled how, during a recent visit to Australia, he saw a good number of buildings that resembled the mosques that one sees in Muslim lands. However, they were being put to secular uses, such as office space, meeting halls, and the like. He was informed that there was once a large population of Afghani immigrants to Australia and that the now-converted mosques are the last remnants of a community that had been completely assimilated by the dominant culture. Dr. Badawi used this example to highlight the urgent need for Islamic schools in America.

Islamic schools may help Muslim children preserve their religious identity, but there looms the larger issues of what and how they are taught. Many an agnostic or atheist today attended church or synagogue schools as children. If a religious community is to produce leading scholars and scientists, its approach towards education will have to be compatible with modern critical analytical methods of study; this, I feel, is absolutely necessary. It requires an environment of free inquiry and expression, where self-criticism and objectivity are encouraged and questioning and doubt tolerated. If the approach to general education conflicts with that of religious education, then the students will be left with a choice, perhaps a perpetual one, between alternative modes of thinking. In this way, religion for its children will be delimited—westernized, so to speak; it will become a compartment of thought to be entered into in limited situations and abandoned in others.

For Muslim children, this dilemma is particularly acute. If Islam can not be shown to be in harmony with rational thought, then faith for the western Muslim, like many adherents to other religions in the West, becomes solely a personal, experiential, and spiritual matter. It loses much of its persuasiveness. Reasoning can be communicated quite effectively, but not spiritual experiences. We cannot really share our mystical encounters; we can only interpret and approximate them. I am not saying that faith can exist on an exclusively rational level or that it cannot exist in disharmony with reason. What I am saying is that if a rationally compelling case is not made for Islam, one that Muslim young people in the West can relate to, then Islam will be seen by many of them as just another religion, a religious option among more or less equal options. In addition, in an environment where their religion is greatly feared, where of all the great world religions theirs is the most despised, where its rituals and practices are the most demanding, where its constraints seem to go against the larger society's trends and lifestyles—in such an environment, we should not at all be surprised if a significant fraction of children born to Muslim parents leave aside the faith they inherited.

A few years ago, I read an article in a Muslim American magazine that stated, according to a study it had conducted, that nine out of ten children born to Muslim parents in America either become atheists or claim allegiance to no particular religion by the time they reach college age. The article did not state what statistical methods were used to obtain this fraction, so I doubted its reliability. But even if only half as many of these children ultimately leave Islam, it will still be a crisis for Muslims in America. Yet perhaps such a statistic should not be such a shock. Why should American children born of Muslim parents be very different from those born of Buddhist or Hindu parents or of any religion unfamiliar to the West, especially in consideration of some of the above-mentioned special obstacles they face?

It is said that it takes about three generations before an immigrant family becomes fully assimilated into American society. I have not conducted
a scientific study, but I have met through my teaching at the university a
good number of third-generation Americans of Muslim descent, and so far,
I have not found a single one who professes belief in Islam. When I ask
these students if they are Muslims, the typical response I obtain is "My parents are," which is exactly the same answer I used to give when asked if I
was a Christian. This may paint an excessively pessimistic picture, since
the grandparents of these young people were part of an infinitesimally
small Muslim minority group. Now that there are suddenly several million
Muslims in America and Canada, we should expect that a large number of
their grandchildren will identify themselves as such, although it remains to
be seen to what extent this will reflect an active religious commitment. In
my travels to various Islamic conferences in America, I always ask about
the participation of young people in the local Muslim communities; I
inevitably find that it is extremely small.

I first became interested in the relevance of Islam to American Muslim
children a little over ten years ago when I lived in San Francisco. One night,
after the evening ritual prayer, about a dozen of us sat in a circle on the floor
of the *masjid* engaged in chitchatting. We had been led in the prayer that
night by Muhammad, who, at forty, was the oldest among us and one of the
most loved and respected members of our community. Someone asked him
how his son was doing, as we had not seen him in some time. He answered
that he had turned sixteen that day, and the little room was immediately
filled with smiles, laughter, and congratulations, for our *oldest* boy had
become a man. However, Muhammad was not sharing in our joy, and we
suddenly all fell silent, because we saw large, round teardrops falling from
Muhammad's downcast face. He looked up and his voice cracked as he
exclaimed, "Brothers, I lost him—I lost my son!"

No explanation was necessary. We had seen or heard of too many similar cases in the neighboring communities. If his son, at sixteen, was still
attached to the religion, he would have been an exception; it was only that
our confidence and esteem for Muhammad was so great. All we could do
was sit there, speechless, belittled by an irresistible and unfeeling power.

As I drove home from the *masjid* that night, I could not rid myself of
the expression on Muhammad's face or the desperation in his plea. I
thought about my first child, who was soon to be born, and how I would be
feeling sixteen years from now. The more I thought about the whole matter, the less I found myself in agreement with Muhammad. I was not con-

vinced that he had lost his son, because I was not sure that he had really found him.

Muhammad was a truly devout Algerian Muslim who had done everything to raise a good Algerian Muslim son. But his son was not an Algerian; he was as American as apple pie, and whatever used to work back in Algeria had failed in America, as it did for so many others.

We used to remark how very quiet Muhammad's boy was at our community functions. A child's silence may be a sign of respect or assent, but it could also represent indifference to what is being said. I wondered if Muslim American children had as much difficulty relating to the perspectives and traditions of the mosque as I did.

Through the years, conversations with Muslim children and parents supported this suspicion and led me to conjecture that if the Americanness that I shared with Muslim young people was alienating many of us from the viewpoint of the mosque, then perhaps at some stage in their lives these children may come to relate to what other Americans and I discovered in Islam. As I discussed the matter with other converts, it emerged that our reflections intersected at many key points that approximate a certain characteristic path to Islam. Therefore, I would like to take you, the reader, along that path. I would like to invite you to a journey: *A Journey to Islam in America*.

You need to know what to pack and how we will get to our destination. To the first of these the answer is: as little as possible. You are requested to leave behind as much religious baggage as you can; ideally, you should pretend you are an atheist, with perhaps many objections to belief in God, yet open-minded enough not to dismiss a point of view without at least considering it. As for the second question, our guide will be the Qur'an, the principle source of guidance and spiritual compass of billions of Muslims, and, for many newcomers to Islam, their main introduction to the faith.

CHAPTER 2

Setting Out

Approaches to the Qur'an

It would probably be better to delay this discussion for the appendices, so as not to lose many readers before even getting started, because I expect that the majority will be Muslims and that many of them find this subject upsetting. It has to do with the role of symbolism in revelation. The appendices may be more appropriate, because the main conclusions reached in this chapter will hardly be affected by these remarks, but my principle concern is with a smaller readership, which, while attempting to reconcile religion with modern thought, might be dissuaded by its own excessive literalism.

Muslims assert that the Qur'an is a revelation appropriate for all persons, times, and places, and it is not difficult to summon Qur'anic verses to support this claim. If they held to the opposite, there would not be much point in considering their scripture. In order to entertain this premise sincerely, we certainly should allow for, even anticipate, that the Qur'an would use allegory, parables, and other literary devices to reach a diverse audience. The language of the Qur'an would have to be that of the Prophet's milieu and reflect the intellectual, religious, social, and material customs of the seventh-century Arabs. But if the essential message is universal, then it must transcend the very language and culture that was the vehicle of revelation. Since a community's language grows with and out of its experiences, how then are realities outside that experience communicated? There appears to be only one avenue: through the employment of allegory, that is, the expression of truths through symbolic figures and actions or, as the famous Qur'an exegete Zamakhshari put it, "a parabolic illustration, by means of something which we know from our experience, of something that is beyond the reach of our perception."[5]

---

[5] Muhammad Asad, *The Message of the Qur'an* (Gibraltar: Dar al Andalus, 1980), 989-91.

For example, the Qur'an informs us that Paradise in the hereafter is such that "no person knows what delights of the eye are kept hidden from them as a reward for their deeds" (32:17). Yet it also provides very sensual images of Paradise that are particularly suited to the imagination of Muhammad's contemporaries. These descriptions recall the luxury and sensual delights of the most wealthy seventh-century Bedouin chieftains. If the reader happened to be a man from Alaska, he may be quite apathetic to these enticements. He may prefer warm sandy beaches to cool oases; sunshine to constant shade; scantily clad bathing beauties to houris, with the issue of whether or not they are virgins of no real consequence. This reader will probably take these references symbolically, reinforced by the Qur'an's frequent assignment of the word *mathal* (likeness, similitude, example) to its eschatological descriptions.

Similarly, though God is "sublimely exalted above anything that men may devise by way of definition" (6:100) and "there is nothing like unto Him" (42:11) and "nothing can be compared to Him" (112:4), the reader nonetheless needs to relate to God and His activity. Thus we find that the Qur'an provides many *comparative descriptions* of God. For instance, while human beings are sometimes merciful, compassionate, generous, wise and forgiving, God is The Merciful, The Compassionate, The Generous, The Wise, and The Forgiving. The Qur'an mentions God's "face," "hand," "throne" and other expressions

> which at first sight have an almost anthropomorphic hue,
> for instance, God's "wrath" (*ghadab*) or "condemnation";
> His "pleasure" at good deeds or "love" for His creatures;
> or His being "oblivious" of a sinner who was oblivious of
> Him; or "asking" a wrongdoer on Resurrection Day about
> his wrongdoing; and so forth.[6]

To disallow the possibility of symbolism in such expressions would seem to imply contradictions between some statements in the Qur'an. To do so is entirely unnecessary, especially in consideration of the following key assertion:

> He it is Who has bestowed upon you from on high this
> divine writ, containing messages clear in and of them-
> selves (*ayat muhkamat*)—and these are the foundation of

---

[6] Ibid.

the divine writ—as well as others that are allegorical (*mutashabihat*). Now those whose hearts are given too swerving from the truth go after that part of it which has been expressed in allegory, seeking out confusion, and seeking its final meaning, but none save God knows its final meaning. (3:7)

Therefore the Qur'an itself insists on its use of symbolism, because to describe the realm of realities beyond human perception—what the Qur'an designates as *al ghayb* (the unseen or imperceptible)—would be impossible otherwise. This is why it would be a mistake to insist on assigning a literal interpretation to the Qur'an's descriptions of God's attributes, the Day of Judgment, Heaven and Hell, etc., because the *ayat mutashabihat* do not fully define and explicate these, but they relate to us, due to the limitations of human thought and language, something similar. This helps explain the well-known doctrine of *bila kayf* (without how) of al Ash'ari, the famous tenth-century theologian whose viewpoint on this matter became dominant in Muslim thought. It states that such verses reveal truths, but we should not insist on, or ask, how these truths are realized.[7]

Throughout Muslim history, the literalist trend in Qur'an exegesis was one among a number of approaches. Today, in America and Canada, it has emerged as the most prevalent. It appears that the majority of Muslim lecturers in America tend to take every narrative or description in the Qur'an as a statement of a scientific or historical fact. So, for example, the story of Adam is assumed to relate the historical and scientific origins of Homo Sapiens. This tendency is reinforced by the current widespread excitement over recent Qur'an and Science studies, where many, if not most, of the discoveries of modern science are believed to have been anticipated by the Qur'an.

It is true that some of the descriptions in the Qur'an of the "signs" (*ayat*) in nature of God's wisdom and beneficence bear a fascinating resemblance to certain modern discoveries, and it is also true that none of these signs can be proved to be in conflict with science. But part of the reason for this may argue against attempts by Muslims to subject the Qur'an to scientific scrutiny.[8] The Qur'an is very far from being a science textbook. Its lan-

---

[7] Annemarie Schimmel, *Islam, An Introduction* (New York: SUNY Press, 1992), 78-81.

[8] See for example, Malik Bennabi, *The Qur'anic Phenomenon*, trans. by A.B. Kirkary (Plainfield, IN: American Trust Publications, 1983); Maurice Bucaille, *The Bible, the*

guage is of the highest literary quality and open to many different shades of meaning. The descriptions of many of the Qur'an's signs that are believed today to predict recently established facts appear to be consistently and intentionally ambiguous, avoiding a degree of explicitness that would conflict with any reader's level of knowledge of whatever era. If the Qur'an contained a precise elaboration of these phenomena (the big bang theory, the splitting of the atom, the expansion of the universe, to name a few), these would have been known to ancient Muslim scientists. A truly wondrous feature of the Qur'an is that these signs lose nothing of their power, beauty, and mystery from one generation to the next; each generation has found them compatible with the current state of knowledge. To be inspired with awe and wonder by the Qur'anic signs is one thing; to attempt to deduce or impose upon them scientific theories is another and, moreover, is contrary to the Qur'an's style.

The relationship between the Qur'an and history is very much the same. Anyone familiar with the Bible will notice that there are many narratives in the Qur'an that have Biblical parallels. In the past, Orientalists would accuse Muhammad, whom they assumed to be the Qur'an's author, of plagiarizing or borrowing material from Jewish and Christian sources. This opinion has become increasingly unpopular among western scholars of Islam. For one thing, where Biblical parallels do exist, the Qur'anic accounts almost always involve many key differences in detail and meaning. Equally important is the fact that the Qur'an itself assumes that its initial hearers were fairly well acquainted with these tales. It is therefore very probable that through centuries of contact, Jews, Christians, and pagans of the Arabian peninsula adopted, with modifications, each other's oral traditions. It also would not be at all surprising that traditions shared by Jews and Arabs of the Middle East would go back to a common source, since

---

Qur'an and Science (Paris: Seghers Publishers, 1977); and Keith L. Moore, *The Developing Human* (appendix to 3d edition) (Philadelphia: W. B. Saunders Co., 1982). As I remarked in *Struggling to Surrender*, this topic is interesting and sometimes fascinating, but it too often requires complicated and unobvious extrapolations in interpreting certain words and phrases.

This trend exists in other religious communities as well. A speaker informed his audience that the New Testament contains the big bang theory of creation, for in John it states that in the beginning was the "word." Since a word is a single entity in the universe of language that when voiced produces a vibration of sound, we obtain by some isomorphism to the physical universe the theory of a single original point mass of infinite density that explodes!

they shared a common ancestry. Hence, the conjecture that the Qur'an borrows from the Bible is inappropriate.

In addition to biblical parallels, the Qur'an contains a number of stories that were apparently known only to the Arabian peninsula and at least one of mysterious origins.[9] A striking difference between all of the Qur'anic accounts and the biblical narratives is that while the latter are very often presented in a historical setting, the former defy all attempts to do so, unless outside sources are consulted. In other words, relying exclusively on the Qur'an, it is nearly impossible to place these stories in history. The episodes are told in such a way that the meaning behind the story is emphasized while extraneous details are omitted. Thus, western readers who know nothing of the Arabian tribes of 'Ad and Thamud readily understand the moral behind their tales. This omission of historical detail adds to the transcendent and universal appeal of the narratives, for it helps the reader focus on the timeless meaning of the stories.

The Qur'anic stories are so utterly devoid of historical reference points that it is not always clear whether a given account is meant to be taken as history, a parable, or an allegory. Consider the following two verses from the story of Adam:

> It is We Who created you, then We gave you shape, then We bade the angels, "Bow down to Adam!" and they bowed down; not so Iblis; he refused to be of those who bow down. (7:11)

> And when your Lord drew forth from the children of Adam, from their loins, their seed, and made them testify of themselves, (saying) "Am I not your Lord?" They said, "Yes, truly we testify." (That was) lest you should say on the Day of Resurrection: "Lo! of this we were unaware." (7:172)

Note the transition in 7:11 from "you" (plural in Arabic) in the first two clauses to "Adam" in the third, as if mankind is being identified with Adam. These verses seem to demand symbolic interpretations, otherwise from the first we would have to conclude that *we* were created, then *we* were given shape, then the command was given concerning the first man! As for 7:172, I would not even know how to begin to interpret this verse

---

[9] See the discussion on page 14 concerning Dhul Qarnain.

concretely, and it should come as no surprise that many ancient commentators also understood it symbolically.

The Qur'an's eighteenth *surah*, *al Kahf*, relates a number of beautiful stories in an almost surrealistic style. For example, verse 86, from the tale of Dhul Qarnain reads,

> Until, when he reached the setting of the sun, and he found
> it setting in a muddy spring, and found a people near it.
> We said: "O Dhul Qarnain! Either punish them or treat
> them with kindness." (18:86)

This verse has puzzled Muslim commentators, many of whom searched history for a great prophet conqueror that might compare to Dhul Qarnain, who reached the lands where the sun rises and sets. The most popular choice was Alexander the Great, which is patently false since he is well known to have been a pagan. Since the sun does not literally set in a muddy spring with people nearby, a less-than-literal interpretation is forced upon us.

Rather than belabor the point, let me summarize my position. On the basis of the style and character of the Qur'an, I believe that the most general and most cautious statement one can make is: The Qur'an relates many stories, versions with which the Arabs were apparently somewhat familiar, not for the sake of relating history or satisfying human curiosity, but to "draw a moral, illustrate a point, sharpen the focus of attention, and to reinforce the basic message."[10] I would advise against attempts to force or decide the historicity of each of these stories. First of all, because the Qur'an avoids historical landmarks and since certain passages in some narratives clearly can not be taken literally, such an insistence seems unwarranted. Furthermore, imposing such limitations on the Qur'an may lead, unnecessarily, to rational conflicts and obstructions that distract the reader from the moral of a given tale. The Qur'an itself harshly criticizes this inclination in *Surat al Kahf*:

> Some say they were three, the dog being the fourth among
> them. Others say they were five, the dog being the sixth—
> doubtfully guessing at the unknown. Yet others say seven,
> the dog being the eighth. Say, "My Lord knows best their

---

[10] G. R. Hawting and Abdul-Kader A. Shareef, *Approaches to the Qur'an* (New York: Routledge, 1993), from the article by Ismael K. Poonawala, "Darwaza's principles of modern exegesis," p. 231.

number, and none knows them, but a few. Therefore, do
not enter into controversies concerning them, except on a
matter that is clear." (18:22)

Moreover, it would be humanly impossible to definitively decide the
historic or symbolic character of every tale; no one has the requisite level
of knowledge of history and Arab oral tradition—not to mention insight
into the intent and wisdom of the author—to make such a claim. Personal
ignorance should be admitted, but it should not be allowed to place limits
and bounds on the ways and means of revelation.

As we set out on our journey, we will be approaching the Qur'an from
the standpoint of meaning; seeking to make sense of and find purpose in the
existence of God, man, and life. We are now ready to embark. We have
made our preparations and have broken camp. With the Qur'an before us,
we enter the first page.

An Answer to a Prayer

In the Name of God, The Merciful, The Compassionate
1. Praise be to God, Lord of the worlds;
2. The Merciful, The Compassionate;
3. Master of the day of Requital;
4. You do we serve and You do we beseech for help;
5. Guide us on the straight path;
6. The path of those whom you have favored;
7. Not those upon whom is wrath and not those who are
lost. (1:1-7)

Volumes upon volumes have been written on the Qur'an's opening
surah, even though it consists of only seven short verses, but we, my fellow
travelers, have only time enough to pause for a few very brief observations.

The first verse indicates a hymn of praise, to God, "the Lord of the
worlds." The divine names, "The Merciful, The Compassionate," appear-
ing in the second, head every *surah* but one (the ninth) and are among the
most frequently mentioned attributes of God, both in the Qur'an and by
Muslims in their everyday speech. The mood abruptly changes in verse two
as it reawakens deep-seated anxieties and conflicts. No sooner are God's
mercy and compassion emphasized than we are threatened with the "Day
of Requital." Would it not have been more tactful to postpone such considerations, to wait until the reader is a little more comfortable with and confident in the Qur'an? Assertions about God's mercy, compassion, gentle-

ness, or love never drove us from religion, but warnings of a Day of Judgment, of Hell, of eternal damnation that we found impossible to harmonize with mercy and compassion, did.

The fourth verse goes even deeper into the quagmire as it reminds us that service is rendered and pleas for help are directed to the very creator of the predicament from which we seek salvation. Far from allowing us to warm up to its message, the scripture wastes no time recalling our complaints against religion. We will discover that this is a persistent tactic of the Qur'an; that it repeatedly agitates the skeptic by confronting him with his personal objections. We will soon see that this Qur'an is no soft sell nor hard sell; that in reality it is no sell at all; that it is no less than a challenge, a dare, to fight and argue against this book.

We can relate to the last three verses all too readily. Life is a chaotic puzzle, a random and confusing maze of paths and choices that lead no where but to broken dreams, empty accomplishments, unfulfilled expectations, one mirage after another. Is there a right path, or are all in the end equally meaningless? Note the transition from personal to impersonal in verses six and seven, as if to say that to obtain the "straight path" is a divine favor conferred on those who seek and heed divine guidance and that those who do not follow divine guidance are exposed to all of life's impersonal, unfeeling wrath, and utter loss and delusion. This wrath and loss we know well, for we have absorbed life's anger and aimlessness and made it our own; it is our argument for the nonexistence of a personal God and the foundation of our philosophy.

We moved through the seven verses quickly. There was a subtle shift in mood from the first four that glorified God to the last three that asked for guidance. More than likely our first reading of them was so casual that we did not observe the change. It was not until we had finished the opening *surah* that we realized that we had just involuntarily and semiconsciously made a supplication. We were almost tricked into it before we had a chance to resist. The beginning of the next *surah* will inform us that whether we consciously intended it or not, our prayer has reached its destination and that it is about to receive an answer.

That Is the Book

> In the name of God, the Merciful, The Compassionate
> 1. *Alif lam mim*
> 2. That is the book, wherein no doubt, is guidance to those
> who have fear,

3. Who believe in the unseen, and are steadfast in prayer
and spend out of what We have given them,
4. And who believe in that which is revealed to you and
that which was revealed before you, and are certain of the
hereafter.
5. These are on guidance from their Lord, and these, they
are the successful. (2:1-5)[11]

Alif lam mim is a transliteration of the three Arabic letters that open this
surah. Twenty-nine *surahs* begin with such letter combinations of the
Arabic alphabet. They continue to be a mystery to Qur'an commentators,
and opinions differ as to their meaning. Most believe they are abbreviations
of words or mystic symbols, but we will leave such speculation aside.

The second verse declares to us that *that* book, the Qur'an—that we
have before us—is without doubt the answer to the prayer we had just
recited. The tenor of the Qur'an from here on is different from that of the
opening *surah*. In the first *surah*, it was the reader humbly petitioning
God for guidance, while the perspective of the remainder of the Qur'an,
as this verse insists, will be God, in all His supreme power and grandeur,
proclaiming to the reader the guidance that he sought, whether consciously or unconsciously, knowingly or unknowingly. Also observe that
doubt and fear are accentuated in this verse. We should not exclude ourselves so hastily from these attributes, even though we do not fit the full
description continued in verses three through five. We do have doubts,
not only about God's existence but also about our denial of it. If we were
absolutely certain of our atheism, we would not be reading this scripture.
As much as we hate to admit it, we are not quite sure of ourselves; there
exists in us at least a glimmer of doubt—and of fear. The word *muttaqin,*
translated as "those who have fear," comes from the Arabic root which
means to protect, to guard, to defend, to be cautious. It implies an acute
alertness to one's potential weaknesses, a person on his toes, a self-critical awareness. We may not be believers, but we are definitely guarded,
defensive and cautious when it comes to religion, otherwise we would

---

[11] The interpretations of verses from the Qur'an in this book are for the most part my
own, although I have relied heavily on a number of well-known interpreters to guide me:
Asad, *Message of the Qur'an*; Muhammad Ali, *The Holy Qur'an, Text, English Translation
and Commentary* (Lahore, Pakistan: Ahmadiyyah Anjuman Isha'at Islam, 19730; Abdullah
Yusuf Ali, *The Meaning of the Holy Qur'an, New Edition with Revised Translation,
Commentary* (Beltsville, MD: amana publications, 1989); Marmaduke W. Pickthall, *The
Meaning of the Glorious Qur'an* (New York: Muslim World League, 1977).

not be atheists; we would have simply accepted what we inherited from our parents. These are the same qualities that brought us to this journey, because we suspect that we might be wrong, that there is at least a chance that there is a God and if there is, then we are ignoring what would have to be the most important fact in our being.

Verse two also begins a description of the Qur'an's potential audience. Like many a book of knowledge, it describes the prerequisites and predisposition necessary to fully benefit from its contents. The most sincere in their belief in God (2:2-5) will profit the most. They believe in realities beyond their perceptions and are devout and are kind to their fellow man. They have faith in what is currently being revealed to them, which are the same essential truths of all ages.

Verse six refers to the rejecters, who refuse to even consider the Qur'an. The Qur'an in turn promptly dismisses them in the next verse. Verse eight begins a relatively lengthy discussion (2:8-20) of all those in between, who waver between belief and disbelief, often distracted and blinded by worldly pursuits. From the standpoint of the Qur'an, we may be towards the boundary of this category. Verses twenty through twenty-nine outline some of the Qur'an's major themes: Man's need to serve the one God, the prophethood of Muhammad, the hereafter and final judgment, the Qur'an's use of symbolism (2:26), the resurrection of man, and God's ultimate sovereignty.

Verse thirty begins the story of man. We will proceed slowly here, line by line, since this has a strong bearing on our questions. The ancient Qur'anic commentators would endorse such an approach, for they used to speak of the *ijaz* of the scripture—its inimitable eloquence that combines the most beautiful and yet most economical expression. They would advise us not to rush hastily, but to allow each verse, each word, each sound, to penetrate our hearts and minds in order to reap its greatest possible benefit. Otherwise, we may deprive ourselves of essential keys to unlocking truths buried deep within us.

> Behold, your Lord said to the angels: "I am going to place
> a vicegerent on earth." They said: "Will you place therein
> one who will spread corruption and shed blood? While we
> celebrate your praises and glorify your holiness?" He said:
> "Truly, I know what you do not know." (2:30)

The opening scene is heaven as God informs the angels that He is about to place man on earth. Adam, the first man, has not yet appeared. From the verses that follow, it is clear that at this point in the story Adam is free of any wrongdoing. Nevertheless, God plans to place him (and his descendants [6:165; 27:62; 35:39]) on earth in the role of vicegerent or vicar (*khalifah*). There is no insinuation here that earthly life is to serve as a punishment. The word *khalifah* means "a vicar," "a delegate," "a representative," "a person authorized to act for others." Therefore, it appears that man is meant to represent and act on behalf of God in some sense.

The angels' reply is both fascinating and disturbing. In essence it asks, "Why create and place on earth one who has it within his nature to corrupt and commit terrible crimes? Why create this being, who will be the cause and recipient of great suffering?" It is obvious that the angels are referring here to the very nature of mankind, since Adam, in the Qur'an, turns out to be one of God's elect and not guilty of any major crime. The question is made all the more significant when we consider who and from where it comes.

When we think of angels, we imagine peaceful, pure, and holy creatures in perfect and joyous submission to God. They represent the model to which we should aspire. In our daily speech, we reserve the word "angel" for the noblest of our species. Mother Theresa is often called an "angel of mercy" by the press. Of a person who does something very kind we say, "He is such an angel!" When my wife and I look in on our daughters at night, sleeping so beautifully and serenely, we remark to each other, "Aren't they angels?" Our image of an angel is of the perfect human being. This is what gives the angels' question such force, for it asks: "Why create this patently corrupt and flawed being when it is within Your power to create *us*?" Thus they say: "While *we* celebrate your praises and glorify your holiness?" Their question is given further amplification by the fact that it originates in heaven, for what possible purpose could be served by placing man in an environment where he could exercise freely his worst criminal inclinations? All of these considerations culminate in the obvious objection: Why not place man with a suitable nature in heaven from the start? We are not even a single verse into the story of man and we have already confronted our (the atheists') main complaint. And, it is put in the mouths of the angels!

The verse ends not with an explanation, but a reminder of God's superior knowledge, and hence, the implication that man's earthly life is part of a grand design. Many western scholars have remarked that the statement, "I know what you do not know," merely dismisses the angel's question. However, as the sequence of passages will show, this is not the case at all.

Our initial encounter with the Qur'an has been anything but pleasant; it has been distressful and irritating. Either the author is completely unaware of possible philosophical problems and objections, or else he is deliberately provoking us with them! We are a mere thirty-seven verses into the Qur'an and our anxiety and resentment has been aroused to a fever pitch. We ask, "Why indeed subject mankind to earthly suffering? Why not remove us to heaven or place us there from the first? Why must we struggle to survive? Why create us so vulnerable and self-destructive? Why must we suffer broken hearts and broken dreams, lost loves and lost youth, crises and catastrophes? Why must we experience pains of birth and pains of death? Why?" we beg in our frustration. "Why?" we plead in all our sorrow and emptiness. "Why?" we insist in our anguish. "Why?!" we scream out to the heavens. "Why?!" we plead with the angels. "If You are there and You hear us, tell us, why create man?!!"

And His Lord Turned toward Him

We move now to verse thirty-one, where we find that the Qur'an continues to explore the angels' question.

> And He taught Adam the names of all things; then He placed them before the angels, and said, "Tell me their names if you are right." (2:31)

Clearly, the angels' question is being addressed in this verse. Adam's capacities for learning and acquiring knowledge, his ability to be taught, are the focus of this initial response. The next verse demonstrates the angels' inferiority in this respect. Special emphasis is placed on man's ability to name, to represent by verbal symbols, "all things" that enter his conscious mind: all his thoughts, fears, and hopes, in short, all that he can perceive or conceive. This allows man to communicate his experience and knowledge on a relatively high level, as compared to the other creatures about him, and gives all human learning a preeminent cumulative quality. In several places in the Qur'an, this gift to mankind is singled out as one of the greatest bounties bestowed on him by God.[12]

> They said: Glory to you: we have no knowledge except what You taught us, in truth it is you who are the Knowing, the Wise. (2:32)

---

[12] See p. 26.

In this verse, the angels plead their inability to perform such a task, for, as they plainly state, it would demand a knowledge and wisdom beyond their capacity. They maintain that its performance would, of course, be easy for God, since His knowledge and wisdom is supreme, but that the same could not be expected of them. In the next passage, we discover that Adam possesses the level of intelligence necessary to accomplish the task and hence, though his knowledge and wisdom are less than God's, it is yet greater than the angels.

> He said: "O Adam! Tell them their names." When he had
> told them their names, God said: "Did I not tell you that I
> know what is unseen in the heavens and the earth and I
> know what you reveal and conceal?" (2:33)

Here we have an emphatic statement that man's greater intellect figures into an answer to the angels' question. We are informed that God takes all into account, in particular, all aspects of the human personality: man's potential for evil, which the angels' question "reveals," and his complementary and related capacity for moral and intellectual growth, which their question "conceals." To drive home this point, the next verse has the angels demonstrate their inferiority to Adam and shows that man's more complex personality makes him a potentially superior being.

> And behold, We said to the angels, "Bow down to Adam"
> and they bowed down. Not so Iblis: he refused and was
> proud: he was of the rejecters. (2:34)

We also find in this verse the birth of sin and temptation. The Qur'an later informs us that Iblis (Satan) is of the *jinn* (18:50), a being created of a smokeless fire (55:15) and who is insulted at the suggestion that he should humble himself before a creature made of "putrid clay" (7:12; 17:61; 38:76). Satan is portrayed as possessing a fiery, consuming, and destructive nature. He allows his passions to explode out of control and initiates a pernicious rampage. We are often told that money is at the root of all evil, but here the lesson appears to be that pride and self-centeredness is at its core. Indeed, many terrible wrongs are committed for no apparent material motive.

> And we said: "O Adam! Dwell you and your spouse in the
> garden and eat freely there of what you wish, but come not
> near this tree for you will be among the wrongdoers."
> (2:35)

Thus the famous and fateful command. Yet, the tone of it seems curiously restrained. There is no suggestion that the tree is in any way special; it almost seems as if it were picked at random. Satan will later tempt Adam with the promise of eternal life and "a kingdom that never decays" (20:121), but this turns out to be a complete fabrication on his part. There is not the slightest hint that God is somehow threatened at the prospect of Adam and his spouse violating the command; instead, He voices concern for *them*, because then "*they* will be among the wrongdoers."

This is probably an appropriate place to reflect on what we have learned so far. We saw how God originally intended for man to have an earthly life. We then observed a period of preparation during which man is "taught" to use his intellectual gifts. Now, Adam and his spouse are presented a choice, of apparently no great consequence, except for the fact that it is made to be a moral choice. It thus seems that man has gradually become—or is about to become—a moral being.

> But Satan caused them to slip and expelled them from the
> state in which they were. And we said: "Go you all down,
> some of you being the enemies of others, and on earth will
> be your dwelling place and provision for a time. (2:36)

Once again the Qur'an seems to have a penchant for understating things. The Arabic verb *azalla* means to cause someone to unintentionally slip or lose his footing. But how can one of the most terrible wrongs ever committed be described as a momentary "slip"? Yet perhaps we are letting our own religious backgrounds, even though we rejected them, distort our reading. Perhaps the Qur'an considers this sin as nothing more than a temporary slip. After all, it *is* only a tree! Its only significance may be that it signals a new stage in man's development, that it causes man to depart from a previous state.

The words "some of you being the enemies of others" apparently refer to all mankind and echo the angels' remark concerning man's earthly strife.

Under normal circumstances, we would know now what to expect. We have been terrified by it ever since we were children. It shook us from our sleep and required our mothers to calm our fears and, unlike other nightmares, it never went away when we awoke, because it was confirmed by everyone we trusted. We know that there is about to be unleashed on mankind a rage, a violence, a terror, the like of which has never been known either before or since. Like a huge, thundering, black, and terrifying storm cloud, looming on the horizon and heading straight for us, mankind is about to be engulfed by an awesome fury. And when the smoke clears, man will find himself sentenced, TO LIFE, on earth, where he and all his descendants will suffer and struggle to survive by their sweat and toil. There they will experience illness, agony, and death. There they will suffer endless pain and torment and, in all probability, more of the same and worse in the life to come.

And the WOMAN!!!! To her belong the greater punishment and humiliation, for it was she who duped Adam with her beauty and her charms. It was she who allied herself with Satan—an alliance for which Adam was, of course, no match. It was she who corrupted his innocence and exposed his weaknesses. So it is she who will ache and bleed monthly. It is she who will scream out in her labor pains. It is she who will bare the brunt of greater humiliation and drudgery, because the man will be made to rule over her, in spite of the fact that he is obviously her intellectual inferior, since he was unequal to her cleverness and guile.

So we wince and shudder as we turn to the terror we have always known. We cringe and cower as we peek to the next verse.

> Then Adam received words from his Lord, and He turned
> to him (mercifully). Truly He is Oft-returning, the Mer-
> ciful. (2:37)

What is this? What is this talk of mercy and turning compassionately towards man? Where is the passion, the jealousy, the anger, erupting out of control?

In this verse, those that follow, and others in the Qur'an that relate the same episode (see, for example, 20:116-24), the tone is first and foremost consoling and assuring. God immediately pardons Adam and Eve, with no greater blame assigned to either of them. Adam receives "words," which some commentators interpret to be words of inspiration and others see as divine assurances and promises. The next verse supports the latter viewpoint, while there are others that include him in the community of prophets (for example, [3:32]) which sustain the first.

> We said: Go down from this state all of you together; and
> truly there will come to you guidance from Me and who-
> ever follows My guidance, no fear shall come upon them,
> nor shall they grieve. (2:38)

The command issued in 2:36 is repeated here, but this time with special emphasis put on God's assurances and promises to mankind, thus further precluding the interpretation that man's earthly life is a punishment. This explains why the Qur'an has man remain on earth even though Adam and Eve are immediately forgiven. Nonetheless, the Qur'an will insist, as we read through it, that life serves definite aims and, as the next verse warns, it has grave consequences and must be taken seriously.

> But those who are rejecters and give the lie to our signs,
> these are the companions of the fire; they will abide in it.
> (2:39)

The story of Adam ends here to be taken up in bits and pieces later. Many questions and problems have been raised, but we have obtained only some clues and clarifications. This is another characteristic of the Qur'an: It interweaves themes throughout the text, rather than provide several distinct and complete discourses on various topics. In this way it baits the reader, luring him or her into its design, so that its different approaches are allowed to exert their influence frequently and repeatedly. It would be naive of us to expect long uninterrupted dissertations on metaphysics or theology, for such would be understandable to few and of interest and inspiration to far fewer. On the other hand, if the Qur'an is a guidance, as it claims to be, then we should anticipate suggestions, guideposts, and touchstones that help us along the way. Be assured, the Qur'an will not simply translate us to our goal; it will provide directions at different stages, but the traveling and the discovery will have to be ours, because the questions we ask are not only about God—they are about ourselves as peculiar individuals and we are the only persons who have real access to our souls. Thus, as the Qur'an might say, we must be willing not only to search the horizons, but also our own selves, until we know as much as we can grasp of the truth (41:53).

"When Will God's Help Come?"

Although the picture is still far from clear, some themes that invite further reflection and elaboration have emerged. The most striking fact that we observed is that the Qur'an does not maintain that life on earth is a punishment. Long before Adam and Eve enter the story, the angels raise the troublesome question: Why create man? A series of verses supplies pieces of an answer. Man has a relatively higher intelligence than other creatures. His nature is more complex and he has a greater degree of personal freedom. Thus, he has not only potential for growth in evil but, reciprocally, he has the potential for growth in virtue. We witness a period of preparation, wherein man learns to use his intellectual strengths. Adam and Eve are then ready to become moral beings. They are presented with a somewhat innocuous—although from the standpoint of their development critical—moral choice. They slip and enter a moral phase in their existence, which is symbolized in other Qur'anic passages that have the couple now conscious of sexual morality and modesty (7:19-25; 20:120-23). Thus they depart from a state of ignorance, innocence, and bliss. Man's higher intellect, freedom of choice, and growth potential will inevitably involve him in conflict and travail. The last of these is the focus of the angels' question. As we continue along our journey, the Qur'an will stress repeatedly these three features of the human venture: reasoning, choice, and adversity. We will consider each separately.

Reason. That the Qur'an gives a prominent place to reason in the attainment of faith is well known and frequently mentioned by western Islamicists. Many western scholars view this as a defect, because they see faith and reason as being inherently incompatible. For example, H. Lammens sarcastically states that the Qur'an "is not far from considering unbelief as an infirmity of the human mind!"[13] His reaction, however, is more cultural and emotional than rational, having its roots in the West's own struggle with religion and reason. Yet not all western scholars are so cynical. While certainly no advocate for Islam, Maxime Rodinson sees this aspect of the Qur'an as somewhat in its favor and writes:

> The Koran continually expounds the rational proofs of Allah's omnipotence: the wonders of creation, such as the gestation of animals, the movements of the heavenly bodies, atmospheric phenomena, the variety of animal and vegetable life so marvelously well adapted to men's needs. All those things "are signs (*ayat*) for those of insight" (3:187-190) . . . . Repeated about fifty times in the Koran is the verb *'aqala* which means "connect ideas together, reason, understand an intellectual argument." Thirteen times we come upon the refrain, after a piece of reasoning: *a fa-la ta'qilun* "have ye then no sense?" (2:41-44, etc.) The infidels, those who remain insensible

---

[13] H. Lammens, "Caracteristique de Mohomet d'apres le Qoran," *Recherches de science religieuse*, no. 20 (1930): 416-38.

to Muhammad's preaching, are stigmatized as "a people of no intelligence," persons incapable of the intellectual effort needed to cast off routine thinking (5:63-58, 102-103; 10:42-43; 22:45-46; 59:14). In this respect they are like cattle (2:166-171; 25:44-46).[14]

The Qur'an insists that it contains signs for those who are "wise" (2:269), "knowledgeable" (29:42-43), "endowed with insight" (39:9), and "reflective" (45:13). Its persistent complaint against its rejecters is that they refuse to make use of their intellectual faculties and that they close their minds to learning. The Qur'an asks almost incredulously: "Do they not travel through the land, so that their hearts may thus learn wisdom?"(22:44), "Do they not examine the earth?"(26:7), "Do they not travel through the earth and see what was the end of those before them?"(30:9), "Do they not look at the sky above them?"(50:6), "Do they not look at the camels, how they are made?"(88:17), "Have you not watched the seeds which you sow?" (56:63).

Muslim school children throughout the world are frequently reminded of the first five verses of the ninety-sixth *surah*:

> Read in the name of your Lord, who has created—created
> man out of a tiny creature that clings! Read and your Lord
> is the Most Bountiful One, who has taught the use of the
> pen, taught man what he did not know. (96:1-5)

These verses are believed to comprise Muhammad's very first revelation. "Read!" It commands, as the skill of written communication is presented as one of the great gifts to mankind, because it is by use of the pen that God has taught man what he did not or could not know. Here again, the Qur'an highlights man's unique ability to communicate—this time in writing—and to collectively learn from the insights and experiences of others.

Repetition is indicative of the importance given to certain topics. It should be observed that the Arabic word for knowledge, *'ilm*, and its derivatives appear 854 times in the Qur'an, placing it among the most frequently occurring words. It should also be noted that in many of its stories, where the Qur'an presents a debate between a believer and disbeliever, the believer's stance is inevitably more rational and logical than his opponent's.

---

[14] Maxime Rodinson, *Islam and Capitalism* (Penguin Books, 1974), 79-80.

Choice. The Qur'an presents human history as a perennial struggle between two opposing choices: to resist or to surrender oneself to God. It is in this conflict that the scripture immerses itself and the reader; it could be said to be the very crux of its calling. This choice must be completely voluntary, for the Qur'an demands, "Let there be no compulsion in religion—the right way is henceforth clearly distinct from error" (2:256). The crucial point is not that one should come to know and worship God, but that one should freely choose to know and worship God. Thus we find the repeated declaration that God could have made all mankind rightly guided, but it was within His purposes to do otherwise.

> Had He willed He could indeed have guided all of you. (6:149)

> Do not the believers know that, had God willed, He could have guided all mankind? (13:31)

> And if We had so willed, We could have given every soul its guidance. (32:13)

> Had God willed He could have made you all one community. But that He may try you by that which He has given you. So vie with one another in good works. Unto God you will all return, and He will inform you of that wherein you differ. (5:48)

The Qur'an categorically affirms that God is not diminished nor threatened by our choices, yet they do carry grave consequences for the individual, as the primary beneficiary of a good deed and the primary casualty of an evil act is the doer.

> Enlightenment has come from your God; he who sees does so to his own good, he who is blind is so to his own hurt. (6:104)

> Indeed they will have squandered their own selves, and all their false imagery will have forsaken them. (7:53)

> And they did no harm against Us, but [only] against their own selves did they sin. (7:160)

> And so it was not God who wronged them, it was they who wronged themselves. (9:70)

> And whosoever is guided, is only (guided) to his own gain,
> and if any stray, say: "I am only a warner." (27:92)

> And if any strive, they do so for their own selves: For God
> is free of all need from creation. (29:6)

> We have revealed to you the book with the truth for man-
> kind. He who lets himself be guided does so to his own
> good; he who goes astray does so to his own hurt. (39:41)
> (Also see (10:108; 17:15; 27:92).)

These statements are hardly easy on the reader. At first glance they
seem to indicate a detachment from and indifference to man's situation.
Philosophically, such a stance may be consistent with God's transcendence,
but only at the expense of attempting any possible relationship with God.
Yet such an interpretation would be inappropriately severe. The Qur'anic
God is anything but impartial to mankind's condition. He sends prophets,
answers prayers (2:186; 3:195), and intervenes in and manipulates the
human drama, as in the Battle of Badr (3:13; 8:5-19; 8:42-48). All is under
His authority, and nothing takes place without His allowing it (4:78-79).

The Qur'an's "most beautiful names" of God imply an intense involvement in the human venture. These names, such as The Merciful, The
Compassionate, The Forgiving, The Giving, The Loving, The Creator,
etc., reveal a God that creates men and women in order to relate to them
on an intensely personal level, on a level higher than with the other creatures known to mankind, not out of a psychological or emotional need but
because this is the very essence of His nature. Therefore, we find that the
relationship between the sincere believer and God is characterized consistently as a bond of love. God loves the good-doers (2:195; 3:134, 3:148,
5:13, 5:93), the repentant (2:222), those that purify themselves (2:222;
9:108), the God-conscious (3:76; 9:4; 9:7), the patient (3:146), those that
put their trust in Him (3:159), the just (5:42; 49:9; 60:8), and those who
fight in His cause (61:4). And they, in turn, love God.

> Yet there are men who take others besides God as equal
> (with God), loving them as they should love God. But
> those who believe love God more ardently. (2:165)

> Say: "If you love God, follow me, and God will love you,
> and forgive you your faults; for God is The Forgiving, The
> Merciful. (3:31)

> O you who believe! If any from among you should turn
> back from his faith, then God will assuredly bring a peo-
> ple He loves and who love Him. (5:54)

On the other hand, tyrants, aggressors, the corrupt ones, the guilty,
rejecters of faith, evil-doers, the arrogant ones, transgressors, the prodi-
gal, the treacherous, and the unjust will not experience this relationship of
love (2:190; 2:205; 2:276; 3:32; 3:57; 3:140; 4:36; 4:107; 5:64; 5:87;
6:141; 7:31; 7:55; 8:58; 16:23; 22:38; 28:76; 28:77; 30:45; 31:18; 42:40;
57:23).

There are Muslim and non-Muslim scholars who view God in the
Qur'an as virtually indifferent to humanity, establishing the cosmos with
fixed laws of cause and effect in all spheres (physical, psychological, spiritual, etc.), and then setting it to run subject to them. Others have seen Him
as so completely involved in and in control of creation that all is totally
determined, even our choices. Many believe that shades of both viewpoints
are present and that they may be irreconcilable. The latter is perhaps closest
to the truth, although the irreconcilability is not necessary. Certainly, the
Qur'an maintains God's absolute sway over all creation, which He cease-
lessly and continuously sustains, maintains, and influences. Nothing exists
or takes place without His permission. Yet He empowers us with the ability
to make choices, act them out, and see them, most often, to their expected
conclusions. In fact, He frequently leads us to such critical choices. In particular, He allows and enables us to make decisions that are detrimental to
ourselves and others:

> Say: "All things are from God." But what has come to
> these people, that they fail to understand a single fact?
> Whatever good befalls you is from God, but whatever evil
> befalls you, is from yourself. (4:78-79)

The assertion here is that our ability to experience true benefit or harm
comes from God, but to do real injury to ourselves, in an ultimate and spiritual sense, depends on *our* actions and decisions, which God has empowered us to make.

As noted above, our acts and choices in no way threaten God and it is
the individual who gains or loses by them. However, on the collective level,
the Qur'an shows that God intends to produce through this earthly experience persons that share a bond of love with Him. While any individual may
or may not pursue this, the Qur'an acknowledges that there will definitely

be people who will, and their development is apparently the very object of man's earthly life (15:39-43;17:64-65).

Our vision is still quite blurry, but it seems somehow a little clearer than when we started, although we still have far to go. Questions persist about the need for this earthly life as well as the roles of human choice, intelligence, and suffering in the creation of individuals. It also feels as if we are slipping into the difficult topic of predestination. We will reserve that subject for the end of this chapter, for it will take us too far afield at this stage. However, we need to discuss one more Qur'anic statement that relates to divine and human will, because it is very often misunderstood and has a strong bearing on the theme of human choice.

The Qur'an frequently states that God "allows to stray whom He will, and guides whom He will" (2:26; 4:88; 4:143; 6:39; 7:178; 7:186; 13:27; 14:4; 16:93; 35:8; 39:23; 39:36; 40:33; 74:31). This phrase is typically rendered in most English interpretations as "God misleads whom He will, and guides whom He will." Grammatically, both renderings are possible, because the verb *adalla* could be used in either sense. It could mean either "to let someone or something stray unguided," or equally, "to make someone or something lose his/its way." Ignaz Goldziher, the famous Orientalist and scholar of Arabic, strongly argues in favor of the first rendition. He writes,

> Such statements do not mean that God directly leads the latter into error. The decisive verb (*adalla*) is not, in this context, to be understood as "lead astray," but rather as "allow to go astray," that is, not to care about someone, not to show him the way out of his predicament. "We let them (*nadharuhum*) stray in disobedience" (6:110). We must imagine a solitary traveler in the desert: that image stands behind the Qur'an's manner of speaking about guidance and error. The traveler wanders, drifts in limitless space, on the watch for his true destination and goal. Such a traveler is man on the journey of life.[15]

His observation is given further support by the fact that almost all of the statements in the Qur'an of this nature are immediately preceded or followed by others that assert that God guides or refuses to guide someone

[15] Ignaz Goldziher, *Introduction to Islamic Theology and Law* (Princeton: Princeton University Press, 1981), 79-80.

according to his/her choices and predisposition. We find that "God does not
guide the unjust ones," "God does not guide the transgressors," and God
guides aright those who "listen," are "sincere," and are "God-conscious"
(2:26, 258, 264; 3:86; 5:16, 51, 67, 108; 6:88, 144; 9:19, 21, 37, 80, 109; 12:52;
13:27, 16:37, 107; 28:50; 39:3; 40:28; 42:13; 46:10; 47:8; 61:7; 62:5; 63:6).
Thus we find that "when they went crooked, God bent their hearts crooked"
(61:5). This demonstrates that receiving or not receiving guidance is affected by sincerity, disposition and willingness; it recalls the saying of Muhammad: "When you approach God by an arm's length, He approaches you by
two, and if you come to Him walking, He comes to you running."[16]
Therefore, the phrase "God allows to stray whom He wills" illumines what
we have already concluded: while God, according to the Qur'an, could
guide all mankind uniformly, He has other purposes and hence does not.
Instead, He has created man with a unique and profound ability to make
moral decisions and He monitors, influences, and guides each individual's
moral and spiritual development in accordance with them.

Suffering. The great divide between theist and atheist is their reactions
to human suffering. Often the first views it as either deserved or an impenetrable mystery, while the second sees it as unnecessary and inexcusable.
The Qur'an advocates neither viewpoint. Trial and tribulation are held to be
inevitable and essential to human development and both the believer and
unbeliever will experience them.

> Most assuredly We will try you with something of danger,
> and hunger, and the loss of worldly goods, of lives and the
> fruits of your labor. But give glad tidings to those who are
> patient in adversity—who when calamity befalls them,
> say, "Truly unto God do we belong and truly, unto him we
> shall return. (2:155)
>
> Do you think that you could enter paradise without having
> suffered like those who passed away before you? Misfor-
> tune and hardship befell them, and so shaken were they
> that the Messenger and the believers with him, would
> exclaim, "When will God's help come?" Oh truly, God's
> help is always near. (2:214)

---

[16] From *Sahih al Bukhari* as translated in Imam Nawawi, *Riyad al Salihin*, trans. by
Muhammad Zafrullah Khan (London: Curzon Press Ltd., 1975), 28.

You will certainly be tried in your possessions and yourselves. (3:186)

And if we make man taste mercy from Us, then withdraw
it from him, he is surely despairing, ungrateful. And if
we make him taste a favor after distress has afflicted him,
he says: The evils are gone away from me. Truly he is
exultant, boastful; except those who are persevering and
do good. For them is forgiveness and a great reward.
(11:9-11)

Every soul must taste of death. And we try you with
calamity and prosperity, [both] as a means of trial. And to
Us you are returned. (21:35)

O man! Truly you've been toiling towards your Lord in
painful toil—but you shall meet Him!(84:6)

Man, however, does not grow only through patient suffering, but also
by striving and struggling against hardship and adversity. This explains
why *jihad* is such a key concept in the Qur'an. Often translated as "holy
war," the word *jihad* literally means "a struggle," "a striving," "an exertion," or "a great effort." It may include fighting for a just cause, but it has
a more general connotation as the associated verbal noun of *jahada,* "to
toil," "to weary," "to struggle," "to strive after," "to exert oneself." The following verses, revealed in Makkah before Muslims were involved in combat, bring out this more general sense.

And those who strive hard (*jahadu*) for Us, We shall certainly guide them in Our ways, and God is surely with the
doers of good. (29:69)

And whoever strives hard (*jahada*) strives (*yujahidu*) for
his self, for God is Self-Sufficient, above the need of the
worlds. (29:6)

And strive hard (*jahidu*) for God with due striving (*jihadi-
hi*). (22:78)

So obey not the unbelievers and strive against them
(*jahidhum*) a mighty striving (*jihadan*) with it [the
Qur'an]. (25:52)

The last verse occurs in a passage that encourages Muslims to make use of the Qur'an when they argue with disbelievers.

The Qur'an's attitude towards suffering and adversity is not passive and resigned, but positive and dynamic. The believers are told that they will surely suffer and to be patient and persevering in times of hardship, but they are also to look forward and seek opportunities to improve their situation and rectify existing wrongs. They are told that while the risks and struggle may be great, the ultimate benefit and reward will be much greater (2:218; 3:142; 4:95-96; 8:74; 9:88-89; 16:110; 29:69).

> Those who believed and fled their homes, and strove hard in God's way with their possessions and their selves are much higher in rank with God. And it is these—they are the triumphant. (9:20)

Life was never meant to be easy. The Qur'an refers to a successful life as an "uphill climb," a climb that most will avoid.

> We certainly have created man to face distress. Does he think that no one has power over him? He will say: I have wasted much wealth. Does he think that no one sees him? Have We not given him two eyes, and a tongue and two lips and pointed out to him the two conspicuous ways? But he attempts not the uphill climb; and what will make you comprehend the uphill climb? [It is] to free a slave, or to feed in a day of hunger an orphan nearly related, or the poor one lying in the dust. Then he is of those who believe and exhort one another to patience and exhort one another to mercy. (90:4-17)

Wishful Thinking

"Why create man?" The angels' question echoes through our reflections. We can at least attempt a partial explanation based on what we have learned from the Qur'an so far.

It seems that God, in accordance with His attributes, intends to make a creature that can experience His being (His mercy, compassion, love, kindness, beauty, etc.) in an intensely personal way and at a level higher than the other beings known to mankind. The intellect and will that man has been given, together with the strife and struggle that he will surely face on earth, somehow contribute to the development of these individuals, this subset of humanity that will be bound to God by love.

We need to travel on and delve deeper in this direction in order to gain greater insight. But before we do, we should consider the possibility that we may be deluding ourselves. By this I mean that we may have been reading into the Qur'an something that is not really there; we may have been projecting onto the scripture our own personal conflict, one that the Qur'an never insists on explicitly nor even intentionally raises the issue of an ultimate purpose behind the creation of man. Yet here again we meet with the persistently provocative method of the scripture. Just when we are prepared to doubt our first impressions and to revert to the familiar and comforting corner of cynicism from which we have come, the Qur'an reopens the topic.

> Those [are believers] who remember God standing and sitting and lying down and reflect upon the creation of the heavens and the earth [and say]: Our Lord, You did not create all this in vain. (3:191)

> We have not created the heaven and the earth and whatever is between them in sport. If We wish to take a sport, We could have done it by Ourselves—if We were to do that at all. (21:16-17)

> Do you think that We created you purposely and that you will not be returned to Us? The true Sovereign is too exalted above that. (23:115)

> We did not create the heavens and the earth and all that is between them, in play. (44:38)

So for us there is no easy escape. The Qur'an apparently will not back out of the challenge. It is up to us to either continue on in this search or to resign and avoid a decisive engagement. Our numbers now are almost surely less than when we started. For those willing to continue, we should consider what would be the next natural step. Since the Qur'an undoubtedly claims that life has a reason and since, as we observed, it has to do with the nurturing of a certain relationship between God and man, it would seem quite appropriate to seek more information about the nature of man and what the Qur'an requires of him as well as about the attributes of God and how mankind is affected by them.

Except Those Who Have Faith and Do Good

The key to success in this life and the hereafter is stated so frequently and formally in the Qur'an that no serious reader can miss it. However, the utter simplicity of the dictum may cause one to disregard it, because it seems to ignore the great questions and complexities of life. The Qur'an maintains that only "those who have faith and do good" (in Arabic: *allathina aaminu wa 'amilu al saalihaat*) will benefit from their earthly lives (2:25; 2:82; 2:277; 4:57; 4:122; 5:9; 7:42; 10:9; 11:23; 13:29; 14:23; 18:2; 18:88; 18:107; 19:60; 19:96; 20:75; 20:82; 20:112; 21:94; 22:14; 22:23; 22:50; 22:56; 24:55; 25:70-71; 26:67; 28:80; 29:7; 29:9; 29:58; 30:15; 30:45; 31:8; 32:19; 34:4; 34:37; 35:7; 38:24; 41:8; 42:22; 42:23; 42:26; 45:21; 45:30; 47:2; 47:12; 48:29; 64:9; 65:11; 84:25; 85:11; 95:6; 98:7; 103:3). This statement and very similar ones occur so often that it warrants careful analysis.

Wa 'amilu al saalihaat (and do good). The verb *'amila* means "to do," "to act," "to be active," "to work," or "to make." It implies exertion and effort. Thus the associated noun *'amal* (pl. *a'maal*) means "action," "activity," "work" or "labor," as in the verse, "I waste not the labor (*'amala*) of any that labors (*'amilin*)" (3:195). The noun *al saalihaat* is the plural of *saalih,* which means "a good or righteous act." But this definition does not bring out its full meaning. The verbs *salaha* and *aslaha,* which come from the same Arabic root, mean "to act rightly and properly," "to put things in order," "to restore," "to reconcile," and "to make or foster peace." Hence the noun *sulh* means "peace," "reconciliation," "settlement" and "compromise." Therefore, the phrase *'amilu al saalihaat* ("do good") refers to those who persist in striving to set things right; to restore harmony, peace, and balance.

From the Qur'an's many exhortations and its descriptions of the acts and types of individuals loved by God, it is not difficult to compose a partial list of "good works." Not unexpectedly, it will consist of those acts and attributes that are universally recognized as virtuous. One should show compassion (2:83; 2:215; 69:34), be merciful (90:17), forgive others (42:37; 45:14; 64:14), be just (4:58; 6:152; 16:90), protect the weak (4:127; 6:152), defend the oppressed (4:75), seek knowledge and wisdom (20:114; 22:54), be generous (2:177; 23:60; 30:39), truthful (3:17; 33:24; 33:35; 49:15), kind (4:36), and peaceful (8:61; 25:63; 47:35), and love others (19:86).

> Truly those who believe and do good will the Most Merciful endow with love and to this end have We made this

> easy to understand in your own tongue, so that you might
> convey a glad tiding to the God-conscious and warn those
> given to contention. (19:86)

One should teach and encourage others to practice these virtues (90:17;
103:3) and, by implication, learn and grow in them as well. The stories of
the prophets have God's messengers bidding their communities and families to adopt such ethics, although many of them remain contemptuous.

It is not surprising that the Qur'an upholds the so-called golden rule.
Many do feel that it is better to give than to receive, to be truthful rather
than to live a lie, to love rather than to hate, to be compassionate rather than
to ignore the suffering of others, for such experiences give life depth and
beauty. I believe that in the winters of our lives, our past worldly or material achievements will seem less important to us than the relationships we
had, loves and friendships that we shared, and times we spent giving of ourselves and doing good to others. In the end, according to the Qur'an, these
are what endure.

> But the things that endure—the good deeds—are, with
> your Lord, better in reward and better in hope. (18:46)

> And God increases the guided in guidance. And the deeds
> that endure—the good deeds— are, with your Lord, better
> in reward and yield better returns. (19:76)

These are the themes of songs, poems, novels, plays, and films not only
because of their sentimental appeal, but because they are part of our collective human experience and wisdom. Some would say that life is really
not about taking, but about giving and sharing, and that this is what gives
life meaning and purpose. The Muslim, however, would not fully agree. If
human intellectual, moral, and emotional evolution was the sole purpose of
life, then belief in God might be helpful, but not entirely necessary, for a
humanistic ideology may suffice. But the Qur'an does not state that the successful in life are only "those who do good"; rather, they are only those who
unite faith with righteous living, those who "have faith and do good."

Illa-l lathina aamanu (except those who believe). The verb *aamana*
means "to be faithful," "to trust," "to have confidence in," and "to believe
in." It is derived from the Arabic root, *AMN*, which is associated with the
ideas of safety, security, and peace. Thus *amina* means "to be secure," "to
feel safe," "to trust"; *amn* means "safety," "peace," "protection"; *amaan*
means "safety," "shelter," "peace," and "security." The translation of

aaminu as "believe" is somewhat misleading, because in modern times it is usually used in the sense of "to hold an opinion" or "to accept a proposition or statement as true." The Arabic word has stronger emotional and psychological content, for "those who believe" implies more than an acceptance of an idea; it connotes a personal relationship and commitment and describes those who find security, peace, and protection in God and who are in turn faithfully committed to Him.

Like the phrase we are analyzing, the Qur'an maintains the utter indivisibility between faith and good works. The mention of the first is almost always conjoined to the second. Faith should inspire righteous deeds, which, in turn, should nurture a more profound experience of faith, which should incline one to greater acts of goodness, and so on, with each a function of the other, rising in a continuous increase. From this viewpoint, all of our endeavors acquire a potential unity of purpose: ritualistic, spiritual, humanitarian, and worldly activity are all brought into the domain of worship. Good deeds become simultaneously God-directed and man-directed acts. For example, the spending of one's substance on others becomes an expression of one's love of God.

> But piety is to . . . spend of your substance out of love for
> Him. (2:177)

Hence the relationship between God and man is inextricably bound to man's relationship with fellow man.

Repeatedly, we come upon the Qur'anic exhortation, "Establish salah [ritual prayers] and pay zakah [the annual financial tax]." We normally think of the first as God-directed and the second as community, and hence man, directed. While this may be so, the line between them is extremely faint in Islam, for both are ritual obligations and both require and contribute to a high level of community discipline and cohesion.

Many a non-Muslim has been impressed with the synchronous, almost military, precision of a Muslim congregation in prayer. At the call to the prayer, the congregation quickly arranges itself in tight formation, with no one possessing a fixed or privileged position, so that even the prayer leader is frequently elected on the spot from those present. In this way, the prayer becomes not only a powerful spiritual exercise, but, secondarily, also trains the community in leadership, organization, cooperation, equality, and brotherhood. The physical and hygienic advantages of preparing for and performing the ritual prayer have also been noted frequently by outsiders. This is not to say that Muslims would list these gains as the primary benefits of prayer—indeed they would not—but it does exemplify how the spiritual and worldly intersect and complement each other in Islam.

The ritual of zakah illustrates the same point but from the reverse angle. It is the yearly tax—something like a social security tax—on a Muslim's wealth, which is distributed to the poor and needy and others as stipulated in the Qur'an (9:60). The social concerns behind this tax are obvious, but the Qur'an underlines its personal and spiritual sides as well. The word zakah, which means "alms" or "charity," is associated with the Arabic verbs *zakka* and *tazakka,* which mean "to purify" or "to cleanse." Muslims have long understood that through its payment one may attain to higher levels of spiritual purity. This is not a coincidental or forced association, because the Qur'an clearly makes the connection between alms-giving and self-purification.

> So take of their wealth alms, so that you might purify (*tuzakkeehim*) and cleanse them. (9:103)

> But the most devoted to God shall be removed far from it: those who spend their wealth to purify (*yatazakka*) themselves. (92:18)

The Qur'an's recurring summons to establish salah and pay zakah is indicative of its general attitude towards faith and good deeds: They are interconnected and mutually enriching. The ultimate goal is to perfect harmony between both types of activities, as each is indispensable to our complete development. Thus, giving of oneself strengthens the experience of faith, or, as the Qur'an says, spending in God's way and doing good brings one nearer to God and His mercy.

> And some of the desert Arabs are of those who believe in God and the Last Day and consider what they spend as bringing them nearer to God and obtaining the prayers of the Messenger. Truly they bring them nearer [to Him]; God will bring them into His mercy. (9:99)

> And it is not your wealth nor your children that bring you near to Us in degree, but only those who believe and *do good*, for such is a double reward for what they do, and they are secure in the highest places. (34:37)

The vision of the "face of God" refers to the intense mystical encounter obtained in the hereafter by those who attain the highest levels of spirituality and goodness. Here too the Qur'an connects this divine vision with our concern and responsibility towards others.

> So give what is due to kindred, the needy and the way-
> farer. That is best for those who seek the face of God, and
> it is these, they are the successful. (30:39)

As these verses show, virtuous acts augment faith and spirituality. More than acceptance of dogma or a state of spiritual consciousness, faith in Islam is comprehensive, an integrated outlook and way of living that incorporates all aspects of human nature and that increases with the level of giving and self-sacrifice.

> By no means shall you attain piety unless you give of that
> which you love. And whatever you give, God surely
> knows it. (3:92)

> Those who responded to the call of God and the
> Messenger after misfortune had befallen them—for such
> among them who do good and refrain from wrong is a
> great reward. Men said to them: surely people have gath-
> ered against you, so fear them; but this increased them in
> faith, and they said: God is sufficient for us and He is an
> excellent guardian. (3:172-173)

> When the believers saw the confederate forces, they
> said: "This is what God and His messenger had pro-
> mised us, and God and His messenger told us what was
> true." And it only increased them in faith and in sub-
> mission. (33:22)

Conversely, the spiritual experiences of faith should intensify one's commitment to goodness:

> And those who give what they give while their hearts are
> full of awe that to their Lord they must return—*These has-
> ten to every good work and they are foremost in them.*
> (23:60-61)

> The believers are those who, when God is mentioned,
> feel a tremor in their hearts, and when His messages are

recited to them they increase them in faith, and in their
Lord do they trust; who keep up prayer and *spend out of
what We have given them*. These, they are the believers
in truth. (82:3-4)

Doctrine, ethics, and spirituality overlap to such a degree in the Qur'an,
that they are frequently interwoven in its definitions of piety and belief.

Piety is not that you turn your faces towards the East or
West, but pious is the one who has faith in God, and the
Last Day, and the angels, and the scripture, and the messengers, and gives away wealth out of love for Him to the
near of kin and the orphans and the needy and the way-
farer and to those who ask and to set slaves free and keeps
up prayer and practices regular charity; and keep their
promises when they make a promise and are steadfast in
[times of] calamity, hardship and peril. These are they who
are true [in faith]. (2:177)

The sacrificial camels We have made for you as among
the symbols of God: in them is (much) good for you: then
pronounce the name of God over them as they line up (for
sacrifice). When they are down on their sides (after
slaughter), eat thereof and feed such as those who live in
contentment and such as beg in humility: thus have We
made animals subject to you that you may be grateful. It is
not their meat nor their blood that reaches God: It is your
piety that reaches Him. (22:36-37)

Prosperous are the believers, who are humble in their
prayers, and who shun what is vain, and who are active in
deeds of charity, and who restrain their sexual passions—
except with those joined to them in marriage, or whom
their right hands possess, for such are free from blame, but
whoever seeks to go beyond that, such are transgressors—
those who faithfully observe their trusts and covenants,
and who guard their prayers. (23:1-9)

The second passage refers to the day of sacrifice at the annual pilgrimage to Makkah. The pilgrimage is one of Islam's five ritual "pillars" and it
is, even today, perhaps the most physically demanding of all of them. It is

stunning in its religious imagery, emotion, and drama. And yet, here too, the Qur'an interconnects its social and spiritual benefits.

Non-Muslims are often surprised by the spirit of optimism and cele- bration that pervades Muslim rituals, especially during Ramadan (the month of fasting) and the pilgrimage, which they assume are performed mostly as atonement for past sins. Muslims, however, perceive their rituals positively—as spiritually and socially progressive. They understand them to be a challenge and an opportunity, as is life itself.

Islam means "surrender" or "submission," a giving up of resistance, an acquiescence to God's will, to His created order and to one's true nature. It is a lifelong endeavor and trial, an endless road that opens to boundless growth. It is a continuous pursuit that leads to ever greater degrees of peace and bliss through nearness to God. It engages all human faculties and its terms are unconditional. It seeks a voluntary commitment of body and mind, heart and soul. Its comprehensives may be brought to light by exam- ining one of the great questions of Christianity: "Is salvation obtained by faith or good works?"

First, the question needs to be rephrased, because it is unnatural to Muslims. Islam has known nothing similar to Christianity's soteriology. If a Muslim is asked: "How do you know you are saved?" he or she will likely respond: "From what or from whom?" Earthly life for Muslims is an opportunity, a challenge, a trial, not a punishment from which one must be rescued. In the Qur'an, all creation, knowingly or unknowingly, serves God's ultimate purposes. Thus it would not be obvious to a Muslim that we needed to be saved from some entity. Even Satan is stripped of his power in the Qur'an and reduced to the function of eternal tempter, a catalyst for ethical decision making and, hence, for moral and spiritual development. If anything, Muslims feel that they may need to be saved from themselves, from their own forgetfulness and unresponsiveness to God's many signs.

In a Muslim context, it would be more natural to ask, "How does one achieve *success* in this life: through faith or good works?" In consideration of what we have already observed, the answer becomes immediately obvi- ous: both are essential. Otherwise, human existence would not make sense and much of life would be superfluous. For the Muslim, such a question would be analogous to asking, "What element in water—hydrogen or oxy- gen—is necessary to quench one's thirst?"

Before considering what the Qur'an tells us about God, let us recapit- ulate. The Qur'an claims that man's earthly life is not a punishment and that it does not satisfy some whim of its creator. Rather, it is a stage in God's creative plan. Mankind has been endowed with a uniquely complex nature with contrary inclinations. Through the use of his/her faculties (intellectual, volitional, spiritual, moral, etc.) and the trials he or she is guaranteed to face, an individual will either grow in his or her relationship with God—or as the Qur'an says "in nearness to God"—or squander himself or herself in misdirected pursuits. The Qur'an asserts that this earthly life will indeed produce a segment of humanity that will experience and share in God's love; these are called in the Qur'an *Muslimun* (Muslims; literally, "those who surrender"), for they strive to submit themselves— heart, mind, body and soul—to this relationship. They are those who find peace, security, and trust in God and who do good and strive to set things right. To better understand how the lives we lead facilitate closer communion with God, we turn now to God in the Qur'an.

The Most Beautiful Names

The Qur'an presents two obverse portraits of God and His activity. On the one hand, He is transcendent and unfathomable. He is "sublimely exalted above anything that men may devise by way of definition" (6:100); "there is nothing like unto Him" (42:11); and "nothing can be compared to Him" (112:4). These statements warn of the limitations and pitfalls in using human language to describe God, especially such expressions as are commonly used to describe human nature and behavior, for man's tendency to literalize religious symbolism often leads to the fabrication of misguiding images of God. Nevertheless, the above statements serve only as cautions in the Qur'an, since it too, of necessity, contains such comparative descriptions. If we are to grow in intimacy with God, then we need to know Him, however approximately, in order to relate to Him, and toward this end speech is an obvious and indispensable tool.

Thus, in addition to declarations of God's complete incomparability, we find His various attributes mentioned on almost every page. Often used to punctuate passages, they occur typically in simple dual attributive statements, such as, "God is the Forgiving, the Compassionate" (4:129), "He is the All-Mighty, the Compassionate"(26:68), "God is the Hearing, the Seeing (17:1). Collectively, the Qur'an refers to these titles as *al asmaa al husnaa*, God's "most beautiful names" (7:180; 17:110; 20:8; 59:24).

Say: Call upon God, or call upon the Merciful, by which-

ever you call, to Him belong the most beautiful names.
(17:110)

God! There is no God but He. To Him belong the most
beautiful names. (20:8)

He is God, other than whom there is no other god. He
knows the unseen and the seen. He is the Merciful, The
Compassionate. He is God, other than whom there is no
other God; the Sovereign, the Holy One, the Source of
Peace, the Keeper of Faith, the Guardian, the Exalted in
Might, the Irresistible, the Supreme. Glory to God! Above
what they ascribe to Him. He is God, the Creator, the
Evolver, the Fashioner. To Him belong the most beautiful
names. Whatever is in the heavens and on earth glorifies
Him and He is exalted in Might, the Wise. (59:23-24)

The Divine Names are a ubiquitous element of Muslim daily life. They
are invoked at both the inception and completion of even the most common
tasks, appear in persons' names in the form of *Servant of the Merciful,
Servant of the Forgiving, Servant of the Loving,* etc., cried out in moments
of great joy and sorrow, murmured repeatedly at the completion of ritual
prayers, and chanted rhythmically in unison on various occasions. Because
Muslims insert them into conversations so frequently and effortlessly, some
outsiders have accused Muslims of empty formalism. But this reflects a
lack of understanding, for the truth is that the Divine Names play such an
integral role in the lives of the faithful that their use is entirely natural and
uninhibited.

The Divine Names are, for Muslims, a means of turning towards God's
infinite radiance. Through their recollection, believers attempt to unveil and
reorient their souls towards the ultimate source of all. A knowledge of them
is essential if one is to comprehend the relationship between God and man
as conceived in the Qur'an and as experienced by Muslims.

In his *Concordance of the Qur'an,*[17] Kassis renders in English most of
the titles and adjectives applied to God in the scripture, together with some
of their different shades of meaning. His list is not exhaustive. Other Qur'an
scholars have obtained longer lists and other possible meanings in English

---

[17] Hanna E. Kassis, *A Concordance of the Qur'an* (University of California Press,
1983).

could have been added, as it is hard to do justice to the Arabic original. For example, *rabb* which Kassis renders as "Lord," conveys the idea of "fostering," "sustaining," and "nourishing." According to the famous scholar of Arabic, al Raghib al Isfahani, it signifies "the fostering of a thing in such a manner as to make it attain one condition after another until it reaches its goal of completion."[18] Clearly, the word "Lord" does not bring out this idea. The following list of divine attributes is taken from Kassis.

Divine Names and Attributes:

Able (*qadir*); **Absolute** (*samad*); **One Who Answers** (*ajaaba*); **Aware** (*khabeer*); **Beneficent** (*rahmaan*); **Benign** (*barr*); **Bestower** (*wahhaab*); **Blameless** (*haasha*); **Bountiful** (*akrama, tawl*); **Clement** (*'afoow, haleem, ra'oof*); **Compassionate** (*raheem*); **Compeller** (*jabbaar*); **Creator** (*badee', bara'a, fatara, khalaqa, khallaq*); **Deliverer** (*fattaah*); **Disposer** (*wakeel*); **Embracing** (*wasi'a*); **Eternal** (*qayyoom, samad*); **Everlasting** (*qayyoom*); **Everlasting Refuge** (*samad*); **Evident** (*dhahara*); **Exalted** (*ta'aala*); **the Exalter** (*rafee'*); **Faithful** (*aamana*); **Fashioner** (*sawwara*); **First** (*awwal*); **Forgiver** (*ghaffaar, ghafuur*); *Gatherer* (*jama'a*); **Generous** (*kareem*); **Gentle** (*lateef, ra'oof*); **Giver** (*wahhaab*); **Glorious** (*'adheem, akrama, majeed*); **God** (*Allah, ilaah*); **Gracious** (*lateef, rahmaan*); **Grateful** (*shakara*); **Great** (*kabeer*); **Guardian** (*hafeedh, wakeel, waleey*); **Guide** (*had'a*); **He** (*huwa*); **Hearing** (*samee'*); **High** (*'aleey*); **Holy** (*quddoos*); **Honorable** (*akrama*); **Informed** (*khabeer*); **Inheritor** (*waritha*); **Inward** (*batana*); **Irresistible** (*jabbaar*); **Most Just Judge** (*hakama*); **Kind** (*lateef, ra'oof*); **King** (*malik, maleek*); **Knower** (*'aleem, 'alima, khabeer*); **Last** (*aakhir*); **Laudable** (*hameed*); **Light** (*nuur*); **Living** (*hayy*); **Lord** (*rabb*); **Loving** (*wadood*); **Majestic** (*jalaal, takabbara*); **Master of the Kingdom** (*malaka*); **Merciful** (*rahmaan*); **Mighty** (*'azeez, 'adheem*); **Omnipotent** (*iqtadara, qadeer, qahara, qahhaar*); **One** (*ahad, waahid*); **Originator** (*fatara*); **Outward** (*dhahara*); **Overseer** (*aqaata*); **Pardoner** (*'afoow*); **Peaceable** (*salaam*); **Powerful** (*qadira, qadeer, aqaata*); **Praiseworthy** (*hameed*); **Preserver** (*haymana*); **Protector** (*mawl'a, wala', waleey*); **Provider** (*razzaaq*); **Quickener** (*ahyaa*); **Reckoner** (*haseeb*); **Sagacious** (*khabeer*); **Seeing** (*baseer*); **Shaper** (*sawwara*); **Splendid** (*akrama*); **Strong** (*qaweey*); **Sublime** (*takabbara*); **Subtle** (*lateef*); **Sufficient** (*ghaneey, istaghn'a, kaf'a*); **Superb** (*takabbara*); **Sure** (*mateen*); **Tender** (*lateef*);

---

[18] Quoted by Ali, *The Holy Qur'an, Text, English Translation and Commentary.*

Thankful (*shakara, shakoor*); **True** (*haqq*); **Trustee** (*wakeel*), **one who Turns towards others** (*tawwaab*); **Watcher** (*raqeeb*); **Wise** (*hakeem*); **Witness** (*shaheed*).

There is great variance in the number of times these attributes are applied to God in the Qur'an. For example: God is called *Allah* (the God) approximately 2698 times, *Rabb* (Lord, the Sustainer) almost 900 times, *al Rahmaan* (the Merciful) 170 times, *al Raheem* (the Compassionate) 227 times, *al Ghaffaar* (the Forgiving) and *al Ghaffoor* (the Forgiving) a total of 97 times, and *al Lateef* (the Kind, the Gentle) 7 times. This repetition and variation have an important influence on Muslim religiosity. To appreciate this, one first needs to realize just how often a believer is in contact with the Qur'an.

A practicing Muslim will recite the Qur'an at the very least five times per day during his/her obligatory prayers. Many Muslims listen to the Qur'an on cassette tapes similar to the way westerners listen to music, very many read some portion of it daily for guidance and study, and a significant number have memorized it in its entirety. As they continue through the Qur'an, Muslims are constantly recalling the Divine Names and Attributes, which appear again and again on virtually every page. Through this continuous recollection, a certain spiritual vision or image of God writes itself on the Muslim heart and mind, with the more frequently mentioned attributes attaining a certain position of priority over those less frequently stated. If we were to attempt to visualize this effect, we might picture a pyramid of the Most Beautiful Names: *Allah* would be at the apex and then the attribute of *Rabb* (Nourisher, Sustainer, Lord) connected to and proceeding from Allah somewhat below; then the attributes of Mercy, *al Rahmaan* and *al Raheem*, further on down, proceeding from and manifesting the attributes above them, like rays of light flowing from a lamp; then Forgiveness, *al Ghafaar* and *al Ghafoor*, and Creator, *al Khallaaq*, proceeding from Mercy; and so on (see the diagram below).

In this way, a Muslim develops a completely immaterial conception of God; he or she approaches God through mind, heart, soul, feelings, and intuition, not through physical imagery. This, I feel, is the main source of Islam's famed iconoclasm. It is not a harsh fanaticism that has its roots in a culturally and artistically primitive desert community; it is a corollary to the way Muslims conceive of and relate to God through concepts that express intrinsic qualities and activities rather than through visual images. Thus we have the unique Muslim religious art of calligraphy, which does not consist of portraits and statues, but of words, often the Divine Names and Qur'anic

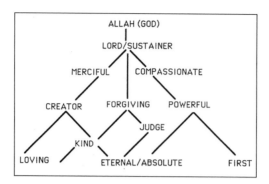

verses, beautifully and elegantly written and producing wondrous and intricate symmetries and designs that must be studied very carefully to decipher
the hidden meanings and discover the truth behind the beauty.

Another look at the Divine Names reveals a perplexity. Since the
names *al Rahmaan* (the Merciful), *al Raheem* (the Compassionate), *al
Rabb* (the Sustainer, Nourisher), *al Mawla/al Waleey* (the Protector,
Guardian), and *al Ghaffaar/al Ghafoor* (the Forgiving) appear so frequently, we would expect that the seemingly closely related name, *al Wadood*
(the Loving), would appear more than twice. If we include the large number of references to God's loving or withdrawing His love from others, then
we might feel it appropriate to increase this total. But on close examination
of such instances, we notice that God's love in the Qur'an is not universal,
and this is in fact what sets this attribute apart from the others just mentioned. His mercy, for example, embraces all creation and includes even
the worst sinners (7:156; 30:33; 30:36; 30:46; 40:7; 42:28), and His sustaining and nourishing extend to all. God is the only true protector of every
soul (2:107; 6:62; 10:30) and He immediately accepts all sincere repentance (4:110; 13:6 39:53). But when the Qur'an speaks of God's love, it is
pointing to a very special *relationship*, willfully entered into by God and
man, a relationship that the Qur'an says most of humanity will reject
(17:89; 25:50; 27:73). Although God's mercy, compassion, and care shine
on all mankind, only those who turn to Him and strive throughout their
lives to surrender themselves to Him will attain a bond of love with Him.
This love signifies a love shared—a love received and given—and a mutual involvement. Since relatively few will choose to enter into it, we should
probably not be at all surprised at the limited use of the name *al Wadood* in
the Qur'an, for while a loving relationship with God is available to everyone, most will not enter into one.

Let us turn again to the Divine Names, this time recalling our discussion of what Islam requires of man. As we make our way through the Qur'an, we are reminded persistently of the attributes of God and the qualities that we are supposed to cultivate in ourselves. It is not long before it dawns on us that there is considerable intersection between the two, for almost every virtue that we are to develop in ourselves through our actions toward others has its origin and perfection in God. For example, we are to grow in beneficence, benignity, bountifulness, clemency, compassion, faithfulness, our willingness to forgive, generosity, gentleness, givingness, graciousness, honorableness, justice, kindness, knowledge, love of others, mercy, peacefulness, protectiveness of the weak, truthfulness, trustworthiness, and wisdom. Yet, these originate in God as His attributes of perfection. Thus, by developing these attributes in ourselves, we are actually growing *nearer*—to use a Qur'anic term—to their infinite source. Hence, the more we come to possess these qualities, the more we may come to know God. Since it is possible for human beings to experience and acquire these virtues at higher levels than other creatures, they have the potential to relate to God in a uniquely intimate way.

An analogy may help elucidate this point. Assume that I have a pet gold fish, a dog, and three daughters. The gold fish, being the most limited in terms of intellect and growth, could only know and experience my love and compassion at a relatively low level no matter how much kindness I direct toward it. The dog, who is a more complex and intelligent animal than my fish, can feel warmth and affection for another on a much higher level and therefore can experience the love and compassion I shower on him to a much greater degree. Yet my daughters, as they mature, have the potential to feel the intensity of my love and caring for them on a plane that my dog could never conceive of, because they have the capacity to know first hand, through their own emotions and relationships, deeper and richer feelings than my dog. And I would have to say that the love I now have for my parents is greater than the love I had for them when I was a child, because by having children of my own, I came to better know and understand the power of the love my mother and father gave to me.

Pushing the above analogy a bit further, we see that it is not enough for my daughters to invest themselves only in other human relationships, as they will never experience the intensity of my feelings toward them unless they also acknowledge and turn to me as their father, that is, unless they accept and enter into that parent–child relationship. I could have all the fatherly feelings for them in the world, but if by some strange set of circumstances they totally rejected or were oblivious of them, then they would never enter into a relationship of love with me. All the caring and kindness I had for them would be of little benefit to them. This, I believe, is why the Qur'an insists on both faith in God and good works toward our fellow man, because both are necessary if we are to come to know God. If an atheist is a great humanitarian, he may gain the love and admiration of neighbors and friends and perhaps great self-satisfaction and meaning in life, but he will still be spiritually empty. I am not insisting that such a person would be destined for eternal suffering, for that would depend on factors that are impossible for us to know or measure, such as his personal limitations, the environment in which he lived, the opportunities that were presented to him, and many others. However, the purpose of the Qur'an is not to discuss such precarious, borderline cases as possible options; it guides toward what will most benefit man and warns of what will destroy him.

"Every soul must taste of death; then to Us you will be returned" (29:57). This truth reverberates throughout the Qur'an. It reminds the reader that the end and purpose of all earthly endeavor is this reunion. Ultimately, it is our relationship with God that matters. However, it would be wrong to say that it is all that matters, for, as we discovered, our relationship with God is bound intimately to our responses to our fellow man. Rituals, inspiration, contemplation, and remembrance (3:191; 4:103) all play integral parts in bringing us nearer to God, but so does our growth in virtue. The more a believer grows in the attributes that originate in God, the closer and more intense is his/her bond with Him and the greater is his/her capacity to receive and experience His infinite beauty and power, both in this life, and incomparably more so in the next life, where earthly distractions and masks are removed.

This is much more than having our own personal experiences of goodness to approximate God's transcendent goodness; it involves a kind of intimacy and knowing that cannot even be shared by two human beings. There is the well-known expression, "In order to begin to understand me, you have to walk a mile in my shoes." This means that we cannot truly know another person unless we could somehow fully enter into his life and experience it from his personal perspective. As this is not really possible—since we are always, in a sense, outside that experience—the implication is that we are very limited in our ability to sympathize with others. Certainly, we can never fully know God, but yet we can experience His being in a uniquely profound way.

The Prophet once told his companions that one percent of the mercy that God bestows on creation is manifested in human behavior.[19] The saying is meant to impress upon us the greatness of God's mercy. However, it also indicates that the mercy we demonstrate and feel is but an infinitesimal fragment of God's limitless mercy. Thus, God grants us the ability to participate in and experience His mercy firsthand in our earthly lives, not only as recipients, but as givers of mercy as well, for when we are merciful toward another creature, that being receives something of God's mercy through us.

The same holds for almost all of the other Most Beautiful Names of God: if we are truthful, we are experiencing a fraction of the truth that comes from God; if we attain wisdom, all wisdom flows from God; if we obtain power, there is no power but in God. A mother participates in creation on a level that will always be a mystery to men, and hence her experience of the attribute of Creator is especially profound. Perhaps the same can be said of her experience of the Merciful and the Compassionate. Many ancient Muslim scholars felt that the female is more sensitive to certain divine attributes than the male and conversely. Such names as the Powerful, the Protector, the Provider, were believed to be more suited to the male.

The Qur'an informs us that God breathes something of His spirit into every human soul (32:9). This seems to indicate that every human has a seed of the Divine Attributes within him/her or, in other words, that the virtues he/she experiences are but a breath of the Divine Names. The concept, that the more one pursues virtue the greater becomes his or her capacity to experience the divine, is brought to light by the saying of Muhammad that asserts that the more a believer persists in worship and doing good, the clearer his heart becomes so that it is better able to receive the divine light, and that if someone is negligent in these, his heart becomes rusted and incapable of receiving divine illumination.[20] The goal of the devout Muslim is to grow continually as a receiver and transmitter of God's infinite radiance, to be drawn ever nearer to the source of all that is beautiful, to accept the office of delegate of the Possessor of the Most Beautiful Names, and, hence, to serve as a *khalifah* (vicar) of God on earth as described in 2:30.

It appears that we have returned to where we first started. This entire discussion of the purpose of life in the Qur'an was launched by the story of

---

[19] From *Sahih al Bukhari* and *Sahih Muslim* as translated in *Riyad as Salihin* of Imam Nawawi, 94.

[20] From Ibn Majah and Tirmidhi as translated in Mazhar U. Kazi, *Guidance from the Messenger* (Jamaica, NY: ICNA Publications, 1990), 84.

man as told in verses thirty through thirty-nine of the second *surah*. One might assume that it began with the angels' question and, hence, with a doubt or criticism, but this would be an oversight. In fact, our investigation was inspired by an astounding affirmation that was so positive and optimistic that the angels' question had to be raised: "Behold, your Lord said to the angels: 'I am going to place a vicegerent on earth.'"

How can man, this most destructive and corruptible creature, serve as a deputy and representative of God? Of all beings, how can man act as an agent and emissary of his Lord? Human history and human nature seem to be at odds with this election. But when we look at mankind from this viewpoint, we, like the angels, are seeing only one side of reality and are neglecting man's potential for goodness and self-sacrifice as well as his ability to strive to live by the highest standards of virtue. Every person has it within himself to receive, represent, and impart to others the mercy, compassion, justice, truth, bounty, and love that originate in God and thus to act in this way as His emissary on earth. The Qur'an maintains that human nature contains this inclination and potential (30:30), but it requires a choice that must be faced continually and remade. The office of *khalifah* is not simply conferred; it must be accepted voluntarily and it must be a lifelong commitment. The Qur'an does not ask for human perfection, but rather asks that we persevere in striving for self-improvement and that we never become complacent (2:197; 5:2; 7:26) or despondent (15:56; 39:53; 15:55) about our progress.

First Objection

It may be that the Qur'an's concept of life has a certain appeal and coherence. However, let us not allow ourselves to be romanced into accepting it. The idea that growth in virtue leads to inner peace and well-being, and that it contributes an abiding beauty to life, is easy to admit. The notion that it also allows us to receive and experience God's infinite attributes to ever greater degrees is sensible. Yet, is there not an obvious and glaring problem with this conception? Cannot this divine plan be charged with gross inefficiency? Why did not God simply create us with these virtues from the start? Why did He not program mercy, truthfulness, compassion, kindness, and the rest into us and bypass this earthly stage in our existence? Thus, we never really got beyond the angels' question: Why not make man someone greater than he is—someone like the angels?

To answer this, we need not search far, but only have to look within our own selves. If we know nothing else of the virtues under consideration, we certainly know they cannot exist in a being at very high levels if they were merely programmed into it. Virtue, if programmed, is not true virtue as we conceive of it, but something less. We can program a computer to be always correct, but we could not describe it as a truthful computer. We do not consider a stethoscope to be merciful although it aids the sick. The Qur'an presents angels as creatures without free will, but man can rise to heights much higher or sink to depths much lower than them.

Virtues are abstract concepts and difficult to define, but I believe that we can agree that to grow in virtue at least three things are needed: *Free will*, or the ability to choose; *intellect*, so that one is able to weigh the consequences of his or her choices and learn from them; and third, and equally important, *suffering and hardship*. As we saw, the Qur'an emphasizes strongly all three of these while discussing man's spiritual evolution. To grow in compassion, for example, is inconceivable without suffering. It also requires choice, the ability to choose to reach out to someone in need or to ignore him. Intellect is necessary so that one can estimate how much of oneself will be invested in showing compassion to the sufferer. Similarly, to be truthful involves a choice not to lie and is heightened when telling the truth may lead to personal loss and suffering, which can be predicted through the use of one's reason.

How often do we hear in plays, movies, and songs statements like, "You never really loved me, because when I was down and out and my life was falling apart you only thought of yourself and you left me!" Such a statement acknowledges the essential roles of hardship, choice, and intellect in love. The same could be said of the famous wedding vow that asks two people if they are ready to commit themselves to each other "for richer or poorer, in sickness and in health, until death." It is the same with all the virtues: these three elements are crucial to our growth in them.

When my oldest daughter, Jameelah, was a baby, she became very ill one night. The only way I could get her to sleep was to carry her on my shoulder while I paced the apartment and sang softly to her. If I stopped singing or tried to put her down, she would immediately wake up crying. So all night long, about eight straight hours, I carried my little girl and kept on singing. Her fever broke around dawn and she was then able to sleep on her own. Of course, by this time I was exhausted. My back was killing me, my throat was hoarse, and I had to be at work in an hour.

When I recently recalled this episode for her, Jameelah asked me, "Weren't you mad at me, daddy?"

I was surprised by her question, because the feeling never at any moment that night entered my heart.

"Mad at you!" I told her: "Sweetheart, I couldn't have loved you more! It is a memory that I will always cherish."

Love, compassion, and caring are born of such experiences. They have a beauty and value that is, to use an expression of the Prophet, "worth more than this world and all it contains."[21] They also frequently contain opportunities for healing previous wounds and recovering past losses.

Sarah, my second daughter, broke her leg when she was only a year old, and I had to stay that night with her in the hospital. She came so quickly after Jameelah—only a year separates them—and my work load at the university had increased so much, that I had spent hardly any time with Sarah until then. When Jameelah was a baby we were inseparable, but now a year had past in Sarah's life and I hardly knew her.

Sarah gripped my hand through the night; if I let go of it she would scream. The muscle spasms in her leg were keeping her awake. I had to lean over her bed rail to reach her hand and the rail was digging into my side. It was another sleepless, uncomfortable night.

As I watched this little child fight and struggle through the hours with her pain, I discovered Sarah for the first time. As I gazed into her big brown eyes and studied her expressions and reactions to my touch and my voice, I found how much this child and I were alike—how similar our personalities were. I was so ashamed that I had not taken the time before this to get to know her and I realized how much I had lost and how much we both needed each other. I vowed that evening to begin to work on my relationships with all my children and not to wait for crises to bring us together.

These incidents were two minor trials in my life from which I learned so much. I wonder how much greater must be the experience of motherhood, for if I could gain so much benefit from these two moments, how much greater must be the potential personal gain from carrying a child for nine months? Perhaps this is why the Prophet Muhammad told his companions that motherhood puts paradise at a woman's feet.

---

[21] An expression used frequently by Prophet Muhammad. See *Riyad as Salihin* of Imam Nawawi, 221-22.

It also helps me understand why Islam places so much emphasis on family ties, since these relationships are for us the most intense and demanding and thus provide some of the most important opportunities for personal growth. The Prophet stated that "marriage is half of faith," since men and women only attain the fullness of their personalities as spouses and parents. Consider also the verse in the Qur'an that states that marriage provides spouses with a special way to experience love and mercy and that we should reflect on this most important sign:

> And among His signs is this, that He created for you spouses from among yourselves, that you may dwell in tranquillity with them, and he has placed love and mercy between you. Truly in that are signs for those who reflect. (30:21)

As parents and as children, we may experience the widest range of the Divine Names as givers and receivers, respectively. When we attain middle age and are simultaneously parent and child, we reach a point in our lives that allows us to learn of God through both perspectives. The following two passages highlight this stage in our lives.

> Your Lord has decreed that you worship none but Him, and that you be kind to parents. Whether one or both of them attain old age in your life, never say to them even "Uff!" (a minor expression of contempt) nor repel them, but address them in terms of honor. And out of kindness, lower to them the wing of humility and say, "My Lord! have mercy on them even as they cherished me when I was a little one." (17:23-24)

> We have enjoined on mankind kindness towards parents. In pain did his mother bear him and in pain did she give him birth. The carrying of the [child] to his weaning is thirty months. At length when he is fully grown and attains forty years he says, "O my Lord! Grant me that I may be grateful for the favor which You have bestowed upon me, and upon both my parents, and that I may work righteousness such as You may approve; and be gracious to me in my children. Truly I have turned to You and truly I do bow in Islam. (46:15)

The first of the above passages links worship of God with kindness toward parents. It recalls their care and tenderness, their self-sacrifice is clearly implied, and thus they deserve our utmost respect. The second passage shows that honoring one's parents is an expression of gratitude toward God. It especially honors the mother's role because of the greater degree of pain and suffering she goes through in raising children.

Islam sees a unity and harmony between body, mind and soul, and unifying principles that govern all three. Coaches often tell athletes "no pain, no gain," by which they mean that in order to develop our physical strengths, we must be willing to suffer. Teachers inform students that they must work hard in order to grow intellectually. Muslims understand that the same law applies to spiritual development. Moral and spiritual growth requires the discipline of one's will, the use and development of one's mind, and the experience of hardship and suffering. The last of these should never discourage the Muslim, for the Prophet told his followers that a believer should always thank God in good times and in hard times, because he or she can benefit from both.[22]

Second Objection

Let us agree that virtues, like love, compassion, truthfulness, and kindness, are not programmable and, furthermore, that in order to grow in these qualities we must possess the ability to choose and to reason and that we need to face adversity. Is there not then an obvious counter-example? Does or did God grow in these qualities? Does He weigh and choose between alternatives? Does He need to reason things out? Did He have to learn these attributes? Can He experience suffering?

This objection confuses creator with creature and bestower with receiver. God, the Creator, is described as eternal, absolute, perfect, transcending time and space. He is not diminished nor improved by His activity. He is the continuous source and preserver of all existence. His Most Beautiful Names indicate that He is the perfect and only real source of the attributes in which we must increase our capacity to receive and experience. He is the absolute source of all the mercy, compassion, wisdom, truth, etc., that flows through creation.

Man as a creature, by definition, becomes. He experiences growth and decline. Creation, according to the Qur'an, passes from one state into another (13:5; 28:88; 32:10). Hence man, in particular, is a changeable being.

---

[22] From *Sahih Muslim* as translated in Kazi, *Guidance from the Messenger*, 151-52.

The fact that God is not is a Qur'anic axiom (33:62; 35:63). God is the sole origin of—the explanation behind—all virtue, as His being accounts for its very existence. He does not grow in His ability to experience mercy; He provides the mercy in which we share. He does not increase in wisdom; He guides us to the wisdom that originates in Him. He does not develop His power; He empowers others. Far from providing a counter-argument, His being accounts for the attributes that we are to pursue.

To Live and Learn

We have seen how the Qur'an underscores the learning ability of man and the instructional value of life in human moral and spiritual growth. That man will err along the way in his choices is inevitable, but God, in the Qur'an, does not expect us to be infallible; instead, He has granted us the ability to learn and gain from our mistakes. The Qur'an warns of the dangers of sin but also explains that if someone realizes his errors, repents, and believes and does good thereafter, God transforms his once-destructive deeds into beneficial ones.

> He who repents and believes and does good; for such God
> changes their evil deeds to good ones. And God is ever
> Forgiving and Merciful. (25:70)

This verse seems to include the notion of the positive value of our acknowledged and amended errors. It is certainly good to avoid an evil solely out of obedience, but if one has also experienced personally its destructive and painful consequences, the wisdom and benefit behind its avoidance become inculcated in his heart and mind. It is like the child who avoids the kitchen stove after having been burned by it: he is no longer simply obeying his parents but is avoiding what he knows intrinsically to be harmful.

The Qur'an describes how even God's elect grew from past errors: Abraham discovers monotheism through a sequence of mistaken attempts (6:75-82); Moses commits involuntary manslaughter but repents and learns from it (28:15-19); and David is taught an important lesson that helps him realize a past wrong (38:21-26). The Qur'an's several criticisms of Prophet Muhammad are clearly meant to instruct him and his community.

God does not require us to become perfect before admitting us into His grace. Rather, the more we grow in goodness and in faith, the more we avail ourselves of it—the more our hearts become opened to receiving it. This is the lifelong effort of the believer: to refine his spirituality and thus to enter into an ever more intimate relationship with God. As long as we are alive, our personal growth has no reachable upper limit, for we can never reach a stage at which we can no longer gain from doing good. A Muslim believes that no good deed is superfluous. No matter how small it is, it will benefit him in this life and the next.

> Then anyone who has done a speck of good, will see it. And
> anyone who has done a speck of evil will see it. (99:7-8)

In the Qur'an, God does not seek to bar men and women from His grace; He desires to guide them to it and He pursues them incessantly and aggressively. He invites, reminds, challenges, argues, shames, entices, and threatens. He inflicts calamities upon the sinful so that "perhaps they will return [to God]" (7:168; 30:41; 32:21, 43:28).

To those won over to its calling, the Qur'an provides much of what may be termed practical spiritual advice. First of all, one should avoid the heinous sins (murder, adultery, cheating the poor, etc.). In conjunction with faith in God, this will insure paradise in the next life.

> If you avoid the great sins of the things which are forbid-
> den you, We shall expel out of you all the evil in you, and
> admit you to the gate of great honor. (4:31)

> That which is with God is better and more lasting for those
> who believe and put their trust in their Lord; those who
> avoid the great sins and indecencies and when they are
> angry even then forgive. (42:36-37)

> Those who avoid great sins and indecencies, only [falling
> into] small faults—truly your Lord is ample in forgive-
> ness. (53:32)

After repentance, one should try to make amends in order to guard against a spiritual decline. In the same vein, the Qur'an states that good deeds offset evil ones (11:114; 13:22; 28:54). The idea here seems to be that if we take a step backward, we should try to counter it immediately by taking several steps forward so as not to lose progress. A key related eschatological symbol is that of the Balance on the Day of Judgment, which will weigh a person's good deeds against his evil ones. If the former outweigh the latter—if the individual is essentially a good person—then he or she will enter eternal bliss. We should keep in mind, however, that God has made it so that the positive rewards of righteousness far outweigh the negative consequences of wrongdoing (28:84; 40:40).

All this may seem too empirical, since it is impossible for us to detect precisely and accurately measure our good and sinful doings. However, the Qur'an is not providing an exact science of spiritual growth, but rather a helpful conceptual model. The Muslim is the first to admit his utter dependence on and trust in God's mercy and kindness, for he knows that he is on earth for a purpose. This conceptualization helps him to pursue it, even if it is not entirely clear to him what life's purpose is or has never agonized over its meaning.

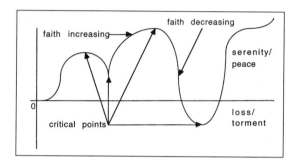

Muslims say that if your faith is not increasing, then it is about to decrease or else it already has. If we were able to plot a person's spiritual growth against time, a Muslim would envision it as a continuous curve that, at any point, is either ascending, descending or at a critical turning point. According to this perspective, faith is not a steady state. A believer must be on guard against unwittingly slipping into a downward slope, and so he must always review the current state of his religiosity.

"How is your faith?" One Muslim will ask another. There is no precise measure, but there are a number of diagnostic checks that may help: "Do I feel closer to or farther from God in my five daily prayers lately?"; "Am I giving more or less in charity these days?"; "Was I at greater or lesser peace with myself and with others in the past?" With such self-analysis a Muslim hopes to stay on what the Qur'an describes as "the uphill climb" (90:11).

> Surely he thought that he would never return (to God). But surely his Lord is ever Seer of him. But no, I call to witness the sunset redness, and the night and that which it drives on, and the moon when it grows full, you will certainly travel stage after stage. But what is the matter with them that they believe not? (84:14-20)

Trial and Error

Life is often described as a great classroom—the ultimate learning environment. This description accords well with the Qur'an. As the best of all teachers, God not only provides us with the essential tools for learning but guides us to learn and grow through personal discovery as well. Thus the Qur'an states that God "taught [mankind] by the pen—taught man that which he did not know" (96:4-5), even though man's acquisition of reading and writing skills was a slow and gradual human development, one in which God's influence is easily missed. So subtle and effective is God's teaching that man often attributes his intellectual achievements entirely to himself. So the Qur'an continues:

> No, but man is overbold, in that he views himself as independent. (96:6-7)

Earthly life provides us with a sense—a false one actually—of independence of and distance from God, a sense that drives us to learn and apply what we learn seemingly on our own. This is somewhat like when a teacher leaves the classroom and then watches through a one-way mirror to see how his students interact when faced with solving problems: no longer able to appeal to their teacher, the pupils are forced to solve the problems independently, while all the while the teacher monitors their progress and intercedes only when he deems it necessary. This is an extremely effective teaching device, for there is no substitute for first-hand experience.

In such a setting, one of the principle ways in which we learn is through trial and error. When I speak of trial and error here, I am referring not only to tests and mistakes we meet with on the intellectual plane, but also on the moral and spiritual plane, although the two overlap and are complementary. When a mistake we make has moral implications, it becomes a sin, the gravity and harm of which increases with our awareness of its wrongfulness (4:17-18). But if we repent and avoid it thereafter, it could, as we have seen, assist our spiritual growth. Thus we can learn and grow from our mistakes. Without the potential for error, realization, and reform, our spirituality would stagnate. So vital are these to our development in this earthly stage that the Prophet Muhammad reported that if mankind ceased sinning, God would replace them with other creatures who would continue to sin and repent and gain God's forgiveness.[23]

---

[23] Ibid., 95.

Earthly trial is another key ingredient of the divine scheme: "We will try you with something of fear" (2:155), "God tests what is in your hearts" (3:154), "You shall surely be tried in your possessions" (3:186), "He tests you in what He has given you: so strive as in a race in all virtues" (5:51), "O believers, God will surely test you" (5:97), "We try you with evil and good" (21:35), "He may try some of you by means of others" (47:4). The Qur'an states that God created the entire cosmos in order to test mankind (11:7) and that God created death and life on earth to the same end (67:2). Since these tests can not improve God, they must be for our intellectual and spiritual refinement, and therefore the universe and our existence in it are designed to produce this testing and learning opportunity.

The Day of Judgment (1:4) is depicted as the moment when the results of our efforts are realized. The Qur'an's depiction of it has an unmistakable academic tone. It resembles the end of term or graduation day on a college campus. Mankind will be sorted out into three classes (56:7-56): The Foremost in Faith, those who excelled in their submission to God and are brought nearest to Him; the Companions of the Right Hand, those who did well enough on earth to enter paradise but who do not reach the level of excellence of the Foremost in Faith; and the Companions of the Left Hand, those who failed in life and who face suffering in the life to come. The record of all deeds, however small or great, will be brought out. The sinful will be in great terror this moment as they sense their fate (18:49). The faces of those who failed in life will be humiliated, laboring, and weary, while those who were successful will have joyful, exuberant faces (88:1-16). The successful will receive their earthly records in their right hands and will gleefully show them to others; the failures, consumed by grief and embarrassment, will be given their records in their left hands or will hold them behind their backs (69:19-30; 89:10). When awarded their records in their right hands, the successful will ecstatically run to show them to their families, but the failures will cry out miserably (89:7-11).

These descriptions have penetrated deeply into the consciousness of Muslims, who frequently draw comparisons between life and preparation for an exam. While this imagery lends itself to the most sophisticated and most naive understandings, every Muslim apprehends at least this much: Life presents us with a continual series of tests and our overall success or failure in responding to them will translate either into a state of happiness or suffering in the life to come. It supports the view that earthly life is an educational and developmental stage in our creation.

Sin as Self-Destruction

If the purpose of life is to grow in the virtues that reach their perfection in God so that we may receive and experience His attributes to ever greater degrees—to grow nearer to God in this sense—and if virtuous deeds promote this growth and evil deeds undermine it, then it would follow, as we have already observed, that the one who stands to gain or lose the most from a good or evil act is its doer. This idea is stated explicitly in many places in the Qur'an. Recall, for example:

> Taste suffering through fire in return for what your own hands have wrought—for never does God do the least wrong to His creatures. (3:182; 8:51)

> Enlightenment has come from your God; he who sees does so to his own good, he who is blind is so to his own [hurt]. (6:104)

> And whosoever is guided, is only (guided) to his own gain, and if any stray, say: "I am only a warner." (27:92)

> And if any strive, they do so for their own selves: For God is free of all need from creation. (29:6)

> We have revealed to you the book with the truth for mankind. He who lets himself be guided does so to his own good; he who goes astray does so to his own hurt. (39:41) (Also see 10:108; 17:15; 27:92)

The statements in the Qur'an and in the traditions of the Prophet that state that an evildoer's heart (his spiritual and moral sense) becomes dark, veiled, rusted, hard, and hence impenetrable, and that the hearts of the virtuous become soft, sensitive, and receptive to God's guiding light, immediately come to mind.[24] The verses in the Qur'an that convey this idea most powerfully are those that assert that the sinners destroy themselves by their wrongdoing—that they commit *zulm* (sin, wrong, harm, injustice, oppression) against themselves.

> To Us they did no harm, but they only did harm to themselves. (2:57; 7:160)

---

[24] See note 20 and, for example, 2:74; 5:13; 9:87; 18:57; 22:46; 22:54; 26:89; 33:53; 39:23; 64:11; and 83:14.

> If any transgress the limits ordained by God, then these,
> they wrong themselves. (2:229; 65:1)

> And God did not wrong them, but they wronged them-
> selves. (3:117)

> And so it was not God who wronged them, it was they
> who wronged themselves. (9:70; 16:33; 29:40; 30:9)

> It was not We that wronged them: They wronged their
> own selves. (11:101)

> Oh My servants who have sinned against yourselves,
> never despair of God's mercy. Surely God forgives all
> sins. (39:54)

Therefore sin, in reality, is a form of self-destruction. When we commit it, we oppress and do injustice to ourselves, for we bar ourselves from
spiritual progress and deprive ourselves of that which has real and lasting
worth. As we saw earlier, and as the last verse (39:54) indicates, the damage from wrongdoing does not have to be permanent, for the way to
reform is open. Personal reform involves repentance and making amends,
yet we should not lose sight of the most important element of all: God's
forgiveness.

When God forgives, He does much more than ignore or efface our sins.
He responds to our repentance and comes to our aid (3:30), He helps us
repair the harm that we inflicted upon ourselves (33:71), and guides us to
spiritual restoration (57:28). In the Qur'an, the Divine Name "the Forgiving" is almost always paired with "the Compassionate," and thus God's forgiveness involves embracing the penitent with His compassion, which
soothes the self-inflicted wounds. The verb *tawbah* (to turn toward) from
the root *TWB*, brings out the chemistry between repentance and forgiveness, for it is used with various prepositions to describe both in the Qur'an.
When we repent, we *turn toward* God in repentance, seeking His mercy
and help, and He then turns *toward us* in His mercy, kindness, and forgiveness. Thus God is described as *al Tawwaab*, the one who turns toward
others. God's forgiveness is His personal response to the sinner, as in the
saying of the Prophet which was quoted above: when we go toward God
walking, He comes toward us running.

The initiative, however, must come from the sinner. The first step
toward reform is the admission of wrongdoing, for we have to realize

and acknowledge the wrongfulness of our behavior and admit our need for God's help in order to begin our recovery. This is similar to what Alcoholics Anonymous counselors tell the desperate families of drug addicts: Unless the addict admits that he has a problem and needs help, no one can reform him. Sincerity is the key here. Recuperation from sin is often a hard and painful process assisted by God's forgiving involvement. It means starting over, going through the pains of growth again, and entails work and effort. It is not a singular moment or formula that repairs us, but our honest commitment to turn our lives around and better ourselves. Thus the Qur'an states that repentance at the last moment of life in order to escape suffering in the next is ineffectual, because it is not motivated by a sincere desire to reform and there is no time left for self-betterment.

> And repentance is not for those who go on doing evil deeds, until when death comes to one of them, he says: Now I repent; nor for those who die while they are ungrateful rejectors [of God]. For such we prepared a great chastisement (4:18).

Pharaoh provides the archetypal case:

> And We brought the Children of Israel across the sea. Then Pharaoh and his hosts followed them for oppression and tyranny, till, when drowning overtook him, he cried: I believe that there is no god but He in whom the Children of Israel believe, and I am of those who submit! What! Now! And indeed before this you rebelled and caused depravity! (10:90-91)

Not only is such last-second repentance vain and illustrative of a complete lack of understanding of the purpose of life and of repentance, but it incriminates the sinner all the more, because it proves that he was always conscious of the existence of God, or at least of the possibility of His existence, but preferred to live a selfish and destructive life rather than seek a relationship with Him.

Three Signs

> And indeed He has created you by various stages. (71:14)

The Qur'an presents three related analogies which have a bearing on the meaning of human earthly existence. These are the *life in the womb–life on earth*, *birth–resurrection*, and *death–sleep* analogies.

Life in the womb–Life on earth

The Qur'an parallels two stages in our creation: our prenatal development and our maturation after birth.

> Then certainly We create man of an extract of clay, then We place him as a small quantity (of sperm) in a safe place firmly established, then We make the small quantity into a tiny thing that clings, then We make the tiny thing that clings into a chewed lump of flesh, then We fashioned the chewed flesh into bones and clothed the bones with intact flesh, then We cause it to grow into another creation. So blessed be God, the best of creators! Then after that you certainly die. Then on the Day of Resurrection you will surely be raised up. (23:12-16)

> O people, if you are in doubt about the Resurrection, then surely We create you from dust, then a small quantity (of sperm), then from a tiny thing that clings, then from a chewed lump of flesh, complete in make and incomplete, that We may make clear to you. And We cause what We please to remain in the wombs until an appointed time, then We bring you forth as babies, then after that you grow to maturity. (22:5) (Also see 40:67.)

> Does man think that he will be left aimless? Was he not a small quantity (of sperm) emitted? Then he was a tiny thing that clings (in the womb), and then He created (him), and then made him perfect. (75:36-38)

This parallel leads to a number of important insights. While our prenatal growth is primarily physical, our earthly development is principally moral and spiritual. As our birth into this life fully manifests our physical maturation in the womb, our resurrection into the next life fully manifests our current spiritual maturation in an analogously objective way. Thus we find symbolic descriptions of the Day of Judgment that indicate that our moral and spiritual doings on earth will be manifested by our very being in the next. Our deeds will be fastened to our necks (17:13; 34:33; 36:8).

Our tongues, hands, and feet will bear witness to our doings (24:24; 36:65). We will eat the fruits of our deeds (37:39-68). The spiritually blind in this life will be raised without vision in the next (17:72). Those who lived in God's light in this life will have their lights shine before them on the Day of Resurrection (57:12; 66:8). Every deed of ours will show its effect (99:7-8).

It is important to note that our creation is not presented as a single moment in time, but as one that proceeds in stages. Our physical development in the womb prepares us for our spiritual growth in the next stage, which will determine the state of our being as we enter the hereafter. Will there be opportunities for further growth in the next life? Perhaps, for the Qur'an has the believers in heaven ask God to "perfect for us our light" (66:8).

A popular American saying states that "you are what you eat." In other words, one's diet greatly affects his or her physical well-being. A Muslim might extend this to two more general truisms: "What you do in this life determines what type of person you are," and, "in the next life on the Day of Resurrection, you will be according to what you do right now."

Birth–Resurrection

> And people say: When I am dead, shall I truly be brought
> forth alive? Does not man remember that we created him
> before, when he was nothing? (19:66-67)

The Qur'an contains an interesting reference to the two deaths which we all experience:

> They say: Our Lord, twice you made us die, and twice you
> gave us life, so we confess our sins. (40:11)

Some Qur'an exegetes felt that the first death corresponds to the termination of non-existence at conception, but this is a strained interpretation, since a death must naturally be preceded by a life. Others believed that the first death represented the termination of life in the womb at the moment of birth. This explanation seems much more plausible, especially in light of the verses we just considered and from what embryologists now know about the vast differences between pre- and post-natal existence. (Even our circulatory system reverses itself seconds after birth!) The latter viewpoint also complements the last parallel, for both deaths are transitions to other levels of existence that are tied to our previous developments.

Both stages of development—in the womb and in life—and the corresponding ends of these stages involve pain and suffering. A mother definitely experiences pain and suffering during pregnancy and intense pain during birth. The fetus also experiences times of discomfort in the womb and certainly undergoes great hardship at birth.

What I find remarkable is that only minutes after the birth, the mother, and even much more so the child, appear to forget the tremendous agony that they have just endured. I recall how exhausted and drained I was after each of my daughters' births and yet how quickly my wife and daughters recovered, even though their suffering was incredibly more severe. My children appeared to have no recollection or after effects from the ordeal. Perhaps there is a sign in this concerning those who enter a state of paradise in the next life. Will all their earthly agony and hardship suddenly seem to them like an illusion, a dream, even though it was all very real? The next parallel we consider suggests that this may be so.

Death–Sleep

> God takes souls at the time of their death, and those that do not die, during their sleep. Then He withholds those on whom has passed the decree of death and sends the others back till an appointed term. Truly there are signs in this for a people who reflect. (39:42)

The Resurrection moment, as pictured in the Qur'an, is very much an arousal from a deep slumber. A trumpet blast will awaken the dead (6:73). The disbelievers will rush from their graves, which the Qur'an refers to as their "sleeping places," in terror. People will be groggy and swoon (39:68). They will be disoriented. Their earthly lives will seem like an illusion (27:88). There will be mass confusion over the time spent on earth: to some it will seem like ten days and to others like a day or even less (20:103-104; 23:113), just like when one recollects a dream, details will be very hazy. Peoples' sight will be confused, like when one arises from sleep (75:7), and then their vision will sharpen and they will have a keen grasp of reality (50:20). The righteous appear to have only faint recollection of their earthly struggles, and the damned have only faint recollection of their earthly pleasures. A well-known saying of Muhammad states that if one of the faithful is immersed in Paradise and is then asked about all his suffering on earth, he will not be able to recall any of it, and if one of the sinful is immersed in Hell and then is asked about all his earthly pleasures, he will not remember any of them.[25]

Hence our lives on earth will seem like a dream. All the pain, struggle, and agony, which appeared so hard and enduring, will be no more than a vague, distant, brief memory, something like when one awakens from a nightmare. A bad dream is very real while we are experiencing it, but when we awake, we feel immediate relief because we are now conscious of a greater reality. It seems that the resurrection of the righteous will be a somewhat similar but more intense experience. Our earthly lives are not dreams nor illusions; what we experience is very real and the consequences of our deeds will become marked upon our souls—written and recorded upon our being—but, by the mercy of God, the hardships true believers endured will be erased from their recollection (35:35). Like the newborn child, their previous existence is forgotten, although they carry with them into the next life their earlier development.

"Except That They Should Worship Me!"

> Say: Truly my prayer and my sacrifice and my living and
> my dying-all belong to God, the Lord of the worlds. (6:163)

Islam's concept of worship complements its view of life. I recall a conversation I had not long ago with a friend who asked me how Muslims worship. I told her that we go to work to provide for our families, attend school functions that our children are involved in, take a few pieces of cake we just baked over to our neighbor next door, drive our children to school in the morning.

"No! No!" She said. "How do you worship?"

I said we make love to our spouses, smile and greet someone we pass on the street, help our children with their homework, hold open a door for someone behind us.

"Worship! I'm asking about worship!" She exclaimed.

I asked her exactly what she had in mind.

"You know—Rituals!" She insisted.

I answered her that we practice those also and that they are a very important part of Muslim worship. I was not trying to frustrate her, but I

---

[25] From *Sahih Muslim* as translated in *Riyad as Salihin* of Imam Nawawi, 103.

answered her in this way in order to emphasize Islam's comprehensive conception of worship.

A famous tradition of the Prophet states that a Muslim is responsible for at least one *sadaqah* daily for every joint in his/her body. The word *sadaqah* is often translated as "charity." It is derived from the same root as the Arabic verb "to be truthful or sincere" and thus most generally signifies an act of fidelity or sincerity towards God. Hence, to Muslims, an act of *sadaqah* is a form of worship.

When Muhammad made this statement to his Companions, they felt overwhelmed, for how can anyone perform so many acts of piety each day? He responded to them that to act justly is a *sadaqah*, to help a rider on his mount is a *sadaqah*, and to remove a stone from the road to ease the way for other travelers is a *sadaqah*.[26] On other occasions, he mentioned that smiling at another person, bringing food to one's family, and making love to one's spouse are all pious acts.

Muhammad's Companions expressed shock at the last of these, since it brings such carnal satisfaction. So he asked them if they did not consider adultery sinful and harmful, and when they responded that they did, he asked them why were they surprised that marital romance was a meritorious act in the service of God.[27] The Prophet's followers wondered what, then, were the greatest acts of faith? He included on different occasions: fighting in a just cause, standing up to a tyrant, taking care of your parents in their old age, giving birth to a child—and if a mother should die while giving birth, then she ranks amongst the highest witnesses of faith.

To the Muslim, almost every moment of life presents an opportunity for worship, and he or she aspires to transform all of his/her earthly life into a type of continuous prayer as verse 6:163 has the Muslim say: "Truly my prayer and my sacrifice and my living and my dying—all are to God." This idea is ingrained deeply in the Muslim character, and so we find believers dedicating even their simplest actions to God with the formula, "In the name of God, the Merciful, the Compassionate."

An Egyptian cab driver about to start his car, a Moroccan mother reaching to pick up her crying child, and a Pakistani worker raising a glass of water to his lips, will pronounce *"bismillah-ir-rahman-ir-raheem"* (In the Name of God, the Merciful, the Compassionate). Every healthy and wholesome activity has the potential to be a worshipful act. Any good deed,

---

[26] Ibid., 59.
[27] Ibid.

performed by one who strives to surrender his/her life to God, can become a moment of devotion. A believer knows that his/her inner peace, happiness, growth, and prosperity correspond to the level of self-surrender he/she attains. To him or her, worship then becomes synonymous with doing what is good and ultimately personally beneficial.

Many western scholars of Islam have objected to the verse in the Qur'an where God states "I have not created *jinn* (beings beyond human perception) nor man except that they should worship me" (51:56), seeing an infinitely jealous and capricious narcissism—the worst side of the Old Testament depictions of God. Yet a Muslim, possessing his/her understanding of the purpose of life and possessing this very general and broad concept of worship, will read the very same verse and respond: "But of course, for what other purpose could there possibly be?"

Additional Questions

We have traveled far, yet in some ways, it seems as if we never needed to leave. Like Dorothy in the Wizard of Oz, we had to venture over the rainbow in order to discover that the key to happiness is within ourselves. To many of those who have recently accepted Islam, its view of life is so holistic and natural that they are astonished that they had not conceived of it themselves.

We saw that the Qur'an claims that earthly life is an essential stage in our creation. It represents a learning stage in which we can develop our intellectual and spiritual qualities and increase in our capacity to know, receive, and experience the attributes of God so that we can enter into a relationship of love with Him that no human relationship could approximate. We observed that human reason, choice, and suffering are key ingredients in this stage and that our relationship with others is organically linked to our relationship with God. We witnessed that human error, sin, and repentance, together with God's forgiveness and His continuous, pervasive influence, aid us in our growth. For many of us, most of the objections we raised initially have dissolved along the way and, although we may still have unanswered questions, we are coming to realize that they are due to the limitations of our own reasoning—our inability to fully comprehend the truth before us—and that given enough time, thought, and study of the Qur'an, we may be able to find satisfactory answers.

We are not at our journey's end. The remainder of the book is devoted to sharing as best its author can the rest of that travel to Islam in America. Ahead, we will meet the inevitable decision that the Qur'an demands of us. Then we will consider the five pillars of Islam and the support they provide to those who have made the decision to convert. We will also meet the community of believers and the tests that its members can bring to one's sincerity. Finally, we look briefly at the future of Muslims in America. Before we continue on, however, we will consider a few more of the theodicy questions that are often raised by modern-day Muslims and non-Muslims interested in Islam. I chose to discuss those about which I am most often asked. Answers to some of them follow as easy corollaries of what we already discovered, while others require a fresh look at the Qur'an from different angles. Some of them are discussed elsewhere,[28] and I will repeat—sometimes word for word—what I wrote there. They are included here for the sake of completeness.

On Omnipotence

If God is all-powerful, can He become a man, terminate His existence, tell a lie, be unjust, or create a stone too heavy for even Him to move? These somewhat silly riddles most often arise from imposing unnecessary and contradictory assumptions on certain attributes of God or by assigning unwarranted additional attributes to Him. For example, the Qur'anic concept of omnipotence is not that God can do any arbitrary thing at all, even though it defies all laws of logical truth. Instead the Qur'an states that God "has power over all things" (2:20; 3:29; 55:17; 6:17; 16:77; 67:1) and thus it is impossible that a created object could exist beyond or independent of His power, such as a stone too heavy to be moved.

Creation is also subject to and in harmony with His attributes. While God does "whatsoever He wills" (2:253; 5:1; 11:107; 22:14), what He wills is not arbitrary or capricious but in accord with His Most Beautiful Names. Hence, it is outside of His perfection to do ridiculous or stupid things. Similarly, His attributes are not in conflict with each other. If omnipotence included the ability to become a man, to terminate oneself, to lie, or be unjust, then His name the All-Powerful would be in conflict with the names the Absolute (*al Samad*), the Everlasting (*al Qayyum*), the Truth (*al Haqq*), or the Most Just Judge (*al Hakeem*), respectively. Therefore, the obvious

---

[28] Lang, *Struggling to Surrender.*

answer to each of the above riddles is that the Qur'anic concept of omnipotence does not include these acts.

The problem of predestination involves similar but more subtle logical traps that arise from imposing time constraints on God.

Predestination

The concepts of time and eternity and their relationship to God have been the subject of diverse philosophical speculation throughout the history of religion. This is amply demonstrated in Muhammad Iqbal's *Reconstruction of Religious Thought in Islam*,[29] where he attempts a new interpretation in conformity with modern thought and doctrinal sources of Islam. The attempt itself has been widely praised by Muslim and non-Muslim scholars, although there is considerable disagreement in both camps about the validity of his ideas. We should, Iqbal asserts, not underestimate the importance of such efforts, since many theological paradoxes arise from our understanding of these concepts. On the one hand, we cannot, as scriptures themselves cannot, resist relating time to God. On the other hand, we must alert ourselves to the deficiencies of our understanding.

The greatest perplexities arise by attributing to God human restrictions in relation to time. As God transcends space, we naturally would not associate with Him spatial limitations. For instance, we would not say that God literally descends to earth or walks in the garden. Equally, we would not insist that God is a three-dimensional being or that He travels from one point in space to another. In the same way, we should not demand that God have a past, present, and future, for this assumes that His existence is as ours, *in time*, and again this conflicts with His transcendence. Even the most rabid atheist, in an effort to prove the illogic of the concept of God, would not suppose that God might be on a bus from Chicago on His way to New Orleans, because he knows that such a hypothesis is unacceptable to a believer. It is equally erroneous to assume God's being was confined to a particular point or interval of time.

We have little difficulty accepting the idea that God's knowledge can encompass two different points in space simultaneously. This is perhaps because we assume that the attribute of transcending space implies a unique vantage point. We could compare it, however imperfectly, to the experi-

---

[29] Muhammad Iqbal, *The Reconstruction of Religious Thought in Islam* (Lahore, Pakistan: Sh. Muhammad Ashraf Publ., 1982).

ence of being high above the ground and having simultaneous knowledge of very distant events. With respect to time, unlike space, we are immobile. We can not travel forward or backward in time. An hour from now, we will be at an hour from now. That can not be changed. Therefore, it is more difficult to comprehend that God's existence is independent of or beyond time, as indeed it must be, for it is impossible to conceive that His being is contained within or constrained by any of the dimensions of the very space–time environment that He created for us to live and grow in. Once again, because of His unique vantage point, His knowledge encompasses all events, regardless of their distance in space or time.

Another key point, well established in the Qur'an, is that our perception of time is not objectively real. As noted earlier, the Day of Judgment is portrayed as a different order of creation, one in which we suddenly comprehend that our former perceptions of time are no longer valid.

> The Day they see it, (it will be) as if they had tarried but a single evening, or the following morning. (79:46)

> One Day He will gather them all together: (it will seem) as if they had tarried but an hour of a day. (10:45)

> It will be on a Day when He will call you, and you will answer with His praise, and you will think that you tarried but a little while. (17:52)

> In whispers will they consult each other: "You tarried not longer than ten (Days)." (20:103)

> "You tarried not longer than a day." (20:104)

> He will say: "What number of years did you stay on earth?" They will say, "We stayed a day or part of a day: ask those who keep account." He will say: "You stayed not but a little, if you had only known!" (23:112-13)

> On the Day that the Hour will be established, the transgressors will swear that they tarried not but an hour: thus were they used to being deluded. (30:55)

Interpreters will always render all references to the Day of Judgment in the future tense, because from our perspective that is when it will take place. Several of the passages, however, actually employ the present and past tenses. Commentators assert that this is a literary device that stresses the inevitability of these happenings, but it seems that the use of the present and past tenses in referring to the Day of Judgment also reinforces the notion that it will take place in a very different environment, one in which our current conceptions of time and space no longer apply.

The illusory character of time is further supported by the Qur'an's comparisons of the "days of God" with earthly days, where a "day of God" is said to be as "a thousand years of your reckoning" (32:5) and like "50,000 years" (70:4). I will not attempt here to provide a model or to interpret the precise relationship between God and time, or for that matter God and space, but rather I suggest the futility of such an endeavor. It cannot be otherwise, since our perceptions of time are not objectively real. Conflicts arise precisely because a given interpretation is assumed.

The question "What is the value of prayer if God has already predestined the future?" assumes that in some way God has a future. That is, it assumes that God is situated in time, as we are, and that as we pray, He is peering into a preordained future. But in order to have a future, one's existence must be contained within—and hence finite—in time. The reason this question leads to contradictions is that it assumes a contradiction in the first place: that God both transcends and is finite in time.

Any question that assumes two mutually incompatible premises will always result in conflicting conclusions. Assume, for example, that a circle is a square. We may ask if a circle has corners. If we emphasize the circle's roundness, the answer is no. If we concentrate on the properties of a square, the answer is yes. When two assumptions lead to a contradiction, at least one of them must be false. Thus, in such a situation, it should be asked if the question itself makes sense and if all premises are necessarily true.

The word "predestination" is itself problematic. If we mean by it that God in the past had programmed the events of the future, the assumption is that God exists in time. If instead we mean that God's wisdom, knowledge, and power encompass all and nothing in creation can conflict with that, then that has to be admitted. However, this is not the primary sense of "predestine," which means "determine in advance," and it does not conflict with the notion that God responds to our prayers.

The words *qadar* and *taqdir* in the Qur'an have come to mean, for many Muslims and Orientalists, the "absolute decree of good and evil by

God." That is, that God has preordained all our acts, even our moral choices. But as Muhammad Ali argues, this doctrine is

> neither known to the Holy Qur'an, nor even to Arabic lexicology. The doctrine of predestination is of later growth, and seems to have been the result of the clash of Islam with Persian religious thought.[30]

According to Raghib,[31] *qadar* and *taqdir* mean "the making manifest of the measure of a thing" or simply "measure." In the Qur'an they signify the divine laws regulating and balancing creation.

> Glorify the name of your Lord, the Most High, Who creates, then makes complete, and Who makes things according to a measure (*qaddara,* from *taqdir*), then guides them to their goal. (87:1-3)

> Who created everything, then ordained for it a measure (*qadar*). (54:49)

> And the Sun runs on to a term appointed for it; that is the law (*taqdir*) of the Mighty, the Knowing. And as for the moon, We ordained (*qaddarna* from *taqdir*) for it stages. (36:38-39)

> Of what thing did He create him [man]? Of a small lifegerm He created him, then He made him according to a measure (*qaddarahu*). (80:18-19)

This is not to claim that God has subjected the universe to certain scientific laws and abandoned it to let it run its course. No reader of the Qur'an gets this impression. In the Qur'an, God is *al Rabb*: the Sustainer, Cherisher, Regulator, and Governor of all. He is the omnipresent source of the harmony and balance of nature. His influence and sway over creation is continuous and all-pervading. However, none of this conflicts with the fact that we are empowered to make moral decisions and to carry them out or that God comes to our aid when we seek Him.

---

[30] Muhammad Ali, *The Religion of Islam* (New Delhi: S. Chand & Co., 317-18.
[31] Ibid.

On the Origins of Evil and Temptation

Where does evil come from? If it comes from God, then it implies that God is imperfect; if it does not, then it implies that something can come into existence independent of Him. Since we already touched on this question when we considered human choice, we will summarize quickly our earlier observations and include some additional comments.

As we have seen, evil is not absolute, existing independent of and in eternal conflict with God. It arises from human nature, which is suited to moral and spiritual growth. What we consider to be evil—tyranny, oppression, deceit, injustice, greed, indifference to the suffering of others—is an outcome of human choice. It is a rejection of and opposition to the divine attributes and our own best interests. This helps explain the Qur'an's description of the disbelievers as *kuffar*, a term that connotes one who shows ingratitude or rejects a gift. Human intelligence and volition, when confronted with the challenges presented by earthly life, frequently will choose evil. However, the same key ingredients combine in some of us to produce remarkable exemplars of goodness. As the Qur'an states, man's capabilities—in particular, his ability to sin and do evil—are from God. He empowers us to choose evil just as He empowers us to choose good. But the choice is ours, and it is in that choice that good or evil occurs:

> Say: "All things are from God." But what has come to these people, that they fail to understand a single fact? Whatever good befalls you is from God, but whatever evil befalls you, is from yourself. (4:78-79)

To choose evil is self-defeating, as the wrongdoer sins—commits *zulm*— against himself. But the damage does not have to be permanent, for through sincere repentance, making amends, and with God's forgiveness and help, we can learn and grow from our mistakes. The existence of and our ability to choose evil as well as good is an essential element of this learning phase of our creation. Evil in this life is not in conflict with God, but rather serves His purposes for mankind. The same could be said about the existence of temptation.

Our decisions are based not only on sensory data. All peoples of all times have been aware of extrasensory influences that introduce subtle suggestions into the human mind. In the past, the study of these forces fell exclusively within the province of religion, while today, modern psychology dominates their study. Religions tended to view these psychic influences as independent from man, but modern science believes them to belong to a subliminal region of our minds. I will not attempt here to resolve this difference in viewpoint or to harmonize Islam with any recent theories of psychology. My interest is not in the precise origin, development, or location of these influences—frankly, I believe that this will always be a mystery to science—for my aim is only to discuss the role of temptation in man's development. Of course, the Arabs of the Prophet's era had their own pneumotology and vocabulary for describing psychic phenomena and, quite naturally, the Qur'an adopted and adapted this system to its calling. In order to better understand the purpose of temptation, it will be helpful to review some terminology.

The word *jinn* was to the ancient Arabs a comprehensive term for beings and powers outside of their immediate experience or perception. It is derived from the Arabic verb *janna,* meaning "to cover, conceal, hide, or protect." To Muhammad's contemporaries, it denoted "a being that cannot be perceived with the senses."[32] The Arabs, as pointed out by Muhammad Ali, commonly referred to other humans as *jinn*. He quotes famous Muslim lexicologists who explain that it could be used to designate *mu'zam al nas,* i.e., "the main body of men or the bulk of mankind."[33]

> In the mouth of an Arab, the main body of men would
> mean the non-Arab world. They called all foreigners *jinn*
> because they were concealed from their eyes.[34]

Through the centuries a tremendous amount of superstition and folklore grew around this word in the Middle East and the Far East, as well as the two other terms that we are about to discuss. Although these developments make it difficult to know exactly what it meant to the Qur'an's first hearers, it appears that any imperceptible being might be referred to as a *jinn*. From its use in the Qur'an and the Prophet's traditions, however, it seems that the term was used most often to refer to a world of spirits, one of sentient beings who were invisible to mankind but yet influenced and sometimes interacted with men.

A close relative of *jinn* is the word *shaitan*, usually translated as "satan." In general, *shaitan* stands for any rebellious being or force. In his famous commentary on the Qur'an, al Tabari states that

---

[32] Ibid., 188.
[33] Ibid., 191.
[34] Ibid., 191-92.
[35] Al Tabari, *The Commentary on the Qur'an*, trans. by J. Cooper (Oxford: Oxford University Press, 1987), 1:47.

> *Shaitan* in the speech of the Arabs is every rebel among
> the *jinn*, mankind, beasts, and everything . . . . The rebel
> among every kind of thing is called a *shaitan*, because its
> behavior and actions differ from those of the rest of its
> kind, and it is far from good.[35]

It derives its meaning from a verb which means to be remote or banished.

> It is said that the word is derived from [the use of the 1st
> form verb *shatana*] in the expression *shatana dar-i min
> dari-k* (=My home was far from yours).[36]

As al Tabari points out, *shaitan* can be applied to humans. He quotes
Ibn 'Abbas in his commentary on 2:14:

> There were some Jewish men who, when they met one or
> several of the Companions of the Prophet, may God bless
> him and grant him peace, would say: "We follow your
> religion." But when they went in seclusion to their own
> companions, who were their satans, they would say: "We
> are with you, we were only mocking."[37]

He also quotes Qatadah and Mujahid, who claimed that these satans were
"their leaders in evil" and "their companions among the hypocrites and
polytheists."

The key difference between a *jinn* and a *shaitan* is that while the former could be benign or destructive, the latter is always evil. In particular, in the pneumatic realm, a *shaitan* is an evil or rebellious *jinn*. However, the power of Satan in the Qur'an is rather limited: He is a source of
evil suggestions that enter a person's hearts (114:4-6) and the notorious
tempter, but beyond that the Qur'an states that he has no authority over
man (14:22; 15:42; 16:99; 17:65) and that his guile is weak (4:76).

> And Satan will say, when the matter is decided: Surely
> God promised you a promise in truth, and I promised you,
> then failed you. And I had no power over you, except that
> I called you and you obeyed me; so don't blame me, but
> blame yourselves. I can not come to your help, nor can you
> come to my help. I reject your associating me with God

---

[36] Ibid., 47.
[37] Ibid., 131.

before. Surely for the unjust is a painful chastisement.
(14:22)

Satanic temptation is counterbalanced in Islamic pneumotology by angelic inspiration. The angels (in Arabic, *malaa'ikah*; sing. *malaak*), among other things, encourage and support virtuous deeds in men and women. From the Qur'an, the sayings of the Prophet, and ancient dictionaries, it seems that, unlike the two previous terms, the word *malaak* (angel) applied only to spiritual beings. The Arabs also had a number of firmly held beliefs concerning angels that the Qur'an rejects: that angels are daughters of God (16:57) and hence semidivine, or that angels are female creatures (17:40; 37:150; 53:21).

These three terms characterize the pneumatic powers that influence the psyche. Angels, satans, and *jinn*s account for many of the virtuous, harmful, and ambivalent psychic urgings to which we are exposed. Angels inspire magnanimity and self-sacrifice. Satans are a source of evil and self-destructive suggestions. The influence of jinns could be either positive or negative depending on how we deal with them, for they excite our lower or more animalistic tendencies, such as our drives for self-survival, power, wealth, security, and the respect of others. Their relationship and function is described succinctly in a well-known saying of Muhammad. He stated that every human is created with a companion *jinn*, who excites his lower passions, and a companion angel, who inspires him with good and noble ideas. When Muhammad's audience asked if he too had a companion *jinn*, he responded, "Yes, but God helped me to overcome him, so that he has submitted and does not command me to anything but good."[38]

The virtuous and base promptings we receive could balance and complement each other. Magnanimous urgings, which stimulate our moral and spiritual growth, would, if surrendered to completely, be self-destructive, for they would cause us to ignore our personal needs. Base desires are necessary for our earthly survival, but if we gave in to them entirely, we would become utterly selfish. The two work together to stimulate our moral and spiritual growth, since what makes an act virtuous is that it involves overcoming or putting aside our lower needs for a while. The successful person, as Prophet Muhammad's saying shows, is the one who can discipline these lower (*jinn*ic) influences and balance them against angelic ones. Then both serve his growth in goodness.

---

[38] Ahmad ibn Hanbal, *Al Musnad* (Cairo: al Maimanah Press, n.d.), 1:385, 397, 401.

When a person inclines too far towards these lower (*jinnic*) suggestions, he makes himself or herself easy prey to evil (satanic) influences. For example, our need to survive gives way to exploitation of others and avariciousness, our need for power gives way to tyranny, our need for wealth gives way to greed, our desire for security gives way to violence, and our wish for respect gives way to arrogance. Such a person, as we saw earlier, becomes spiritually self-destructive, thereby making satanic influences an "obvious enemy" to man (2:168; 7:22; 12:5; 35:6).

These three psychic influences usually act upon us simultaneously. Thus they pinpoint and heighten the morality of many decisions and together provide a stimulus and catalyst for spiritual development. From the standpoint of Islam, what we call temptation is only one type of extrasensory influences to which we are exposed, and, in combination with the others, it perpetuates and hastens our growth. Like all other aspects of our earthly lives, it is in harmony with God's plan for us.

It has been pointed out to me on occasion that this outline compares to certain theories in modern psychology, in particular, to Freud's description of the id, ego, and superego. This may be the case, but I find it neither surprising nor something to be excited about. First of all, if there are similarities between the two systems, there are obviously major differences. Second, I do not consider Freud's ideas to be truly modern nor a discovery in the strictest sense, because the viewpoint just presented is part of ancient wisdom and is contained in many religious traditions. What Freud attempted to do was to construct a secular context for explaining and investigating psychic influences. I, on the other hand, am writing as a convert to Islam from a definite religious perspective.

Don't We Need Another Prophet?

> This day have I perfected for you your religion and completed My favor to you and chosen for you Islam as a religion. (5:3)

> Muhammad is not the father of any of your men, but he is the Messenger of Allah and the Seal of the prophets. And Allah is ever Knower of all things. (33:40)

The second verse, revealed in the fourth year after Muhammad's emigration to Madinah, turned out to contain a prophecy as well as a statement of current fact. Muhammad would leave no male heirs and thus no natural candidate to whom the community might look as inheritor of the prophetic mantle. The deep emotional and psychological need for such a person was indeed felt. On the day of the Prophet's death, Umar, one of his leading Companions, and many others refused to accept that the Prophet had truly passed on until Muhammad's closest friend, Abu Bakr, brought them to their senses. In the succeeding years, there were many others who sought from Muhammad's family a divinely guided leader, one who, through kinship, would be endowed with charismatic authority. But the Qur'an, history, and the Prophet's decisions in his last days made such a search difficult.

Not only did he leave no sons, but Muhammad outlived all of his daughters except Fatimah, the youngest, who died very shortly after he did. Had the Prophet designated Fatimah's husband and his nephew, Ali, as his successor, he might very well have been raised to divinely ordained status in the eyes of most of the Muslims. Muhammad, however, apparently left it to the community to select their next leader, and Ali would not be elected until three political successors to Muhammad (Abu Bakr, Umar, Uthman) had already reigned and then died. Either of Ali and Fatimah's two sons would have been likely candidates, but both of them died—the younger, tragically, while opposing the sixth ruler after Muhammad— without attaining political rule. Nonetheless, various lines of descent from Ali came to be viewed by a significant Muslim minority as inheriting a prophetic charisma, although most viewed the leadership of Muslims as simply a political appointment having religious significance and responsibilities but no divine mandate.

If Muhammad had been outlived by a son or perhaps a daughter—for the Arabian peninsula had known queens in pre-Islamic times—for a sufficient length of time, or if a grandchild of his had obtained political leadership, Muslim political history could possibly have been very different. But as it was, Muhammad's refusal to appoint a political successor and the fact that no direct descendent rose to power in the first few decades after his death, helped to insure that the majority of Muslims would understand the designation, "the Seal (*al khaatam*) of the Prophets," in the most obvious and conservative sense.

The Qur'an states that from every people God chose at least one prophet at some time in their history (10:47; 13:7; 16:36; 35:24). It also contains examples of nations to which prophets were sent repeatedly, because the divine message they conveyed would inevitably be distorted or forgotten. In some traditions of Muhammad, the number of prophets chosen by God for mankind is said to number as many as one hundred thousand. We are told that Muhammad's mission was also corrective and restorative: the revelation he communicated confirms the fundamental truths contained in other sacred books—principally the Jewish and Christian scriptures—and corrects key errors (2:91; 6:92; 35:31).

This is a rather pessimistic appraisal of mankind's spiritual and moral resolve. Since its very beginnings, the human race has been consistently guilty of forgetfulness and perversion as well as of an inability to preserve and adhere to God's revelations. So that even if the Qur'an, as Muslims claim, is the same revelation proclaimed from Muhammad's lips, preserved in its original language, and free from later editing and revision, are we not, like most of humanity throughout history, in need of another prophet? In other words, does it make sense that God would suddenly leave humanity, with its proven propensity for deviation from revelation, to itself until the end of creation after guiding man so directly up to and including the time of Muhammad?

The Muslim might counter that the Qur'an is distinguished from all other sacred scriptures by its purity; others may contain sayings close to what earlier prophets preached—maybe even some verbatim statements —but these are mixed so thoroughly with folklore, poetry, interpretation, commentary, along with errors in translation, copying, editing and transmission, and with other accretions, that sifting out the actual revelation has long been impossible. The Muslim insists that the Qur'an, on the other hand, contains nothing but the words proclaimed by Muhammad during the times when revelation descended upon him. Most modern non-Muslim scholars of Islam are willing to admit this much, or at least something very close to this. Thus, this argument goes, we now possess the unadulterated word of God to guide us, making another revelation or prophet unnecessary. Other religions, of course, have developed viewpoints on the purpose and means of revelation and scripture quite different from the Muslim understanding. It is not my intention to contrast or debate them; I only wish to present a common explanation for the finality of Muhammad's mission.

Does this explanation fully answer the above question? What about the need to interpret and apply the revelation in an ever-changing world and the many difficulties which are bound to arise in time not explicitly addressed by the scripture? The Muslim replies that we have the Prophet's life example, his *Sunnah*, the multitudinous recollections of his sayings and doings that were collected, collated and subjected to meticulous historical criticism during the first three Islamic centuries.

Yet certainly we will encounter situations not dealt with in the Prophet's lifetime—after all, it has been over fourteen hundred years since his demise. How do we respond correctly to these? The Muslim answers that we have the sacred law, the Shari'ah, based on the Qur'an and the Prophet's *Sunnah*: a complete code of living, developed over several centuries by jurists to meet every possible contingency.

Is it any longer tenable to claim that the ancient jurists foresaw every possible future problem? Of course not, admits the Muslim, but we can study their methodologies, repeat their effort, and derive Islamic rules and regulations to address our current circumstances.

This is the inevitable response, but the farther we move away from the Qur'an, the greater our dependence on human choices and judgments, which, it seems, are bound to differ and to include errors. Today, Muslims are debating and often quarreling among themselves over hundreds of issues as they strive to adapt to modern living. Admittedly, these arguments are not over concepts central to Islam—they involve almost exclusively what non-Muslims would regard as mundane issues: men's and women's roles in the community, banking and investment practices, relations with non-Muslims, Muslim involvement in western political systems and similar concerns—but they are extremely important to the community. Such controversies create a great deal of strain and dissension. As one Muslim student attending the University of Kansas once told me, "If only the Prophet, peace be upon him, were here today to settle these issues for us!" From this perspective then, do we not need another prophet?

Any answer is purely speculative, because the Qur'an does not explicitly respond to this question. There very well may be many reasons rather than a single rationale. It is possible that the collective attempt to work out a program of living guided by the Qur'an and Muhammad's life example is in itself a valuable social, intellectual, and spiritual exercise requiring cooperation, tolerance, humility, and sincerity. The possibilities for growth that such an endeavor holds may outweigh the benefits of having a prophet to decide every small point of difference.

Another factor might be that the current environment is incapable of producing an individual having the level of purity and simplicity needed to be a prophet. Perhaps life has become so complicated and corrupting that no one of us is any longer capable of attaining the spiritual sensitivity and

---

[39] *Sahih al Bukhari: The Early Years of Islam*, trans. and explained by Muhammad Asad (Gibraltar: Dar al Andalus, 1981), 19.

receptivity of Moses, Jesus or Muhammad. This interpretation brings to mind the many traditions of the Prophet that predict that life will become increasing corruptive, such as, "The best of my community is my generation, thereafter those who follow them, thereafter those who follow them. Then will come [such] people that one's testimony will outrun his oath, and one's oath his testimony."[39] Recall also the statement in the Qur'an that asserts that while many in Muhammad's era excel in faith, very few will do so in later times (56:10-14) and the verse that predicts that many Muslims will someday shun the Qur'an (25:30).

Further insight into this question might be gained by examining more closely what the Qur'an states necessitated Muhammad's prophethood.

The Qur'an presents itself and Muhammad's apostleship as the culmination and completion of God's direct communication to mankind through divinely inspired persons. Its many narratives about former prophets confirm and reinforce Muhammad's mission. The Qur'an's descriptions of the trials and obstacles faced by these previous messengers very often parallel events in Muhammad's own struggle, and the proclamations they make to their communities echo pronouncements made elsewhere in the Qur'an. This shows that the battle fought by all prophets between good and evil, revelation and rejection, truth and falsity, has always been the same.

The single most important fact governing all creation and preached by all of God's messengers is that "there is no god but God" (in Arabic, la illaha illa Allah). It implies that the many different objects of worship chosen by men have no real authority or power and that the divisions and hatreds to which such misdirected veneration lead are totally unnecessary and a result of nothing more than evil and self-destructive man-made illusions. It means there is but one spiritual and moral standard governing humanity and but one measure of a person's worth.

> O mankind! Lo! We have created you male and female
> and have made you nations and tribes that you may know
> one another. Lo! the noblest among you in the sight of
> God is the best in conduct. (49:13)

Most importantly, it implies that the barriers we set up between ourselves and others are fallacies, because we all must answer to the same supreme God.

In seventh-century Arabia, each tribe had its own deity from which it sought protection and favoritism and to which it appealed in the self-perpetuating intertribal strife. It took Islam's monotheism to unite the warring factions as the Qur'an so poignantly reminds them.

> And hold fast, all of you together, to the rope of Allah, and
> do not separate. And remember Allah's favor unto you:
> how you were enemies and he made friendship between
> your hearts so that you became as brothers by his grace;
> and (how) you were on the brink of an abyss of fire; and
> he did save you from it. (3:103)

Islamic monotheism not only demands that we accept that there is only
one God, but also that we accept its natural corollary: All men and women
are in fact equal under God's authority. These two demands, the oneness of
God and the unity of humanity, have throughout history been difficult to
uphold in any religious tradition, as the cases of Judaism and Christianity
so powerfully demonstrate in the Qur'an.

The story of the Children of Israel is of a people who are uniquely
receptive throughout much of their history to monotheism despite their
existence within a predominantly pagan milieu. Outside influences frequently penetrate their community and cause them to waver at times
from the teachings of their prophets. In the Qur'an, they appear as a
nation in constant struggle between pure monotheism and heathen pressures, and this in part explains their need to insulate themselves from
their social surroundings and their attempt to preserve and protect their
racial and cultural purity. But they came to see themselves as God's chosen people, to the exclusion of others, and as sons of God in the Old
Testament sense. As a result, they could never accept the final messenger of God because of his non-Jewish origins, even though he confirmed
the essential message in their scriptures. The Qur'an continuously
blames them for their refusal in this regard. In short, Judaism, although
successful in preserving the belief in one God, was unable to accept the
oneness of man under God.

Christianity goes back to the same biblical roots. But much more than
Judaism, it is a universal religion. Its coherence derives from an intense
spiritual yearning to know and be loved by God. Thus, while the Jews and
the pagans of the Arabian peninsula were stubbornly closed to a message
that departed from their traditions, Christians are shown to be more easily
affected by its spiritual force (4:85-89).

The biggest difficulty encountered by such universal faiths is the great
diversity of peoples they absorb. Converts bring their own languages, ideas,
symbols, and cultural practices, all of which could potentially distort the
universal faith in question. From the Muslim view, such was the case with
Christianity: Although it eagerly embraces all mankind, its tenets compro-

mise pure monotheism and lend too easily to associating others with God. In this way, the Judeo–Christian experience exemplifies the dilemma faced by all world religions: Monotheism or universalism were invariably compromised in attempting to preserve one or the other.

Islam also struggled—and still struggles—with these internal tensions. Eventually, extreme measures were taken by the mainstream to protect both implications of monotheism. Philosophical and mystical speculation were discouraged, all aspects of life were systematized into religious law, and innovative thought was forbidden through the adoption of *taqlid* (unquestioning acceptance of earlier scholarly opinion). Pressures continued to rise, but Islamic orthodoxy, for the most part, succeeded in placing the major sources and ideas of early mainstream Islam on ice, preserved in a type of suspended animation, that eventually would be transferred to modern man intact. Whatever the cost to Muslim civilization of the severe steps taken by these Muslim scholars, the two major features of Islamic monotheism— the oneness of God and the oneness of humanity—were united successfully in Islam and passed on to future generations. For Muslims, this is one example of how God, through Islam, completed His favor unto mankind (5:3).

This concern with preserving both aspects of monotheism helps to explain the termination of prophethood with Muhammad. As long as a religion anticipates a future revelation, the door is left open to false prophets. Deceivers and self-deluded individuals invariably emerge to mislead others and divide the community. A powerful source of schism threatens the unity of the believers much more deeply and permanently than any legal disputation. Every major religion, including Islam, has known this danger, but the termination of prophethood with Muhammad has greatly restrained this tendency. A Muslim leader today may gain the admiration and allegiance of very many followers, but it is nearly impossible to obtain their unconditional trust—that type of absolute loyalty obtained by a perception of divine guidance. The moment a leader claims such a status, his movement is invariably doomed to become a relatively insignificant cult disconnected from the community of Muslims.

Recently, many Muslims were very curious about Rashad Khaleefah's organization in Tucson, Arizona. When he declared himself to be another messenger of God, however, virtually all Muslims dismissed and ignored him, and he died with only a handful of disciples. Many Western scholars refer to similar disenfranchised movements, such as the Bahai's or Qadianis, as Islamic sects, although the designation is inappropriate and misleading. The Muslim world does not consider these groups to be alternative or even heretical perspectives within the Islamic community; they are considered entirely outside of Islam. No such movement has attracted a significant number of Muslims, although they may win converts from other populations, because the belief in Muhammad as the last and final prophet is one of Islam's principal dogmas.

The *shahadah* (testimony of faith) is the nearest thing to a creed in Islam. It is recited at least nine times a day by observant Muslims in their prayers. In the first half of the *shahadah*, a Muslim bears witness that "there is no god but God" (*la ilaha illa Allah*), while in the second half he or she testifies that "Muhammad is the messenger of God" (*Muhammadan rasul-lu-Allah*). By the second statement, the Muslim understands not only that Muhammad is God's messenger, but also that he is the last prophet and the only one he should follow. Thus, the *shahaddah* connects Islamic monotheism to the finality of Muhammad's mission. From the viewpoint of Muslims, his prophetic vocation was necessitated by the need for a continual witness on earth to both implications of monotheism—the oneness of God and the oneness of humanity under God—and the sealing of prophethood with him was necessary in order to preserve and safeguard that witness from later fragmentation.

CHAPTER 3

THE DECISION

Umar ibn al Khattab[40] could be your most loyal, valuable friend or your most frightening, merciless adversary. A towering, muscular man in his early thirties, he commanded almost everyone's fear and respect. He was a volatile combination of brilliance and hot-temperedness, perspicacity and impetuosity, so that while others were still struggling to get their facts right, he would have already committed himself to an appropriate course of action. He could execute his judgements with numbing speed and austerity, making them seem more like reflexes than decisions.

To Umar, the matter was completely clear: there could be no compromise—Makkan society as they knew and honored it and the movement of Muhammad could never coexist. Of course, he was well aware of the threat of revenge, of long and costly blood feuds, and that Makkah could easily become another Yathrib, but Muhammad posed a much greater danger and he had to be stopped immediately before it was too late.

The air was hot and dry as Umar marched down the dusty, dirt road that led to the area of town where Muhammad and his associates were meeting. The streets were empty, as all were in there homes under cover from the noonday sun.

How was it that "the truthful one" had became such a menace? he thought to himself. He was always somewhat of a loner, but he never showed any political ambition or signs of instability. And what could have seized the minds of the sons of Quraysh who now followed him?

"O Umar! O Umar!"

---

[40] Umar ibn al Khattab came to be one of Muhammad's most devoted and closest followers. The sources report several different variants of his conversion to Islam. Muhammad H. Haykal, *The Life of Muhammad*, trans. by Ismail Faruqi (Indianapolis: North American Trust, 1976), 103-104.

Of all the tribes of Arabia, Umar wondered, how can its proudest and most powerful one produce this shame? What could have gotten into...

"*Umar!!! Stop!! Where are you heading in such haste!!*"

Umar turned towards the voice that was scurrying to catch up with him. "*What do you want?!*" *He blurted out abruptly.*

It was Nuaym ibn Abdullah, also of the tribe of Quraysh. With sweat dripping down his face he panted, "*Where are you rushing to?*"

Umar resumed his march as Nuaym hurried to keep pace with him.

"*I am going to put an end to this plague that grips our city,*" *he answered, his eyes fixed firmly on the mission ahead of him.* "*I am going to kill Muhammad.*"

Nuaym tried to warn him of the obvious risks, but Umar was determined. "*Then perhaps you should put your own house in order first!*" *Nuaym gasped,* "*because your sister and her husband are among his followers!*"

Umar stopped dead in his tracks. He felt an ache in the pit of his stomach and his chest and neck tightened. His face was livid. "*If you're lying...!*" *he shouted furiously.*

"*Ask anyone! Everyone knows!*" *Nuaym pleaded as he retreated several steps, unsure of what to expect next.*

Without another word Umar stormed toward his sister's house, his anger increasing with every stride. By the time he got to her home he had reached the peak of jahl, the term the Arabs used to describe uncontrollable passions. As he approached its entrance he had his worst fears confirmed in what for him was the worst possible way: he heard his sister and her spouse reciting from a peace of parchment some of the verses which Muhammad had claimed were from God.

Umar burst into the room. He demanded to see the parchment. His sister refused. A scuffle broke out. Blows were thrown. His sister fell to the floor. Blood and tears flowed down her cheek where Umar's fist had just landed.

The sight of his injured sister jolted Umar. He begged her to forgive him. He didn't know what he was doing . . . The rumors . . . Their reputations . . . Their family honor . . . Their futures . . . Her best interest . . . Her husband should know better . . . This will all pass.

"*Can I at least see the parchment?*" *he asked, having finally calmed down a little.*

Umar took the parchment and began to read it as he slowly walked over to another corner of the room. He stopped there, alone, standing, motionless, starring at the words before him. His breathing slowed and his shoulders relaxed. His countenance changed, as he now showed no traces of the violence that had just erupted. The confusion in his eyes was gone and they were now distant and deep in thought. He then glanced over toward his sister, but said nothing, and neither did she nor her husband. He looked down again at the parchment for a few more minutes as he slowly wandered in a small circle. He then walked back across the room. He stood for a moment before his sister, looking again as if he had something he wanted to say. He handed her the parchment and excused himself, stating only that he had to leave.

The next day, Umar set out again in search of Muhammad, but this time his purpose was not to put him to the sword, but to join him, and he would become one of his greatest followers.

Muslim history records many great conversions, but Umar's was certainly one of the most dramatic and important. It was a turning point in Muhammad's movement. It changed the image of Islam in the eyes of the Quraysh from an annoying, mostly discreet cult, to an open, defiant challenge to the establishment. The pagan Quraysh responded with severe persecution of Muhammad and his followers, which led to the Muslim emigration to Yathrib.

It would not be long, however, before conversion to Islam became much easier. Islam quickly spread throughout Arabia and within a few generations after the death of the Prophet, the Islamic empire stretched from the Atlantic coast of northwest Africa to the Punjab region of India. The Arab conquerors were in no hurry to win converts to their faith, and conversion proceeded at a slow but steady pace. But there were now definite protections and advantages for those who embraced Islam. Islamic civilization grew and came to lead the world in science, material prosperity, and learning, so that throughout the greater part of Muslim history, wherever Islam spread, it was perceived as the religion of a superior culture.

The situation of western converts to Islam is quite different from this today. When Europe sank into its Dark Ages, Islamic civilization ascended to its Golden Age; the West eventually recovered, while Muslim culture slipped into a long decline. Thus, the relative positions of the two civilizations at the beginning of this century was almost the reverse of what they had been during the Middle Ages. Many westerners, and Muslims too, see the modern Islamic world as backward and inferior to European and

American civilization. In addition, over a thousand years of tension, conflict, distrust, and built-up prejudice and ignorance now distance the two peoples, with each seeing the other as demonic and decadent. Their media portray each other as their greatest current threat and set the stage for what may turn out to be a self-fulfilling prophecy. The American or European who embraces Islam enters the religion in a milieu largely hostile to his or her choice, an environment that compares more with Makkah in the first twelve years of Muhammad's mission than to any other that produced proselytes to Islam.

Conversions to Islam in the West may not pose as great a threat to their societies as Umar's did to his, but they often elicit similar negative reactions on the parts of families and associates. I have never met a western convert to Islam, or anyone even considering conversion to it, who did not hesitate to embrace this religion because of fears of society's reaction. As the West is perceived to be so anti-Islam, conversion is most often a very slow and gradual process. Very few Americans or Europeans jump into the religion, and when they do, they are not usually Muslims for very long. Most converts recall many key turning points on the road to conversion, long before the final decision to embrace Islam. The following two cases, although they represent persons of very different backgrounds, are typical in this sense.

"Malcolm, don't eat any more pork and don't smoke any more cigarettes. I will show you how to get out of prison."

Who could conceive that this short note at the end of Reginald Little's letter to his older sibling would have such an impact, not only on his brother, but on the lives of so many African-Americans as well? In prison, they nicknamed him "Satan" because by this stage in his life he had become evil incarnate to those who knew him. This brief instruction, however, fanned a flicker of hope that even he had not yet extinguished. Incarcerated, where every detail of one's life seems in someone else's control, "Detroit Red" discovered freedom and self-respect in following these instructions, and he would later remember this letter as his first step in a tempestuous and courageous journey that first brought him to the Nation of Islam as Minister Malcolm X, then to the Pilgrimage to Makkah where he discovered what for him was true Islam, and finally to his violent assassination—which he both anticipated and was resigned to—at the age of forty for refusing to back down from or to compromise what he perceived to be the truth. Malcolm X blazed a trail that many African-American Muslims would eventually follow: he went from the radical teachings of Elijah Muhammad to the prevailing viewpoints of traditional Islam.[41]

In a modest castle in a tiny village along a snow covered mountain pass between Herat and Kabul, Afghanistan, the after-dinner conversation turned to the story of David and Goliath.

"David was small, but his faith was great," remarked the host. Leopold Weiss, Middle East correspondent for the Frankfurter Zeitung, responded: "And you are many, but your faith is small."

Leopold was not referring specifically to his three companions, but the world Muslim community. Embarrassed that he probably insulted his host, he began a lengthy apology, explaining how if Muslims had remained true to their faith, they would, in his opinion, never have experienced such a miserable decline.

"But you are a Muslim," his host whispered.

Leopold laughed and replied: "No, I am not a Muslim, but I have come to see so much beauty in Islam that it makes me sometimes angry to watch you people waste it."

His host disagreed: "No, it is as I have said: you are a Muslim, only you don't know it yourself."

In his many years of study of the people of the Middle East, he had explored Islam so deeply and personally, that it was now apparent even to strangers that his way of thinking and living was imbued with the religion. The words of his Afghan host never left him in the months that followed and they served to awaken him to the choice he had to face. Within a year, Leopold Weiss would make the shahaadah (testimony of faith). Today, he is best known as Muhammad Asad, whose writings have greatly influenced many Muslims worldwide.[42]

Neither of these men described their conversions to Islam as leaps of faith. For both of them, their coming to Islam was a long development spanning many years.

Many western converts report that they had become rationally convinced of the truth of Islam before they embraced it. Maryam Jameelah, in her letters to Maududi, describes the intellectual appeal that Islam held for

---

[41] Alex Haley, *The Autobiography of Malcolm X* (New York: Grove Publ., 1966).

[42] Muhammad Asad, *The Road to Mecca* (Gibraltar: Dar al Andalus Publishers, 1984).

her.[43] Marmaduke Pikthall's conversion involved an intellectual maturation and discovery similar to Asad's.[44] Aminah Assilmi and Nancy Ali, well-known speakers at American Islamic conferences, describe their choices to become Muslims in essentially rational terms.[45] Gary Miller, best known for his participation in Muslim–Christian dialogues, tells how he became rationally convinced of Islam after reading a copy of the Qur'an that he came upon one day in a bookstore in Canada.[46] Nuh Ha Mim Keller, writer for *The American Muslim* magazine, mentions how his prolonged study of modern philosophers helped him to become a Muslim.[47]

Some other impressions about converts that I have obtained from personal interviews and autobiographical accounts deserve mention. Most often the western convert was not on a spiritual quest when he or she became interested in Islam, or at least not on one of which he or she was aware. There may be several reasons for this. First, Islam does not view faith as principally a spiritual experience. As we saw earlier, the spiritual side of Islam is only one aspect of a comprehensive and holistic understanding of life. Second, Islam does not offer persons instant sainthood: spirituality matures by patiently sticking to a religious program and discipline. Third, the stress Muslims place on abiding by Islamic law may discourage those who emphasize the spiritual side of faith; they may consider Islam to be overly legalistic.

Most American and European converts were initially curious about the beliefs and practices of the Muslims they had met. Often they mention that the media's portrayal of Muslims and the perceptions they obtained through personal contact with them were very different and that this served to heighten their interest in the religion. Many admit that they were influenced greatly by Muslim friends or romantic interests, but they often add that while they were encouraged strongly to learn about the religion, they were usually discouraged from accepting it without being totally convinced (The

---

[43] *Correspondence between Abi-L-A'la Al-Maududi and Maryam Jameelah*, printed and distributed by IFTA, Islamic Trust, 1982.

[44] Peter Clark, *Marmaduke Pickthall: British Muslim* (London: Quarter Books, 1986).

[45] Amina Assilmi, I*slam in My Life–Sixteen Years as a Muslim*, Ghazali Islamic Video, No. 231, 1993; Nancy Ali, *My Journey From Islam to Christianity*, Ghazali Islamic Video, No. 141, 1990.

[46] Gary Miller, *Impressions on the Christian–Muslim Debate*, Ghazali Islamic Video, No. 207, 1993.

[47] Nuh Hah Mim Keller, "Becoming Muslim," *The American Muslim Magazine* II, No. 11-12 (1994):17-21.

general feeling among Muslims is that a hypocrite is more dangerous to himself and the community than a truthful disbeliever).

Many converts characterize their entry into Islam as an acquiescence to a perceived truth. Very often their decision to become a Muslim is seen as a choice between their material and social interests on the one hand and their relationship with God on the other.

Typically, modern western converts to Islam were non-conformists before entering the religion. Men rejected or were disillusioned by their society's worldview and its goals and dreams. They often associated and identified with unpopular individuals, preferring to avoid the lime-light. Many converts describe themselves as being loners before their joining the Muslim community. They frequently are idealists: wealth, popularity, and power are not as important to them as personal freedom and ideals. Most often they leaned toward the liberal or even radical left end of the political spectrum before conversion. They are usually self-confident individuals who are strongly opinionated and adventurous in their thinking. They are often inquisitive and open to knew ideas, yet tend to seem dogmatic and uncompromising in tone. A few converts, like Maryam Jameelah, report having suffered an emotional crisis short-ly before becoming interested in Islam, but this does not appear to be the norm.

Many converts to Islam were formally atheists or agnostics. Murad Hofmann, Maryam Jameelah, Muhammad Asad, Malcolm X, Nuh Ha Mim Keller, and myself were in this category. In America, a large num-ber of white American converts seem to come from Catholic families. This was my situation as well as better known converts such as Gary Miller, Steve Johnson, Jamaal Zarabozo, Nancy Ali, Aminah Assilmi, Murad Hofmann, and Nuh Ha Mim Keller. Among African–American converts, religious backgrounds appear to be in line with the demograph-ics of the larger non-Muslim black American community.

The following is an attempt at a personality profile of the potential western convert to Islam: Relatively young, between the ages of twenty five and forty. Idealistic. Self-sacrificing. Non-conformist. Periodically reclusive. Prefers the company of society's disenfranchised. Nonmaterialistic to ascetic in nature. An activist. Liberal to radical politi-cally. College educated. Capable of sudden drastic changes in viewpoints. Very curious. Highly opinionated. Stubborn. Argumentative. Confident. Contemplative. Tends toward rationalism as opposed to spiritualism in reli-gion. Critical of others. Loyal to overzealous in commitments.

Some of these qualities can work against an individual once he or she enters the Muslim community. The great emphasis the community puts on emulating the Prophet's habits can be at odds with a non-conformist personality. What many converts perceive as a prevailing misogyny among Muslims will conflict with a liberal western outlook (It is very interesting to note that quite a large number of female converts were feminists before embracing Islam.) The modern Muslim community is quite suspicious of philosophy and is uncomfortable with what it often sees as an overly rational approach to religion among converts.[48] Even though the Muslim community in the West is now fairly large (there are about five million Muslims residing in North America alone), it is still quite politically timid and converts tend to become frustrated by what they see as the Muslim community's extreme passivity.

As already mentioned, the decision to convert formally to Islam is seldom an easy one. However, it seems that the greater the difficulty in coming to that decision, the more steadfast is the convert in his or her commitment to Islam. Perhaps this is because such persons already have considered and accepted most of the difficulties and problems that come with being a Muslim in America or Europe. The time spent studying Islam before actual conversion was long for all of the above mentioned individuals but one, who may be the exception that proves the rule, or maybe not.

At first glance, it appears that the conversion of Malcolm X was a sudden impulse. He seemed to embrace Islam in prison on the spot, after reading his brother Reginald's letter. But this would be a wrong conclusion. Malcolm X's conversion to what he eventually saw as authentic Islam was actually a very long development, lasting more than a decade, that was crowned on his pilgrimage to Makkah. What makes his conversion so outstanding is the resoluteness with which he submitted to Islam: He was fully conscious of the great personal risks that he was taking, but once convinced, he showed virtually no hesitation.

What then are the most salient obstacles to conversion to Islam in the West? What are the main reasons that cause people to hesitate to embrace this religion, even when it appeals to them? For Muslims living in the West, many of whom feel it is their duty to bear witness to their religion,

---

[48] For the history of rationalism and philosophy in Islam see Fazlur Rahman, *Islam* (Chicago: University of Chicago Press, 1979), 85-100; H. R. Gibb, *Mohammedanism* (London: Oxford University Press), 107-27.

these are important questions—yet ones that are seldom asked of converts. If potential converts anticipate harm from their societies, perhaps
the Muslim community could help allay or address these fears. If certain
actions or behaviors of Muslims are discouraging potential converts, then
one would think that the Muslim community would want to know what
these are.

Islam in the West

*I lay in bed—in the dark—on my back—unable to sleep—staring at the
ceiling. I could never tolerate loose ends: a trait I had inherited from my
mother. I needed to get this over with. I could not handle another sleepless
night. I could feel my heart beating as I switched on the lamp beside my
bed. I felt a little queasy as I began to dial the ten digit number. The conversation went uneasily. I was nervous and uncomfortable. "What's wrong,
Jeff," my mother finally asked me.*

*She was the religious pillar of our family. When we were kids my
mom dragged the rest of us to church every Sunday, enrolled us in
Catholic schools up through high-school, donated weekly to the
church, cared for the sick and elderly in our neighborhood, never
uttered a profanity, and with the most powerful love, she fought tooth
and nail to keep her sons from going down the self-destructive paths
that cities like Bridgeport, Connecticut offer children. She was more
than a mother to me: she was my friend and hero. I had only disappointed her once before. She always said how much she admired and
respected me.*

"Mom, I did something and I thought you should be the first to know."

*I sounded and felt like I was divulging something that I should have
been ashamed of, as if I was confessing some crime or sexual perversion.*

"I became a Muslim."

*She was shocked and deeply hurt. For the next quarter of an hour I felt
pinned into a corner, groping for an explanation for how I could come to
do such a thing. I could only think of how ridiculous I must have sounded:
how this was so unlike me! I tried to calm her fears, to demonstrate with a
few jokes that I had not really changed. But I had changed and I knew it. I
then pretended to be surprised by her reaction.*

*"I was an atheist!" I told her. "I thought you would be pleased that I
finally came to believe in God."*

*"But how can you worship Muhammad?!" She exclaimed. "How can
you worship a man?!"*

With my mother's question I suddenly saw an opening. Until then, I had been assailed by feelings of embarrassment and guilt for what I had done to my culture, my heritage, my mother. I was overly concerned with how I would be perceived—with how I would be associated with the many misconceptions and prejudices Americans have of Muslims. But the tables had suddenly turned—now we were on my turf—and I felt a surge of confidence.

I seized the moment and fired back: "I believe we have our roles reversed," I answered her. "Muslims do not worship Muhammad. And should not I be asking that type of question of you?"

For the rest of the conversation, the momentum was on my side and I was in control. My mother and I went several more rounds when I flew to Connecticut over the semester break, but as long as I stuck with my reasons for becoming an atheist at sixteen and then embracing Islam at twenty-eight, I had the upper hand. Eventually, our religious warfare turned into dialogue and we both came to respect each other's perspective.

My mom became very curious about my religion. She asked me to send her videotapes of the public lectures I had given on Islam. On one of her visits to Kansas, she asked me if she could attend a talk on Islam I was scheduled to give at the university.

As we drove home from the lecture, she began to explain to me that most people need to stay in one of the religions of their culture, that not everyone could make the transition I did, and that she was sure that God in His mercy would understand this. What she said caught me off guard. I was not sure what to say and I kept silent.

Looking out the car window she remarked: "I believe that your religion might make more sense than mine, and I understand how Islam would appeal to someone who thinks like you do, but I could never become a Muslim."

"I didn't even suggest . . . ," I quickly began to explain.

"I know," she interrupted me, "I know you didn't."

The biggest obstacle to acceptance of Islam by potential converts is anxiety over society's response to that decision. The questions I am asked most frequently by non-Muslims considering conversion to Islam are about my family's and friends' reactions to my becoming a Muslim.

The first reactions of relatives and friends to new converts to Islam in the West almost always involve some degree of shock and dismay. Some new Muslims meet with blind prejudice and intolerance, and there have been rare cases where parents or friends sever all relations with the convert; but most often the parents and friends come to accept the convert's choice, and quite frequently to respect it, especially if he or she seems happier and more at peace with him/herself in the new-found faith. Usually, if the relationship between a parent or friend and a convert was close before Islam, it will remain so after conversion. In addition, converts can help to reduce tension by being reasonable and non-aggressive when discussing Islam. The latter is no small feat, because the attitudes that confront new Muslims are often prejudiced and combative, making it all too easy to respond in kind. However, the Qur'an disapproves of such tactics:

> And indeed He has revealed to you in the Book that when you hear God's messages rejected and mocked at, do not sit with them until they enter into some other discourse, for then indeed you would be like them. (4:140)

> Invite to the way of your Lord with wisdom and the best of speech; and argue with them in ways that are best and most gracious. (16:125).

> And do not dispute with the People of the Book except with means better, unless it be with those of them who inflict wrong. But say, "We believe in that revealed to us and revealed to you; Our God and your God is One and it is to Him we have submitted ourselves."(29:46)

The requirement to use "wisdom and the best of speech" when representing Islam is well served by broadening one's knowledge of Islam as well as the other world religions. In this way, arguments about issues over which there is already substantial agreement can be avoided and the discussions can focus more clearly on shared values and viewpoints as well as on true points of difference.

Many converts fear job discrimination and keep their faith secret from their employers and co-workers. In my case, some colleagues have displayed ill-feeling and disapproval about my commitment to Islam, but I do not believe it has greatly affected my career. Others have endured much worse, especially women who embrace Islam in the West.

A man can become a Muslim without substantially altering his outer appearance and hence can conceal his religious identity whenever he chooses. The Muslim community, however, puts tremendous pressure on female converts to adopt the most conservative styles of traditional

Islamic dress, even though it often leads to terrible hardship and makes them easy targets for threats and insults. My wife is not a convert, but she has been chased, screamed at, cursed, struck, and refused employment because of her dress.

When a man converts to Islam he may be considered eccentric, a little strange, an independent thinker, a rebel, perhaps even brave; but when a woman converts, the hand that rocks the cradle commits cultural treason. Every society seems to pin its honor, traditions, and stability on its women, so that when a female steps out of line, all hell breaks loose. The female convert to Islam, much more than her male counterpart, becomes caught in a cultural tug of war in which she becomes the rope, as both societies—the dominant western and the traditional Islamic subculture residing in it—fight to assert themselves in opposing directions through her. This felt pressure from both sides causes many women who see much that is positive in Islam to remain non-Muslim and many others who embrace the religion to keep apart from the Islamic community.

The Muslim community in western countries can do much to counter the pressures felt by newcomers to their religion. First and foremost, they could take a much more active role in fighting discrimination. Up to now, the Muslim community is one of the most passive and disorganized minorities in the West. If an American or European Muslim chooses to fight discrimination, it is usually a solitary battle.[49]

Second, the Muslim community in the West should put less pressure on its female members to adhere to strict traditional dress codes. The dangers and hardships that some of these women face can be very severe, and there is no social system established to support and protect them. The enjoining of modest dress and behavior for both sexes should suffice for now.

Third, the mosque must become much more of a haven and buttress to new Muslims—a place where they can turn for comfort and encouragement. In the time of Prophet Muhammad, the mosque certainly served this function; today, however, new Muslims not only feel estranged from their own western cultures, but often from what should be the very center of Muslim community life. This is especially the case with female converts, for they—and women in general—are often made to feel unwelcome in the mosque.

---

[49] However, I must commend the efforts of the American Muslim Council (AMC) and the Council on American Islamic Relations (CAIR) for their outstanding efforts in fighting prejudice and discrimination against Muslims.

I know of one young lady in California who went with her mother to a mosque in order to learn more about Islam. When the man who opened the door saw the two American women standing in front of him, he slammed the door in their faces. A Muslim student at the University of San Francisco once announced that if he saw any women praying in the mosque, he would throw them out bodily. His threat was taken seriously by some recent female converts, and they abruptly stopped attending the evening prayer rituals.

As noted, estrangement from friends and relatives and job discrimination seem to be the two biggest worries that initially confront potential converts to Islam in the West. Overcoming these anxieties can be very difficult. While most converts attest that reactions to their decision to adopt Islam were mostly cool, they also admit that their worse fears were never realized. Surmounting these anxieties is only one of the social obstacles to becoming or remaining a Muslim. Many western apostates—and there have been many—claim that the Muslim community presents a greater problem.

Confirming Misconceptions

> You are the best nation raised up for mankind: you enjoin
> good and forbid evil and you believe in God. (3:110)

Western culture has very definite preconceptions about Islam and its followers that are rooted deeply in its own long experience as the principal rival of the Muslim world.[50] A person in search of God may be ready to concede the possibility of false personal prejudice against a religion and to put them aside for a while, but it does not take much on the part of the faithful to confirm and ignite earlier predispositions, regardless of the religious or non-religious basis of the community's behavior. What follows is a discussion of what I believe are some of the major problems that persons sincerely interested in Islam often have with the Muslim community.

An Arab Religion

> And We sent you to mankind as a messenger. And God is
> sufficient as a witness. (4:79)

---

[50] Norman Daniel, *Islam and the West, The Making of an Image* (Oxford: One World Publications, 1993).

O mankind, the messenger has truly come to you with
truth from your Lord, so believe, it is better for you.
(4:170)

Say: O mankind, surely I am the messenger of God to you
all. (7:158)

This is a message to mankind that they may be warned
thereby and that they may know that He is one God, and
that persons of understanding may bear it in mind. (14:52)

And We have not sent you except as a bearer of good news
and as a warner to all mankind, but most men do not know.
(34:28)

There are many references in the Qur'an to the universal character of
Islam, and its many addresses and exhortations to all mankind (in Arabic,
insaan and *naas*) make it obvious that the Qur'an addresses its message to
all humanity. Of course, Muhammad's immediate audience was the Arabs,
and thus, as the Qur'an explains, the revelation is naturally in Arabic (12:2;
26:195; 42:7; 43:3; 46:12). The unprecedented success that the early community had in protecting and preserving the revelation in its original language and in compiling thousands of details about Muhammad's everyday
sayings and happenings assured that Arabic and seventh-century Arabian
culture would influence Muslim life forever. Every new Muslim needs to
learn at least some Arabic, however little, if only to participate in the ritual
prayers, since Arabic is the liturgical language of Islam. In striving to develop an Islamic lifestyle in western countries, many new Muslims also feel it
advantageous to study Arabic grammar in some depth in order to have firsthand access to the revelation and to the Prophet's *Sunnah* (the Prophet's life
example), the two primary sources of guidance for the community.

Although a few short passages of the Qur'an need to be memorized in
Arabic in order to perform the ritual prayer, and more extensive knowledge
of Arabic is required for scholarly study of Islam's textual sources, by no
means should this imply that Islam is strictly an Arabian religion, which is
the common perception in the West. Actually, the majority of Muslims
throughout the world (about 85 percent) are not Arabs and know virtually
no Arabic. Yet this false perception of Islam may be more the fault of
Muslims than non-Muslims.

Middle-Eastern Arabian culture appears to dominate the Muslim communities of America and Europe far beyond what scholarship, ritual, and

piety demand. At the many Islamic conferences held in western countries, men and women are segregated, many participants dress in middle-eastern costumes (especially the converts), and many speakers frequently interject Arabic words into their lectures, even though the majority of listeners do not speak Arabic and English translations are available and well known. The same often occurs at lectures about Islam presented for the general public and sponsored by Muslim organizations.

I recall a lecture I attended at a university when I first became interested in Islam. The speaker, an American convert dressed in something similar to Saudi Arabian attire, continuously inserted poorly pronounced Arabic terms into his presentation, as if the entire audience should be familiar with them. This created so many gaps in my understanding that his speech became, for me, practically unintelligible. I left the lecture with the feeling that in order to become a Muslim one needed to become an Arab or at least a foreigner. This seems to be the message many non-Muslims are getting, whether or not the Muslim community intends to convey it. Steve Johnson, an American convert who used to lecture extensively on Islam, once related that he overheard his brother say to a friend, "O yeah! My brother Steve became an Arab!" This confusion is understandable.

Most converts take on Arabic names, even though early non-Arab converts to Islam like Salmon the Persian and Bilal from Ethiopia kept their non-Arabic names, with the approval of the Prophet. I also met quite a few converts who developed foreign accents in no time at all, yet they had never left America nor learned a foreign language. On one occasion, I took a Muslim friend of mine from Yemen to a lecture given at our local Islamic center. As we were listening to the speech, he leaned over to me and whispered, "I traveled through India and Pakistan and I recognize that accent. Is the speaker Pakistani?" "No!" I told him. "I know the speaker well. He is a fifth generation American of Scandinavian descent from San Diego."

When devout American Muslims appear in the news, they are usually dressed in middle-eastern garb. The defendants in the World Trade Center bombings trial and their supporters were almost always seen in foreign dress, even though a fair number of them were Americans. Cat Stevens, now Yusef Islam, seems to always appear in public in a turban and long gown. Recently, in Lawrence, Kansas, an American convert with an Arabic name led a hunger strike against the Hallmark Corporation for distributing a greeting card he felt was offensive to Muslims. He appeared frequently on television and in the newspapers dressed in an Egyptian *jallabiyah*. The offending card showed a neurotic American woman convert to Islam, veiled in the traditional Iranian manner, who changed her name to Yasmeen and moved to Tehran. Muslims had every right to protest the card, which involved the word "Mecca" in a tasteless pun, but ironically, the much publicized furor continued to *visually* reinforce the stereotype that the card presented: to be a Muslim one needed to become a middle-easterner.

Melting Pot

There are a number of factors that contribute to the predominance of middle-eastern—primarily Arabian and Pakistani—culture in the Muslim communities of the West. First and foremost is the fact that the majority of Muslims currently residing in western countries are Arab, Pakistani, Indian, Iranian, and Turkish immigrants. They are naturally proud of their own cultures and eager to preserve that heritage within their families and communities. As is the case with other immigrants from non-western lands, western society could often seem to them strange and frightening, which only heightens the need to cling to one's roots.

Islam is a powerful social force in the immigrants' homelands, where, over time, religion and culture have become fused. Thus each immigrant is likely to view his particular culture's understandings and applications of Islam as the truest expression of the faith and to be uncomfortable with Muslim perspectives that differ from these.

We might expect that if the majority of members of a local Islamic community or an Islamic organization come from a certain common culture, then its policies and regulations would reflect that cultural background. Yet this is not always the case. In order to avoid internal conflicts, a Muslim community or organization will often enforce the most conservative cultural option advocated, even if only a minority of its members support it, for, on the whole, Muslims prefer to err on the conservative side. The result is that the subculture of the local Muslim community becomes even more remote from the western culture that surrounds it.

Almost all Muslim communities in America and Europe now include home-grown converts, but their influence on the practices and viewpoints of their communities is usually negligible. In most mosques and Islamic centers, the number of converts is still very small. Also, the criticism converts make of the practices or views of Muslim immigrants are often dismissed as essentially western and, hence, un-Islamic.

Twenty years from now this may all change, since the majority of Muslims in the West will most probably no longer be immigrants or converts. They will not only have been born into Muslim families, but they will be citizens from birth of western countries as well. As they assimilate both cultures, their expression of Islam will likely display strong influences from each. Ideally, they might harmonize their faith with their western cultural backgrounds, but that depends very much on their parents open-mindedness, adaptability, and knowledge of the religion. The more culturally rigid a parent's understanding of Islam is, the more difficulty his or her child will probably have in living as a Muslim in the West.

Imitating the Prophet

Another major element adding to the middle-eastern character of modern Islamic communities in the West is the current prevailing attitude among Muslims toward the Prophet's *Sunnah* (his life example). Muslims have always revered Muhammad and have considered his life to be the perfect exemplification of self-surrender to God. Many Muslims (Ibn Umar is one of the earliest and best known examples) so highly honored the Prophet's habits that they considered the imitation of his most quotidian deeds to be of great spiritual benefit. Thus they would strive to walk, sleep, part their hair, dress, laugh, and so on, exactly as he did, even though these acts are not directly related to ritual or legal concerns. This intensive type of imitation of Muhammad became quite common among Muslims, and it appears to have many zealous advocates today in the Muslim communities of the West. It is often inspired by more than only reverence for Prophet Muhammad.

The Muslim community in America is made up almost entirely of foreign immigrants and African–American converts. Each, in different ways, has felt humiliated and violated by western civilization. African–Americans were the victims of a brutal system of slavery in America, and after emancipation they were long denied even the most basic human rights. Muslim immigrants not only suffer from the dislocation and shock that most newcomers to the West experience, but also from intense feelings of humiliation that come from being surpassed and now dominated by a Judeo–Christian West that has relegated and reduced them to Third World status. This has helped to trigger a passionate desire, in both groups of Muslims in America, for an alternative culture. The wearing of distinctive dress, the possession of non-Jewish and non-Christian names, the frequent use of Arabic words, and the observance of customs that go against the American mainstream become a religious rejection and protest against the dominant western culture and a return to, or at least a reminder of, a more stable and glorious past, when God, through his prophet Muhammad, brought greatness first to the Arabs and then to other peoples who would later embrace Islam.

For many Muslims, the revival of Muhammad's daily habits has a profound spiritual benefit. But it also has psychological and social dimensions, for it instantly provides Muslims with a distinctive culture, history, and tradition. For immigrants, it is a culture with which they have obvious links, and for many converts, it is a culture into which they can enter rather easily by learning a surprisingly small number of expressions and mannerisms. A rational argument cannot be made against this strict and literal application of Muhammad's life example. The fact that so many Muslims gain strength, inner peace, group solidarity, and heightened spirituality through this approach argues for its legitimacy. It is one thing, however, to maintain the appropriateness of meticulously imitating the Prophet's lifestyle, down to his everyday habits, but quite another to insist that any other response to his *Sunnah* is wrong. Yet this is a common stance among Muslims.

A minority of Muslims—and I must confess that I am one of them—believes that we must remain cognizant of the historical context of Muhammad's actions and sayings and that if we are to apply his example correctly, we must be alert to the many differences that exist between his time and ours. These people prefer to search for general ethical and spiritual lessons through the study of the Prophet's biographies, rather than to copy his daily routines. The main assumption behind the stricter approach is that the best and most efficient way to derive moral and spiritual benefit from Muhammad's life example is by imitating him as closely as possible. The principle aim of the more liberal approach is to understand the intentions behind and effects of the Prophet's actions and to duplicate them. This less conservative application of the *Sunnah* seems self-serving and disingenuous to stricter Muslims. The more conservative approach seems illogical and overly restrictive to more liberal believers, who feel that we can easily produce the opposite of what Prophet Muhammad intended by ignoring the historical and societal background of his acts.

I recall an Islamic conference where a member of the audience asked a Muslim speaker, dressed in a business suit, if he was not selling out to the West by wearing European clothing instead of the *Sunnah* (style of clothing worn by Muhammad). The question apparently startled and embarrassed him, for he was unable to formulate a coherent reply. However, his wearing of modest western clothing while lecturing in America could very much be considered in line with Muhammad's example, for the Prophet dressed in the style of his culture. He did not suddenly appear before his contemporaries dressed in foreign or radically unfamiliar clothing. If he had, it probably would have created for them an unnecessary obstacle to considering his message.

I attended a lecture in a mosque in San Francisco in which a speaker stressed the extreme importance of following the *Sunnah* by always and only using your right hand when eating. During the discussion that followed, I asked him in jest what one should do when eating with a knife and a fork. To my surprise, not only did he not laugh, but a serious debate arose over my question. Some advocated holding the knife in the right hand, since it is gets more use than the fork; others felt that the fork belonged in the right hand, since it touched one's mouth more often; some said it did not matter; and still others believed it preferable to not use eating utensils at all, since it was not part of the Prophet's *Sunnah*.

In seventh-century Arabia, much like today, people used their left hand to clean themselves after relieving themselves. They also used water if available, otherwise, a few stones, some smooth bark, or even dry sand. Since the Arabs also ate with their hands from a common dish, it was considered proper etiquette to use only the right hand when dining and to only eat from the food on the platter directly in front of oneself. Many of Muhammad's followers were rough-and-tumble Bedouin, and he often instructed them in proper hygiene and manners.

In the West, people normally eat from their own plates with knives, forks, and spoons and serve themselves with special utensils, so that their hands do not come in contact with the food. This form of dining is both hygienic and polite—matters that greatly concerned the Prophet—but whether to hold the fork with the right or left hand in such a context is of no great consequence. The Prophet might very well have endorsed this eating style if it was well known to and practical for the Arabs. If a Muslim were to insist on eating with his hands while dining with non-Muslims in the West, the latter may be quite offended, especially since a more sanitary option is readily available.

Failing to Communicate

At the Islamic center one evening, I was greeted by an American Muslim who asked me how things were going.

"Very well, thank God. And how are you?" I responded.

"Al hamdu-lillah!" (All praise belongs to God!) he answered. "And how are you?" he asked me again.

"Fine, thank God!" I repeated.

He looked dissatisfied and a few seconds later repeated his question,
and I repeated my answer. Another few seconds of conversation, and then
the same question and answer. I realized he would not give up until he
received a satisfactory reply. I held on a little longer but finally gave him
the answer he wanted: "Al hamdu lillah," I sighed.
With an approving look on his face he nodded, "Al hamdu lillah."

It is not that I mind practicing well-known, traditional, Arabic formulas, which are popular among Muslims, but often I prefer, for emotional and
even spiritual reasons, to speak in my own language, since this is more natural for me, especially when I am talking to fellow Americans. However,
the use of a few specific Arabic expressions has become one of a number
of external measures of a convert's progress in the faith.

A friend of mine, who for a while was very interested in Islam, once
remarked to me that he discovered the key to becoming a fully accepted
member of the Islamic community. He said: "Wear a middle-eastern cap,
grow a long beard, and say '*al hamdu lillah*' (all praise belongs to God),
'*ma sha'a Allah*' (as God wills), '*as salaamu alaikum*' (peace be upon
you), and '*jazaka Allah khairan*' (may God reward you with blessings) in
certain standard situations." Another friend and convert to Islam commented to me on one occasion that Muslims seem to think that God only
understands Arabic.

Since Arabic is the the language of the Qur'an and Islamic rituals, and
is in some sense the lingua franca of Islam, all Muslims should try as best
they could to learn Arabic. But, this should not be confused with memoriz-
ing a few badly pronounced and poorly understood phrases to be parroted
automatically in a finite number of well-rehearsed situations. In particular,
if persons with whom one is trying to communicate do not know Arabic,
then it is better not to use Arabic words they do not understand. The
Prophet exhorted his followers to speak plainly to people and to avoid using
confusing or misleading language.[51]

Superficialities

Two of the most conservative Muslim groups in the West are the
Jamaat Tableegh (a movement that originated in India and Pakistan) and
the Salafi movement (based in Saudi Arabia). A main plank of both groups

---

[51] *Sahih Muslim*, translated in *Riyad as-Salihin* of Imam Nawawi, 1:383.

is a strict return to the *Sunnah* of the Prophet. However, the practices that differentiate members of these organizations from other observant Muslims are very small in number and have mostly to do with matters of dress, grooming, dining habits, and separation of the sexes.[52] Although most Muslims residing in America and Europe do not usually follow the practices promoted by these groups in their day-to-day living, they often admit that it is preferable to do so, and some feel guilty for neglecting them. Persons who do adopt the stricter practices of these organizations are considered by their fellow Muslims to be the most religious of the faithful, and they often rise to leadership positions in their local communities.

With the widespread deference paid to the most conservative viewpoint, and since conservative Muslims usually control the mosques and Islamic organizations in the West, it is not surprising that outsiders and newcomers to the Islamic community come to regard such practices as wearing middle-eastern dress, growing a beard, eating on the floor without utensils, separation of men and women, and taking an Arabic name as essential to Islam. It is also not surprising that many non-Muslims come to think of Islam as an exclusively middle-eastern or foreign religion. Although Muslims say Islam is for all times and places, a non-Muslim can easily get the impression that Muslims want all people to squeeze themselves into a singular moment and place in history.

Religion and Culture

Another element that encourages the western perception of Islam as an exclusively middle-eastern religion is the tendency among Muslims from Islamic societies to attribute various customs from their homelands to Islam. A Muslim graduate student once told me that adultery, when committed by a woman, is a much greater sin in Islam than when committed by a man. His culture may see it this way, but his statement blatantly contradicts explicit pronouncements in the Qur'an and the Prophet's sayings. Recently, a young Saudi Arabian man insisted to me that Islam forbids

---

[52] There are many behaviors of the Prophet which are well documented and quite practicable but which are either unknown to most Muslims or simply ignored. For example, Muhammad was well known to never have raised his voice or his hand to his wives, yet wife abuse is quite common among even religious Muslims. The Prophet was also known to be very punctual, while Muslims today are notoriously dilatory. The Prophet also fought hard against the intrenched pre-Islamic prejudice that sons were a source of great pride while daughters were, for the most part, a liability and a potential source of family dishonor; but it seems that his teachings on this matter never quite caught on. Its easy to produce many more examples of this nature.

women to drive cars. I told him that I knew this was a commonly held opinion in his country, but most Muslims around the world would disagree with him. And not long ago, an American convert blamed me for not dressing according to the Prophet's *Sunnah*. I replied to him that what was good for the goose was good for the gander, because the Moroccan outfit he was wearing was quite different from the style of dress worn by Hijazis (the people of western Arabia) in the lifetime of Muhammad. In fact, I have rarely seen Muslims dressed in seventh-century Hijazi attire.

The mixing of culture and religion is nothing new, unusual, or always undesirable. To some extent it is unavoidable, especially when believers attempt to construct a comprehensive code of proper conduct, for our mores are culturally oriented. One often hears American and European Muslims declare that Islam guaranteed women the rights to vote, to contract and dissolve their marriages, to hold positions in government, and to work centuries before western women won these privileges. Yet on visits to the Arabian Gulf, I discovered that many, if not most, scholars there insist on exactly the opposite. Clearly, the cultural orientations of the western and Gulf states' scholars influence their interpretations. I am not claiming that one set of scholars is wrong and the other right, or that one viewpoint is only culture and the other true Islam; I believe that religion and culture inform both standpoints.

A religious judgement can be appropriate in one cultural context and not in another. Many Saudi Arabian scholars maintain that, in accordance with Islam, women should cover their faces in public. Since there are no explicit pronouncements in either the Qur'an or authenticated traditions of the Prophet to this effect, they base their arguments on somewhat strained analogies and rationalizations about the social disruption that will occur from adopting a less strict dress code.[53] Saudi scholars know best their culture and are in the best position to predict the effects of loosening this standard on Saudi society. However, people in the West will have difficulty relating to many of the points Saudi scholars raise. For example, I doubt that most Westerners, Muslim or otherwise, would agree with the argument that men will become overexcited by the sight of womens' eyes and that this will inevitably lead to extreme jealousy and social unrest. On the other hand, I feel that western men and women will easily accept the counter-

---

[53] It is interesting that in general this type of reasoning is rejected by the Hanbali legal school, the school to which most Saudi scholars belong.

argument that veiling the face is harmful to women because it impairs their vision.

"How do we separate culture from religion?" I am often asked this question by young Muslims in America. I tell them that this is very hard to do. While it is important to watch out for the presence or penetration of cultural influences that run counter to the religion, we must expect that Muslim understanding and behavior will never be completely free of culture. The indigenous culture will inform Muslim religious attitudes, and Islam will influence their own cultural or subcultural development.

These days, when a Muslim living in the West questions a ruling of classical Islamic law or a well-established Muslim custom or perception, he or she will usually be confronted with the accusation: "You are trying to change the religion!" There is a pervasive fear among Muslims living in the West that the surrounding non-Muslim culture will permeate and contaminate their practice of Islam. Yet it is often precisely the same concern that has some of the faithful reexamining long established Muslim viewpoints and conventions: They fear the community may be harming itself by clinging unnecessarily to pre-Islamic ideas and practices that had penetrated the Muslim community long ago. Both are legitimate worries. The most effective way to counter either danger is not to discourage questioning and criticism, but, on the contrary, the Muslim community should encourage both. We are most prone to err when we refuse to be self-critical.

Among all systems of thought, religion is the most vulnerable to the idealization of customs and opinions. In religion, the difference between textual source and interpretation is frequently missed. Too often we equate our understanding of a matter with truth itself and dogma with revelation. There is a tremendous difference in authority between the two statements: "According to Islam, there is no god but the one God" and "According to Islam, women must be segregated from men." Yet many Muslims refuse to see any essential difference.

A Misogynous Religion

I was shopping with my family in Khobar, Saudi Arabia. It was Wednesday—the last day of the workweek. It was just before sunset. The air was thick with dust and humidity and it was still very hot outside, about as hot as the hottest Kansas summer day.

People of every race and color filled the sidewalks. Their mood was sober, determined. These were very serious shoppers, absorbed in the pursuit of bargains. They reminded me a little of gamblers at a sporting event.

I noticed that husbands and wives kept a certain distance from each other here; they did not hold hands nor even exchange affectionate glances in public. I saw pairs of men walking with their arms around each other and women holding hands, but I saw no tenderness between spouses.

I was also struck by the contrast between men's and women's attire. All of the women wore black abayas—elegant, long, black cloaks— that covered the entire body except the hands and head. Most of the ladies wore black scarves that covered their hair. Many Saudi women wore black veils that hid their faces and some of them also wore black gloves. A few American and European women risked leaving their heads uncovered. Most of the men wore western clothing—dress shirts and slacks—except the Saudis, who wore thobes—the finely tailored, sharp looking, long, white gowns that have become the national dress of Saudi men. The children all wore western styles: mostly jeans, T-shirts, sneakers, shorts, short skirts and dresses.

Saudis, Asians, Africans, Europeans, Americans, and American soldiers were moving quickly up and down the sidewalks, stepping in and out of small, disorganized shops, haggling, in Arabic and English, over all kinds of merchandise. Almost anything you might want could be bought in Khobar's shopping district—clothing, electrical appliances, sports equipment, jewelry, housing goods, hardware, watches, eyeglasses, toys, groceries, audio and video tapes, calculators, computers—except books, for book shops had a very limited inventory, even in Arabic.

Cars, half of them luxury, the other half old, beaten-up economy, crawled along the narrow streets beeping their horns to clear a path through oblivious, preoccupied pedestrians.

Suddenly, above the din, rose the call of the adhan from a loudspeaker from a nearby mosque. Then another adhan rang out from another loudspeaker from another mosque a few blocks down the street, then another adhan, and another, and another, from the many mosques scattered throughout the neighborhood. A chorus of adhans rose above the hustle and bustle of the shoppers.

The streets quieted, the shops emptied themselves of patrons, shop doors closed, and iron grills were pulled down and locked. The Muslim men, all of them, immediately made for the mosques, like persons heading for a designated shelter during an air-raid. Non-Muslim men and women, knowing well the drill, took positions outside on the sidewalks, leaning on walls and lampposts, sitting on curbs. Some smoked, some chatted, all waited.

To my surprise, for I had just arrived in the Middle East only a short time ago, the Muslim women did not go to the mosques; instead, they bided their time like the non-believers. While their male counterparts hastened to the prayer, the Muslim ladies stood outside the shops on the sidewalks or sat in their cars and waited for the maghrib prayer to end.

When we reached the mosque, my wife and three daughters entered the ladies' section—a very small, dark room, with a dark plexiglas window that looked out upon the area of the mosque where the men prayed. After I dropped my family off, I entered the men's section of the mosque through the main door. The men's area was huge, packed with row after row of male worshippers. It was brilliantly lit by hundreds of glimmering chandeliers; beautiful, luxurious, thick, red patterned oriental carpets covered the floor; marble pillars, forty feet in height, supported the expansive white ceiling. I took a position in the last row.

When the prayer was over, I met my wife and children outside by the entrance to the ladies' section; about twenty-five other women had prayed with them. My daughters looked confused and a little frightened. My youngest daughter had cried during the prayer: she thought I had gotten lost.

My wife and some of her friends sat chatting on the bus ride back to Dhahran. I was sitting across the aisle with my three daughters; the four of us huddled into two adjoining seats. I leaned over toward the ladies and asked them the question that had been bothering me since the maghrib prayer: Why did so few Muslim women perform the prayer, while virtually all the Muslim men did? In the States, I was always told that the ladies did not come to our mosque because there were hardly any women in our Lawrence, Kansas, community and that the few we did have had small children to care for. My wife had always told me that it was cultural. Now I wanted to get the perspective of these women, who came from several different Muslim countries.

One of my wife's friends mentioned that Muslim women are excused from prayer during certain times of the month. But, I answered, that would only account for less than one-forth of the Muslim ladies present whereas at least ninety-five percent just skipped the Maghrib prayer.

Another of her friends told me that the mutawwa' (religious police) forced the men to go but not the women. When I asked her why that was so, she smiled shyly and said that the women might have an excuse and the mutawwa' have no way of checking it. I mentioned that most of the men seemed eager to get to the mosque for the prayer.

Another lady, sitting in the seat behind my wife, said that most Muslim women hardly ever go to the mosque, for, unlike their brothers, they are not encouraged to go when they are children. The lady sitting next to her added that the women are in fact encouraged not to go, for it is better for them to pray at home. She said that there is a hadith that discourages women from praying in the mosque.

I said that I knew of the hadith, but that I had not found any versions of it in the most respected sources. I said that even if it had been judged authentic at one time, I would still doubt that the Prophet discouraged his female companions from attending prayers at the mosque, for there are a large number of reports in the most respected hadith compilations that show that, throughout his prophethood and the reign of his first four political successors, his female companions attended the prayers in large numbers and were very active in the mosque. I said that it is hard for me to believe that these women, who risked their lives, their wealth, and the love of their families to follow Prophet Muhammad, would so casually ignore his advice to them to make their prayers at home.

A lady on the bus commented in a bitter and defiant tone: "I always felt that God must hate women, because He gave everything to men and almost nothing to us. He even gave His houses of worship to the men!"

In the past fourteen years, I have witnessed many persons who were genuinely interested in Islam and in search of faith turn away from this religion because of disillusionment over Muslim attitudes about women. I have observed this so often that I am inclined to say that this may indeed be the biggest barrier to the spread of Islam in the West.

Of all of the topics related to Islam, the position of women in the Muslim community is among the most written about and debated. On this subject there is a vast range of viewpoints. Among non-Muslim authors, opinions run from Islam "left woman forever inferior to man"[54] to "the Koran's pronouncements on the subject of all women can be recognized as truly revolutionary"[55] to "in their rights as citizen—education, suffrage, and vocation—the Koran opens the way to woman's full equality with man."[56] Islamic scholars seem to be in agreement that Muslim women have a status that is on a par with that of Muslim men, but almost all view the roles

---

[54] Nabia Abbott, *Aishah the Beloved of Mohammed* (Al Saqi Books, 1985),107.

[55] Elizabeth W. Fernea and Basima Qattan, eds., Berzigan, *Middle Eastern Muslim Women Speak*, p. xxiii of the introduction.

[56] Huston Smith, *The Religions of Man* (New York: Harper and Row, 1958), 245.

and privileges of the two sexes as very different. Moreover, there are many differences of opinion about what these roles and privileges are. If nothing else, the great disparity of interpretations and points of view indicates that the position of women in the Islamic community has not been, nor need be, static. The history of Muslim women shows that their roles in the Islamic community have varied greatly over time and place, and there are indications that further—and perhaps dramatic—change is ahead.

A large number of Muslim and non-Muslim scholars concede that there is nothing fundamental to Islam that should prevent Muslim women from attaining the same or even greater rights than those possessed by modern-day women in other societies. If this is correct—and I believe it is—then why are so many searching western individuals discouraged by the treatment of women in the Muslim community?

It seems that I am heading toward a lengthy dissertation on women in Islamic law, but I am not. My first book includes such a discussion, and I have very little to add.[57] Also, I do not feel, for reasons stated in the previous paragraph, that Islamic law is a major deterrent to so many western seekers of faith. Rather, I believe that pervasive Muslim attitudes about women are dissuading them.

Gender Differences

When my family and I spent a year in Dhahran, Saudi Arabia, my three daughters had to attend an Islamic school for girls. On the opening day of classes, the school's principal delivered a brief speech exhorting her students to respect their teachers and work very hard and then reminded them of the *hadith* that states that women are of a lower intelligence than men.[58] The only point my children got from the principal's lecture was that no matter how hard they worked, they could never compete intellectually with men.

On many occasions, I have heard Muslim speakers claim that women were on a lower moral and spiritual plane than men. There is nothing in the Qur'an to suggest this and very little in the *hadith* collections; it also seems to defy common knowledge and experience. As one Muslim foreign student said to me after we listened to a lecture on the greater sinfulness of women, "I just don't buy it! The women in our societies back home are much better than the men and everybody knows it!"

---

[57] Lang, *Struggling to Surrender*, 151-92.
[58] For a discussion on this hadith, see ibid., 153-55.

The irrational nature of females is taken for granted by most Muslim men. It is a common belief among Muslims that women especially lose control of their senses during their periods. Arguments that women should not be placed in leadership positions or that their testimony could not be relied on in a court of law often exploit this perception. I recall a well-attended public lecture entitled "Women in Islam" at the University of San Francisco, in which a Muslim speaker made such an argument. To support his contention that women became incoherent during menstruation, he cited a criminal trial in France, in which a judge dismissed a woman's testimony after he discovered that she was menstruating when she was supposed to have witnessed the crime. A non-Muslim in the seat next to mine commented to his friend: "The only thing that proves is that some Frenchmen are as sexist as Muslims!"

In the eyes of Westerners, the treatment of Muslim women by Muslim men and vice versa is often demeaning and offensive. Muslim men and women generally refuse to greet each other when they pass each other on the street, even though the Prophet always would bid *salaam* to passers-bye of either sex.[59] Women are usually discouraged from going to the mosque, although in Muhammad's time they attended the mosque regularly. Some Muslim female friends of mine were told explicitly not to attend the prayers at the mosque, as if, as one of the women put it, "it is some kind of men's club."

Most non-Muslims and many western converts to Islam find the practice of female seclusion extremely degrading to both sexes. At a dinner at a Muslim friend's house, the wife of my host accidentally pushed open the door from inside the room where the women were secluded, just as I was passing by. She glared at me and then let out a loud, shrill scream and slammed shut the door. She must have acted this way for the benefit of her

---

[59] We should be careful here to note that what Westerners interpret to be insulting may not be viewed that way by Muslims. For example, Westerners feel that the scarf worn by a Muslim woman degrades her, but many Muslim women consider wearing it a source of dignity and pride. On the other hand, Muslims find that many western fashions debase women. Similarly, many middle-eastern Muslim women would be greatly insulted if a strange man saluted them on the street, as if he were somehow familiar with them. Women from some of the stricter Muslim countries view seclusion as a protection and an opportunity to relax away from men, while Westerners find it humiliating. I am not arguing that these practices are indeed demeaning, but rather that they may be to the larger culture in which Western Muslims live. Muslims should be aware of this when they consider imposing their customs on others, especially since they could be promoting a practice in the name of religion that offends others and is not truly necessary from the standpoint of Islam.

female guests, because I had passed her in public many times without her ever once panicking.[60]

Young Muslim women growing up in America have complained to me that their brothers are given much more freedom than they are. One described the condition of post-pubescent Muslim girls as one of being placed under house arrest by their parents.

Every culture has had its share of false and demeaning beliefs about men and women, and, until quite recently, the Christian West was one of the worst in this regard. Dramatic change in western society has brought about a change in perceptions. The industrial revolution and the two world wars sent women from the home into the outside work force, where they proved that they could compete effectively with men. As western women obtained more and better opportunities for education, many stereotypes about the female intellect were shattered. In what were once considered strictly male academic domains, like business, mathematics, and medicine, western women are performing on a par with men. Women are no longer believed to be more emotional than men, but are now believed to display and deal with their emotions differently. Men resort to shouting

---

[60] Verse 33:53 in the Qur'an tells Muhammad's Companions, male and female, not to barge unannounced into the apartments of the Prophet's wives', as was the habit of some of them. Classical commentators on this verse report that a few embarrassing moments occasioned its revelation. The verse then tells the Prophet's Companions that when they need to speak to the Prophet's wives, they should remain outside of their apartments and address them while leaving the curtain at the entrance to their living quarters closed.

Some Muslims argue that this verse instituted the general practice of female seclusion during Muhammad's time. However, this argument has several weaknesses: First, it is not clear that the verse is enforcing the type of strict segregation that is practiced today, even with respect to Muhammad's wives. It may only be protecting Muhammad and his family from uncomfortable situations by assuring them of at least some degree of privacy. It should be kept in mind that, at this stage in Muhammad's mission, there were almost always swarms of people in the courtyard just outside his living quarters; second, the tone of the Qur'an does not suggest a general precept, for the same *surah* contains several regulations that apply specifically and exclusively to the Prophet and his wives; third, we learn from the hadith reports that female seclusion was not practiced by many of the Companions. If some did observe it, that only shows that it was practiced irregularly at best; and fourth, Imam Malik states in his *Muwatta*, written toward the end of the second Islamic century, that he sees no problem with men and women sitting together as long as the women are accompanied by a male relative, for example a father or uncle. He states that this is the long-established custom of Madinah, with the words "this is our *Sunnah*" (In Imam Malik's time, the word *Sunnah* stood for the well-established local practices. In later years, it would come to designate, almost exclusively, the Prophet's sayings and doings).

and acts of violence more often than women, which accounts for the fact that the majority of violent crimes and crimes of passion in America are committed by men.

The West's revision of attitudes about the sexes was brought about almost entirely—if not entirely—by changes that occurred within western culture; there was little foreign stimulus. Traditional viewpoints concerning the sexes are now being challenged and reexamined in the Muslim world, but here the importation and confrontation with western culture is playing a big role. Since modern technology and western concepts have penetrated Muslim societies only recently, we should expect that traditional male and female stereotypes will persist for some time. Also, strong anti-western sentiments in the Muslim world have made the Muslim masses extremely suspicious of western notions. The call for women's rights is often seen as a distinctly western phenomenon and an outside attempt to subvert Islamic culture. Throughout the Muslim world, there is currently a strong counter-action against the modern women's movement, and traditional attitudes about men and women are asserting themselves and should continue to prevail in Muslim society for the immediate future.

The majority of western converts to Islam are socially and politically liberal. This is not surprising, since few conservatives would contemplate something so radical as becoming a Muslim. Many converts—men as well as women—were feminists before conversion, and many continue to be so after becoming Muslims. Their entry into the Muslim community creates a volatile situation.

One of the chief charges western apostates make is that the Muslims are hateful of women. As long as the Islamic community continues to ignore this complaint or to whitewash it with idealized lectures on the superior position of Muslim women, the vast majority of Americans and Europeans will not be inclined to look at Islam favorably. I am not advocating compromising the religion to win converts, but rather the opinion that Muslims need to reconsider those attitudes and practices toward women that are essential to Islam and that may be inessential and barriers to sincere seekers of faith.

A Fifth Column

Approximately two months after I had converted to Islam, the Muslim students at the university where I was teaching began to hold lectures on Friday evenings in the mosque. The second lecture was given by Hisham, a very bright medical student who had been studying in America for almost ten years. I liked and respected Hisham very much. He was rather round and jovial and had a very kind face. He was also a passionate student of Islam.

Hisham spoke that night about a Muslim's duties and responsibilities. He talked at length about the rituals and a believer's ethical obligations. His speech was very moving and had been running about an hour when he closed it with the following unexpected and stern remark.

"Finally, we must never forget—and this is extremely important—that as Muslims, we are obligated to desire, and when possible to participate in, the overthrow of any non-Islamic government—anywhere in the world—in order to replace it by an Islamic one."

"Hisham!" I interrupted. "Are you implying that Muslim American citizens are to commit themselves to the destruction of the U.S. government?— That they are to be a fifth column in America—a secret revolutionary group seeking to overthrow the government? Do you mean that when an American converts to Islam he must commit himself to political treason?!"

I thought that by presenting Hisham with a very extreme scenario, it would force him to soften or qualify his statement. He looked down at the floor as he pondered my question momentarily. Then he looked at me with an expression that reminded me of a doctor about to break the news to his patient that his tumor is malignant.

"Yes," he said, "Yes, that's true."

The belief that Islam promotes violence is so deeply ingrained in the western experience that it can be called a cultural axiom. Almost no one in the West would challenge the notion that Islam encourages Muslims to use force in order to spread the religion. For many centuries this was the perception—or perhaps one should say the fear—of a civilization that was on the defensive, both militarily and culturally.

Shortly after Prophet Muhammad died in 632 C.E., Arab armies surged forth from the Arabian peninsula in one of history's most rapid and startling conquests. By 637 C.E., Syria and Iraq had fallen to the new Muslim state, and then Egypt in 642 C.E. Muslim forces continued to push westward and eastward and, before the end of the first Islamic century, not only would the Islamic empire stretch from the Atlantic across North Africa through the former Persian empire and into India, but it would also include Spain and southern France. Thereafter, Muslims and Europeans would meet repeatedly in battle—with the Muslims having the better of it for several centuries.

Europe made a slow-but-sure comeback and eventually caught up to and surpassed Islamic civilization in science, technology, and military power. The expulsion of the Muslims from Spain in 1492 marked a decisive turning point and served as a notice of things to come. With the occupation of Egypt by Napoleon in 1798, the European colonialist era began. Ultimately, most of the Muslim world fell under European control. After the Second World War and a bitter and sustained struggle, Muslims around the world began to wrestle political independence from their colonizers, which led to the creation of a large number of independent Muslim states. The experience of colonization by the West has left deep wounds of humiliation and resentment in the hearts of many of today's Muslims.

Originally, the western conception of Islam as a religion urging armed aggression might have been mostly an emotional reaction to the threat of a Muslim takeover of Europe. At times, the possibility of such an occurrence must have seemed great (recall that Muslim armies threatened Vienna as late as the seventeenth century). However, during Europe's colonialist era, the portrayal of Islam as a violent faith and of Christianity as a gentle one became one of the Christian missionaries' main tactics in their effort to win converts among the Muslim populations of Africa and Asia. The incongruity of this claim must have been evident to even the most simple-minded Muslims, for it was like having someone hold you at gun point while he insists to you that he is opposed to all use of force.

Today, some western historians are questioning the notion that Islam encourages violence, because the history of Muslims has not been any more violent than that of most other cultures.[61] While most Christians probably would not describe Christianity as a violent faith, it would indeed be very difficult to argue that the history of the Christian West has been more peaceful than that of the Muslim world. The number of atrocities committed by Christian governments and armies in the name of God are legion. The same could be said for the number of forced conversions to Christianity. There were times in history when Muslims were also guilty of religious persecution, but western historians have shown that, on the whole, the record of Muslims compares very favorably with that of Christians in this regard. In particular, state-sponsored persecution or forced conversion of non-Muslims was quite rare in the Islamic world.[62]

---

[61] See, for example, the introduction to Bernard Lewis, *The Jews of Islam* (Princeton, NJ: Princeton University Press, 1984) 3-4.

[62] Ibid., 27-62.

Many western writers, past and present, have pointed to the division in classical Islamic Law of the world into *dar al harb* (the abode of war) and *dar al Islam* (the abode of Islam or peace) as evidence of the essentially aggressive nature of Islam. This legal–political formulation separates the world into two mutually exclusive territories: *dar al Islam*, the lands ruled by Muslims according to the Shari'ah (Islamic law), and *dar al harb*, the lands not under Muslim control which must be subjected, by conquest if necessary, to Islamic rule. According to this theory, a perpetual state of war exists between Muslim and non-Muslim territories. Many in academia and the western media claim that this demonstrates the warlike character of Islam.

This argument is not so easy to dismiss. Muslims can remind Westerners that past Church officials often defended aggressive and brutal government policies on religious grounds. But one can counter that those policies were not essentially Christian, since Church leaders would not endorse them today. Almost all Muslim religious leaders, however, still uphold the classical *dar al Islam/dar al harb* concept (hereafter abbreviated *DIH*), which makes it appear to be fundamental to Islam. This poses a very difficult personal dilemma for many converts, because it seems to them that to become a Muslim, they are required to become enemies of their own countries. We will now explore this issue more carefully.

The taking of another person's life has always been, for almost all people, an extremely grave and terrible act.[63] Therefore, people of virtually every time and place found it necessary—and still do—to find or create moral or religious arguments for their military actions.

As Muslim legal scholars began to elaborate a religious–political theory of warfare, they had to address two great facts: the great Muslim conquests of the past and the persistent threat of hostilities along the boundaries of the Islamic empire. I think it can be said that until perhaps quite recently, every great political power perceived itself to be in a conquer-or-be-conquered situation; that is, if your territory is not expanding, then it is in grave danger of shrinking. Muslim legal scholars pointed to the Prophet's military campaigns and the conquests of Umar as support for the *DIH* theory. They also detailed a comprehensive code of wartime ethics that forbade killing or harassing noncombatants, greatly restricted the destruction of enemy lands and property, prescribed humane treatment of captives, and prohibited the use of excessive force and forced conversion. One of the guiding

---

[63] The Qur'an compares an unjustifiable homicide to the murder of all mankind (5:32).

objectives of the Muslim jurists was to bring non-Muslim lands under the authority of the Shari'ah while minimizing destruction and the loss of life. They were also fully convinced that the Shari'ah offered a system of government far superior to any other and that it provided the conquered people a better and more just way of life, not to mention that it allowed them to be exposed to, and hence to consider, the truth of Islam. H. G. Wells, in *The Outline of History*, makes almost the same case:

> And if the reader entertains any delusions about a fine civilization, either Roman or Persian, Hellenic or Egyptian, being submerged by this flood, the sooner he dismisses such ideas the better. Islam prevailed because it was the best social and political order the times could offer. It prevailed because everywhere it found politically apathetic peoples, robbed, oppressed, bullied, uneducated and unorganized, and it found selfish and unsound governments out of touch with any people at all. It was the broadest, freshest and cleanest political idea that had yet come into actual activity in the world, and it offered better terms than any other to the mass of mankind.[64]

I am not about to defend the *dar al Islam/dar al harb* theory, nor, for that matter, to dispute it. My purpose is not to decide if this formulation by classical jurists was right—although I think that would be a useful exercise—but rather to argue against transcendentalizing it, something that is done by both Muslims and many critics of Islam. By this I mean that many non-Muslim scholars who decry Islam as inherently violent, and also many modern Muslim leaders and scholars, claim that this classical political–military theory is fundamental to the religion and that, from the standpoint of Islam, it must be valid for all times and places. Both groups, but with very different motives, claim that to doubt that this classical formula is appropriate for our time is equivalent to a denial of the validity of Islam. The two main questions that I believe both sides should reconsider are: Is this political–legal construct really essential to Islam? and Is it right for this day and age? Since for Muslims, an affirmative answer to the first question implies the same for the second, we will begin with the first question.

The Qur'an does not preach passivity. While it encourages the believer to be forgiving (2:109; 7:199-200; 42:37; 42:40; 45:14), it also

---

[64] H. G. Wells, *The Outline of History*, 613-14.

asserts that warfare is sometimes necessary. For example, the Qur'an maintains that a war fought in self-defense is justified:

> To them against whom war is made wrongfully, permission [to fight] is given—and truly, God has indeed the power to defend them—: those who have been driven from their homelands against all right for no other reason than their saying, "Our Lord is God!" For if God had not enabled people to defend themselves against one another, all monasteries and churches and synagogues and mosques—in all of which God's name is abundantly extolled—would surely have been destroyed." (22:39-40)

The Qur'an also exhorts the believers to fight tyranny and oppression:

> What ails you that you will not fight in the cause of the utterly helpless men, women and children who are crying, "O our Lord, lead us forth out of this land whose people are oppressors, and raise for us, out of Your grace, a protector, and raise for us, out of Your grace, One who will defend us." (4:175)

But it seems to me extremely difficult to justify, based on the Qur'an, a war that is waged for any reason other than self-defense or on behalf of the oppressed and persecuted.

As Muhammad and his Companions battled the pagans of Makkah for eight years, many verses were revealed during this period concerning warfare and relations with non-Muslims. The great majority of them are very explicit in allowing warfare only for the reasons just stated.

> Fight in God's cause against those who wage war against you; *but do not commit aggression, for truly, God does not love aggressors.* And slay them wherever you catch them, and turn them out from where they have turned you out; for sedition is worse then killing . . . . *But if they cease, God is Ever-forgiving, Most Merciful.* (2:191-192)

> And fight them on until there is no more sedition and religion is for God alone; *but if they cease, let there be no hostility except to those who practice oppression.* (2:193)

> Their shall be no coercion in matters of faith. (2:256).

Others you will find that wish to gain your confidence as
well as that of their people. Every time they are sent back
to temptation, they succumb to it. *If they do not let you be,
and do not offer you peace, and do not stay their hands,
seize them and slay them whenever you come upon them:
and it is against these that We have empowered you.* (4:91)

*But if the enemy inclines toward peace, then you [too]
incline towards peace,* and trust in God: for He is the One
that hears and knows. (8:61)

The above passages clearly allow fighting only in self-defense or in defense
of victims of tyranny or oppression. It is significant that three of them occur
in the second *surah*, which is believed by many Muslim scholars to be a
recapitulation of the Qur'an's major themes. Verses 22:39-40 quoted above
may best illustrate the Qur'an's attitude towards war: cautionary, circum-
spect, and realistic. But one finds little support in the Qur'an for the use of
aggression as a means to force non-Muslim states to accept Islamic rule.

The so-called Verse of the Sword (9:5) is often used to argue that Islam
encourages military expansion. All exegetes agree on the occasion of its revelation: Seven years after the Muslim exodus to Madinah, the Prophet nego-
tiated a truce with the pagan Quraysh, known as the Treaty of Hudaybiyah.
A year later, the Quraysh violated the terms of the treaty and the following
verse, which ordered the Muslims to attack the pagans, was revealed:

And so when the sacred months are over, slay those who
ascribe divinity to other than God wherever you may come
upon them, and take them captive, and besiege them, and
lie in wait for them at every conceivable place. Yet if they
repent, and take to prayer, and render the purifying dues,
let them go their way: behold, God is much forgiving, a
dispenser of grace. (9:5)[65]

---

[65] One of the crucial points to recall about 9:5 is that it actually prevented bloodshed.
It was well known at that time that the pagan Quraysh had many informants in Madinah,
and that these people would relay immediately any information they could obtain of the
Prophet's political plans (Muhammad, in fact, turned this to his advantage several times).
When the Quraysh learned of this very threatening declaration of war, they were so frightened that they immediately sent emissaries to the Prophet to negotiate their own peaceful
surrender. This resulted in the bloodless conquest of Makkah, after which Muhammad
declared a general amnesty for his former enemies. Apparently, one of the main reasons
for the extremely bellicose tone of 9:5 was to intimidate the Quraysh into surrendering.

A quick glance at the context shows that this passage is directed against those who, through treachery, break their treaties with the believers. The preceding verse reads:

> [But treaties] are not dissolved with those pagans with whom you have entered an alliance and who have not subsequently failed you in aught, nor aided any one against you. So fulfill your engagements with them to the end of their term: for God loves the righteous. (9:4)

And later,

> As long as they remain true to you, stand true to them: for God loves the righteous. (9:7)

It would seem then that there is absolutely no conflict between 9:5 and the other verses just cited (2:191-93; 2:256; 4:91; 8:61), which prohibit military aggression; verse 9:5 deals with the issue of an opponent's treaty violations and is not a permission to engage in military expansion.[66]

Yet many Muslim commentators feel that this verse does indeed permit military aggression against a government that refuses to surrender to Islamic rule. In order to reconcile the apparent conflict between this interpretation of the Verse of the Sword and the other verses that forbid aggression, a large-scale abrogation of verses is proposed. As one advocate for this position puts it (see the citation below): "114 verses spread among 54 *surahs* advocating peace were revoked by 9:5."

Muhammad 'Abd al Salam Faraj, who was executed on 15 April 1982 along with others accused of assassinating President Anwar Sadat of Egypt, writes in his *The Neglected Duty*:

> Most commentators on the Qur'an have said something about a certain verse they call the Verse of the Sword (9:5). Here is the verse: "When the holy months are over, kill polytheists wherever you find them; capture them, besiege them, ambush them."

---

[66] Verses from the ninth *surah*, such as 9:123 and 9:29, are sometimes employed to justify conquest of non-aggressive states in order to subject them to Islamic rule. Not only does their use in this way also imply a blatant contradiction of the verses just cited, and thus recourse to hypothesizing a large-scale abrogation, but as Muhammad Ali exhaustively argues, it again ignores both historical and revelational contexts. Ali, *The Religion of Islam*, 405-43.

Ibn Kathir noted in his exegesis of the Qur'an: Al Dahak ibn Muzahim said, "[This verse] annuls any treaty between the Prophet—blessings and salvation be upon him —and any infidel, along with any contract or any accord." Al 'Ufi said about the verse, according to Ibn 'Abbas: "No contract, no defense pact with an infidel was recognized after this dissolution of obligations fixed by treaty was revealed."

The exegete Muhammad ibn Ahmad ibn Juzayy al Kalbi said: "The abrogation of the order to be at peace with the infidels, to pardon them, to be passively in contact with them, and to endure their insults came before the order to fight them. That makes it superfluous to repeat the abrogation of the order to live at peace with the infidels in every passage of the Qur'an. This order to live at peace with them is given in 114 verses spread among 54 surahs. All of those verses are abrogated by 9:5 and 2:216 (you are prescribed to fight)"[67]

The theory—and it is a *theory*—that underlies this discussion of Faraj is that certain verses of the Qur'an revoke for all time and place certain other verses. But as I see it, the theory of abrogation, although widely accepted by Muslim scholars, has several weak points.

To begin with, there is no explicit authenticated saying of Muhammad that either states that this theory or asserts that one verse has annulled another verse permanently. All of the *hadith* (reports of sayings of the Prophet) concerning abrogation are considered weak by Muslim experts.[68] If a Companion of the Prophet felt that one verse cancelled another permanently, that was his or her *personal interpretation*. For Muslims, only a statement of Muhammad that a verse had been abrogated should be authoritative. There are no reliable reports of this nature.

Verses 2:106 and 16:101 are often cited in support of the theory of abrogation, although the context indicates that the annulled revelations referred to are those received by prophets that came before Prophet

---

[67] Mohammad Arkoun, *Rethinking Islam*, trans. by Robert D. Lee (Boulder, CO: Westview Press, 1994).

[68] Ali, *The Religion of Islam*, 28-30.

Muhammad. At the very least, this would be a very natural and plausible interpretation.[69]

Another weakness in the theory is that among those Muslim scholars who accept it, there is wide disagreement on exactly which verses are abrogated and to what extent. In almost all cases where abrogation has been upheld by one writer, there are other writers who argue against the alleged abrogation. Ali shows that even with the Companions of Muhammad we find that:

> In most cases where a report is traceable to one Companion who held a certain verse to have been abrogated, there is another report traceable to another Companion to the effect that the verse was not abrogated.[70]

It is true that when Muhammad and his Companions met new or altered situations, verses were often revealed that addressed the new circumstances. After this, the Muslims would make the appropriate modifications or alterations in their behavior. But there is no reason to conclude from this that one passage of the Qur'an annulled another *permanently*. Sometimes, a particular revelation simply would elaborate on or extend a previously revealed ordinance, as in the case of the verses that prohibit drinking wine. In such cases, the earlier injunction and the new one complement each other. On other occasions, the Qur'an would revise prior instructions in light of *changed* circumstances—as in the case of the revelation of 9:5—but here again, since the different injunctions deal with different situations, there is no reason to surmise a conflict between them.

There is, in fact, no need for the theory of abrogation.[71] It was used to resolve what Muslim scholars felt were certain contradictory Qur'anic injunctions, but if close attention is paid to the context of the Qur'an's precepts, one finds that they do not contradict each other. The Qur'an itself points to the absence of such internal discrepancies as proof of its divine origins (4:82). Cases where some Muslim scholars sensed a contradiction invariably deal with very different situations. Thus, when interpreting the Qur'an's ordinances, the situational context must not be ignored, for then it

---

[69] Ibid., 28-34; John Burton, *The Collection of the Qur'an* (Cambridge: Cambrige University Press, 1977), 237-40.

[70] Ali, *The Religion of Islam*, 30.

[71] For a discussion in favor of the theory of abrogation by one of the great masters of Islamic law, see Imam Shafi'i, *Risalah,* trans. by Majid Khadduri (Baltimore: John Hopkins Press, 1961), 123-46.

becomes easy to mistake an exception for a general rule and vice versa, or to perceive a conflict between passages where none exists.

Finally, the theory of abrogation appears to claim that God placed superfluous information in the last revelation to mankind and that He had to correct Himself frequently during the process of revelation. This perception is very hard to square with the Qur'an's depiction of God. Not surprisingly, quite a number of converts to Islam informed me that they were shocked and had their faith severely shaken when they first discovered this theory.

Therefore, I feel that there is no real need or justification for the classical theory of abrogation. Yet without this theory, the Qur'an cannot be used to support waging war other than in self-defense or against oppression. This is proved by the fact that such a massive application of the theory of abrogation is needed to justify the type of military expansion advocated by the *dar al Islam/dar al harb* formula. Clearly, Qur'anic passages dealing with warfare weigh heavily against such unprovoked aggression.

So far I have criticized only one line of argument often used by Muslim and non-Muslim scholars to show that Islam encourages offensive military action. This argument may be diagrammed as follows.

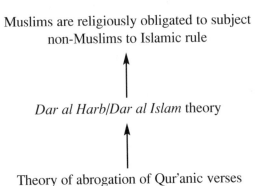

Muslims are religiously obligated to subject
non-Muslims to Islamic rule

Dar al Harb/Dar al Islam theory

Theory of abrogation of Qur'anic verses

There are other lines of argument that support the thesis that Islam obliges Muslims to bring non-Muslims under Islamic rule, but I began with this one because, for Muslims, the Qur'an is their principle source of moral and ethical guidance. For Islam's faithful, the authority of the Qur'an is supreme and takes precedence over all other sources from which the principles and practices of their religion are drawn.[72]

---

[72] Ibid., 117.

Virtually all other attempts to prove that Muslims must subject non-Muslims to Islamic rule intersect at the second stage in the above diagram. That is, the conclusion that Islam encourages the subjugation of non-Muslims is a consequence of—or is at least strongly influenced by—the *DIH* concept. The examples of Muhammad and Umar ibn al Khattab are often cited to support this formulation. But here again, a careful and thorough examination of their political decisions and actions does not lead inevitably to it. Let us begin by considering the Prophet's military career.

Years of severe oppression at the hands of the pagan Quraysh had forced the nascent Muslim community to seek asylum outside of Makkah. At first, Muhammad sent a group of his followers to settle in Abyssinia, where its ruler, the Negus, had guaranteed them religious freedom. Perhaps these emigrants were to prepare for the arrival of the rest of the Muslims if their existence in Makkah became intolerable. The Quraysh responded to this first emigration by stepping up their persecution of those Muslims who remained. Just when it seemed that Muhammad and his followers would all have to obtain asylum somewhere, an unexpected opportunity arose: The people of the north Arabian city of Yathrib, many of whom had come to believe in Muhammad's prophethood, invited the Prophet to come and govern their town, which had been torn by feuds of rival Arab tribes. The city was soon renamed Madinah (short for *madinah al nabi* (city of the Prophet). This migration is known in Arabic as the *hijrah*.

Muslim historians record that both the pagans of Makkah and the fleeing Muslims apprehended the grave implications of the *hijrah*. Both sides knew that this would not be the end of their differences, but that the Muslim exodus to Madinah was equivalent, in their day and environment, to a declaration of war. The records show that warlike threats were exchanged between the Makkan pagans and followers of the Prophet as the latter were departing for Madinah.

When Muhammad remained in Makkah a few more days after the departure of nearly all of his followers, the Quraysh twice attempted to strike a first and decisive blow against the Muslims. First, their plot to murder the Prophet in his sleep failed. Then, on their way to Madinah, Muhammad and Abu Bakr managed to elude the Qurayshi cavalry sent to intercept and kill them. When the Prophet arrived in Madinah, therefore, the Muslims understood full well that they were now at war with the Quraysh and that they would have to defend themselves in battle. The earliest permission from the Qur'an to repel attack and oppression responded to this most tense situation:

> To them against whom war is made wrongfully, permission [to fight] is given—and truly, God has indeed the power to defend them—: those who have been driven from their homelands against all right for no other reason than their saying, "Our Lord is God!" For if God had not enabled people to defend themselves against one another, all monasteries and churches and synagogues and mosques—in all of which God's name is abundantly extolled—would surely have been destroyed. (22:39-40)

As this verse shows, Muhammad's military struggle with the Quraysh was from the very start defensive and retaliatory. The Quraysh had already demonstrated by their words and actions their aggressive intentions. It now would be time to fight back. Eight years later, after a handful of battles with the Quraysh, a great deal of the Prophet's renowned diplomacy and his continuous and tireless efforts to preach Islam, the Prophet subdued the Quraysh. The details of Muhammad's military campaigns against the Quraysh and their allies are readily and easily obtained, so I will not recount them here. I only wish to draw the reader's attention to one crucial fact: Muslim chronicles report not a single case in which Muhammad led an aggressive attack. Historical records show that each tribe with which the Muslims fought had either attacked the Muslims first or else had aided and abetted such an aggressor. In particular, there is absolutely no evidence that Muhammad ever offered a peaceful neighboring tribe the choice between accepting his rule or war. Yet this fact has not deterred Muslim and non-Muslim writers from scouring the *hadith* collections and the Prophet's biographies in search of support for the *DIH* concept.

Muhammad's last expedition, in which he led an army of thirty thousand on a very long and difficult journey to Tabuk, the border region between Byzantium and Arabia, is sometimes cited as evidence of the Prophet's imperialistic plans. However, the expedition was a reaction to reports of Byzantine plans to invade Arabia. Such rumors had been circulating in northern Arabia for some time.[73] When Muhammad reached the

---

[73] A year earlier, Muhammad had sent out an expeditionary force to investigate rumors of a Byzantine invasion of Arabia. At Mu'tah, the Muslims engaged in battle an extremely large Byzantine army and several prominent Companions of the Prophet were killed. As it turns out, the target of the Byzantine incursion into Arabia at this time may not have been the Muslims, but rather certain northern Arab tribes who had been Byzantine allies but who were now defying Byzantine authority. It may be that the Byzantines at first mistook the Muslim contingent for their recalcitrant allies.

frontier and found that the Romans did not contemplate an offensive, he returned without attacking them. His actions on this occasion demonstrate "that the permission to fight against the Christians contained in 9:29 was also subject to the condition laid down in 2:190: that Muslims shall not be aggressive in war."[74]

Similarly, some writers believe that the accounts of Muhammad sending letters to the rulers around him, inviting them to accept Islam, show that something close to the *DIH* concept was implicit in his mind.[75] Yet the letters contain no threats of warfare if the invitations are not accepted. What they do show is that the Prophet was determined to use every available peaceful means of communicating the divine message he had received.

A number of traditions of the Prophet have been used to argue for the *DIH* concept. Typically, these arguments ignore the context of the traditions or draw unobvious or unnecessary implications from them. An important example of the first type of error involves a saying from the collection of al Bukhari, in which the Prophet states: "I have been commanded to fight people until they bear witness that there is no god but God and that Muhammad is the Messenger of God and keep up prayers and pay the zakah."[76] No Muslim jurist applies this saying literally, for such an interpretation would advocate conversion of all non-Muslims— even Christians and Jews—by the sword, which Islamic law does not allow. The statement quite obviously refers to the ninth *surah* of the Qur'an, where, as already mentioned, Muhammad was instructed to fight the tribes that violated the treaty of Hudaybiyyah, but with the added proviso stated in verse 9:11:

> But if they repent and keep up prayer and pay the zakah,
> then they become your brethren in faith: and We make the
> communications clear for a people who know. (9:11)[77]

---

[74] Ali, *The Religion of Islam*, 416.

[75] Ibid., pp. 417-418.

[76] From the collections of al Bukhari and Muslim. See *An Nawawi's Forty Hadith*, trans. by I. Ezzedin and D. Johnson-Davies (Beirut: The Holy Koran Publishing House, 1979), 46.

[77] For the sake of completeness, I will quote the two verses that come after 9:11. They read: "But if they break their oaths after their agreement and openly revile your religion, then fight the leaders of unbelief—for their oaths are nothing—so that they may desist. What! will you not fight a people who broke their oaths and aimed at the expulsion of the Prophet, and they attacked you first; do you fear them?" (9:12-13)

This verse and the above *hadith* reiterate a well-established Islamic principle: If a people at war with Muslims accept Islam, they become protected members of the Muslim community and all combat against them must cease. In several prophetic traditions, various Companions questioned the practicality of this rule, since an enemy could exploit it to their advantage. Yet Muhammad nevertheless insisted on it.[78] Therefore, the Prophet's example does not suggest that Muslims are required to impose Islamic rule on all non-Muslims. His military and political decisions were always in accord with the Qur'an's general prohibition of unprovoked aggression. The same can be said of Muhammad's second political successor, Umar ibn al Khattab.

Muslim jurists recognize four main sources from which all principles and practices of Islam are drawn. Listed in descending order of authority, these sources are the Qur'an, the *hadith* collections (which record the Prophet's life example), *ijma'* (the unanimous agreement of the Muslim community), and *qiyas* (analogical reasoning based on the Qur'an and the Prophet's *Sunnah*).[79] Although the personal opinions and statements of the Prophet's Companions on religious questions are not by themselves a source of Islamic law, Muslims still take them very seriously, especially the decisions and viewpoints of Muhammad's first four political successors: Abu Bakr, Umar, Uthman, and Ali. Their relationships with the Prophet were so close, and their self-sacrifice in the cause of Islam so great, that Muslims assume that their judgments on religious matters could not be opposed to Muhammad's teachings.

The great conquests that took place during the reign of Umar present for many Muslims a strong precedent for the *dar al Islam/dar al harb* conception. However, the wars fought between the Muslims and the Persians and Byzantines did not begin during Umar's rule, but during the reign of his political predecessor, Abu Bakr. In addition, Abu Bakr did not fight these empires because they refused to submit to Muslim rule, but in response to their support of certain rebellious Arab tribes.

After the Prophet's death, a number of Arab tribes rebelled and militarily challenged the political authority of the Muslim state. The insurrections, for the most part, occurred on the western border with Syria and in the east in Bahrain and were supported with equipment and men in the west

---

[78] An Nawawi, *Riyadh Us Saleheen*, trans. by S. M. N. Abbasi, 1:234-38.

[79] Here I am speaking of the Sunni Muslim jurists, which are often referred to as "orthodox" jurists by orientalists. For the sources of Shi'ite scholars: S. M. H. Tabatabai, *Shi'a*, trans. by S. H. Nasr (Qom: Iran: Ansariyan Publ., 1981), 89-122.

and in the east by the Roman and Persian empires, respectively.[80] The newly emerging Muslim nation thus found itself threatened by the two empires, and Abu Bakr's battle with the rebellious tribes was now extended into a full-scale war with Byzantium and Persia.

When Umar came to power, the wars with Rome and Persia were well under way. Under his leadership vast territories quickly fell to the Muslims. Two hundred years of fighting each other had exhausted the Persians and Byzantines, and this, in part, explains the great success of the Arab armies. Another factor contributing greatly to the Muslim conquest was that large numbers of people living in the two empires desired the fall of the government. Most of the population in the conquered territories saw the Arabs as liberators, and many assisted and fought with the Muslim armies.[81]

A few modern Muslim authors claim that both Abu Bakr and Umar directed a purely self-defensive struggle against the two empires. They point out that the Persians and Byzantines were initially the aggressors and that Umar had ordered a halt to Muslim advancement into enemy territories on several occasions. They conjecture that Umar relieved Khalid ibn al Walid of his command of the Muslim armies because he felt that the latter was overly aggressive. They also point out that the Muslim invasion of Egypt had begun against Umar's will.

I do not disagree with these historical facts, but I am not convinced that the Muslims' wars with the two empires were entirely self-defensive. Perhaps during Abu Bakr's reign this was so, and to a degree it may be true of Umar's war with Persia. Even Muir, well known for his animosity toward Islam, concedes in his *History of the Caliphate*: "The truth began to dawn on Umar that necessity was laid upon him to withdraw the ban against advance. In self-defense, nothing was left but to crush the Chosroes and take entire possession of his realm."[82] Yet classical Muslim accounts of the conquest, in particular al Tabari's *History of the Prophets and Kings*,[83] do not show Umar to be a hesitant conqueror. Although a good deal of the material in these accounts of the conquests is not historic, the overall picture of Umar's role seems trustworthy. In the accounts,

---

[80] Ali, *The Religion of Islam*, 416-17; M. A. Rauf, *A Brief History of Islam* (Oxford University Press, 1964), 19-20.

[81] Gregory C. Kozlowski, *The Concise History of Islam* (Acton, MA: Copley Publ., 1991), 29-30.

[82] W. Muir, *History of the Caliphate*, 172.

[83] *The History of al Tabari*, vol. 12 and 13, trans. by Yohannes Freidman and Gautier H. A. Juynboll, 1992 and 1989, respectively.

Umar very deliberately directs the conquests: dispatching armies from Madinah, communicating frequently with his generals at the front, exhorting the Muslim troops, dismissing and appointing officers, and negotiating terms of the enemies' surrender. My own impression is that Umar perceived an opportunity to turn what were originally defensive actions into decisive and perhaps final victories. I also believe that he felt fully justified. After all, in his eyes the Romans and the Persians were originally guilty of aggression, the populations in the conquered territories received the Muslim soldiers warmly as rescuers, the loss of civilian life brought about by the conquest was for the most part very little, and the enemy never sued for peace.

Although I do not see Umar's example as speaking strongly against the *DIH* concept, at the same time I do not see his actions during this period speaking in favor of the concept either. It is one thing to defeat a tyrannous aggressor; it is quite another to declare war on a peaceful neighbor for not submitting to Muslim rule.

We have considered three of the main arguments used by Muslims to justify the *dar al Islam/dar al harb* formulation.[84] The argument based on the Qur'an seems to be extremely problematic, for it requires the acceptance of the very questionable and unnecessary *theory of abrogation* together with a radical application of this theory. A more natural reading of the Qur'an would lead to the conclusion that the scripture is opposed to military aggression. Prophet Muhammad's example also does not support the formulation, for he never led an attack against a peaceful neighbor who refused to accept Muslim rule. We may also note that Muslim historians record that there were pagan tribes who never fought the Prophet, but rather were allies of the Muslims. Moreover, the Muslims fought on their behalf.[85] Finally, the conquests during the caliphate of Umar—and for that matter Abu Bakr—do not fit the scenario assumed by the *DIH* theory and cannot be used to justify it.

---

[84] *Ijma'* is often invoked to support the *dar al Islam/dar al harb* theory. The claim is frequently made that all Muslim scholars accept it. This assertion is untrue, since there are a number of modern Muslim scholars who disagree with the theory. This fact is sometimes gotten around by restricting *ijma'* to a certain period of history or to persons possessing certain qualifications, so as to exclude dissenting scholars. Many rational problems are created by imposing such limitations. For example, in early Islamic history all Muslim scholars were convinced that the world was flat, and, until very recently, Muslim scholars believed that the earth was the center of our solar system. Even though there was a consensus among Muslims on these notions for many centuries, they were nonetheless wrong.

[85] Ali, *The Religion of Islam*, 423.

I do not believe that the *DIH* concept is essential to Islam. The textual sources of Islam do not lead Muslims inevitably to this foreign policy. It may seem that I have gone back on my earlier assertion that I would not attempt to determine whether or not this classical formulation *was* right. But the key word here is "was," for I believe that there may have been extenuating circumstances long ago that justified this division. Did Muslim scholars in the classical period correctly see their non-Muslim neighbors as enemies waiting for the first signs of weakness in order to attack? Was the Muslim nation in those days in a conquer-or-be-conquered political environment? Was the theory only developed in order to justify future Muslim conquests? Was it constructed in an effort to explain and make sense of past conquests? I believe these are important questions, but they require more extensive investigation than we have time and space for here. My purpose in this section has been only to argue against the position that this formulation is fundamental to Islam.

This brings us to the second question: Is the *dar al Islam/dar al harb* concept appropriate for today's Muslims? To the average non-Muslim reader, the answer may seem obvious. To them, the idea that Muslims would be religiously obligated to attack such non-aggressive countries as Switzerland, Luxembourg, Ecuador or Brazil if they were to refuse to submit to Islamic rule is unacceptable. Muslims who do not believe that this classical political division is fundamental to Islam would probably agree. Even more conservative Muslims who uphold the *DIH* formula would most likely hesitate—at least for a moment—to apply it to these hypothetical cases.

Many things have changed since the classical period of Islamic law and most Muslims—liberal, moderate and conservative—acknowledge the need to adapt the Shari'ah to modern times. In particular, there are many elements of the Shari'ah's code of warfare that seem impractical today. For example, the strict limitations it imposes on the destruction of enemy property and the injury of civilians are difficult to uphold in a war fought with today's weapons of mass destruction, as Iranian religious leaders discovered in the recent Iran–Iraq war. In order to succeed against an enemy in modern warfare, it may be necessary to go beyond the restrictions set by classical Islamic law.

Yet if Muslims allow themselves to amend certain aspects of the Shari'ah's theory of politics and warfare, then it seems to me that they should reconsider the *DIH* concept. Since I do not believe it to be essential to Islam, I feel that we Muslims need not insist that it is valid for our time.

However, even if the convert does not accept the *DIH* concept, he has not gotten pass the dilemma of community loyalties. Can he be a good citizen of a western government and, at the same time, a sincere Muslim? The objection may be raised that I just stated that I do not recommend the *DIH* concept to modern Muslims. That is true, but even if a premise upon which an argument is based is rejected, the conclusion of the argument may still be valid.

When leaders of Muslim movements around the world invoke the *DIH* concept today, it is almost always in response to what are perceived as very immediate and real threats to Muslims. That is, the governments that Muslim activists actually apply the *dar al harb* concept to in their political propaganda are ones that they view as real enemies, not only because these governments will not submit to some form of Islamic rule, but also because they are seen to inflict injustice and suffering on Muslim people. Thus, regardless of the theoretical or ethical dilemmas posed by the theory today, the conclusions of the religious leaders who invoke it are, for almost all Muslims, patently correct: These enemies of Muslims should be brought down.

First on the Muslim activists' lists of malevolent "anti-Islamic" governments are the brutal and totalitarian political systems under which most of the world's Muslims currently live. Next are those governments of non-Muslim countries that are now either attacking or actively oppressing Muslims, such as Serbia with respect to Bosnia, the Russian Republic with respect to Chechnia, Israel with respect to the Palestinians, and India with respect to Kashmir. Finally, there are those governments that are believed to be supporting the above political systems in their persecution and suppression of Muslims. Chief among the countries, in the opinion of many Muslims, are the United States, Great Britain, France, Germany and once again, the Russian Republic.

Militant Muslim leaders who plead for the overthrow of these political systems very frequently tie their appeals to the *DIH* concept. However, they would have a stronger case if they focused their arguments solely on the injustice and suffering being inflicted upon the Muslim masses, for, without a doubt, all Islamic textual sources, especially the Qur'an, exhort Muslims to unite in the fight against aggression and tyranny whenever possible.

Of course, it is the third category of anti-Muslim governments that presents the biggest problem for Muslims living in the West. Many Muslims are convinced that the secular West is leagued against them, as evidenced by the fact that secular democracies appear to lower their standards of human rights and justice when dealing with Muslims. For example, the U.N. resolutions against Israel are ignored routinely by western governments, while resolutions against Iraq led quickly to the Gulf War and hundreds of thousands of Iraqi casualties. During the Gulf War, a middle-eastern reporter asked a White House's cabinet member during a press briefing if the United States was not guilty of having a double standard for dealing with Muslim and non-Muslim countries. The reply was a candid, although probably unintentional, admission that the American government has no set standards and has, in fact, a different policy for dealing with each country. To Muslims, this was a frank admission that in international relations the American government—and the same is felt about her western allies—has no moral standards whatsoever when it comes to them.

That the secular governments of the West are united in an effort to destroy Islam or Muslims is probably an exaggeration, but it is true that these governments fear and are opposed to the many Islamic movements that they feel threaten their economic and military interests in the Middle East. It is also a fact that, all too frequently, their political policies have brought great suffering to Muslims. On these grounds alone, are not Muslim citizens of these countries obliged to consider themselves enemies of their governments?

A small minority of Muslims living in the West definitely would say so, while the great majority would prefer not to think about it. But a third alternative is available: Muslim citizens of secular democracies have the ability, and perhaps the obligation, to communicate their community's positions on religious and political issues. Muslims living in the West are often the first to admit that they enjoy greater religious and political freedom than do citizens of Muslim countries. This provides them, as compared to other Muslims around the world, with an unique and important opportunity to influence the societies in which they live. If they unite socially and organize politically—two things that right now they seem reluctant to do—they can greatly affect their society's viewpoints and the future of Muslims everywhere. And this is by far the most practical and effective way they can help their fellow Muslims in distress. To squander this opportunity would be a terrible loss.

The current situation of Muslims living in the West is not, in all respects, similar to that of the Muslims in either the Makkan or Madinan phase of the Prophet's mission. It is true that, at times, Muslim citizens encounter prejudice in western countries, but it is nothing like the persecution that the first Muslims suffered in Makkah. It is also true that western Muslims have many political rights and religious freedom, but they are not politically autonomous, as was the early community in Madinah. Yet as long as this freedom remains, I believe that they should—as every other citizen should—strive to influence their societies according to their conscience. It should not be forgotten that before the Qur'an permitted believers to emigrate to Madinah and retaliate against their oppressors, Muhammad and his Companions exhausted all possible peaceful means of persuading the Quraysh to grant Muslims the freedom to practice and preach Islam in Makkah and that they endured terrible persecution for many years. It seems that a few of the Muslims residing in the West advocate or dream of bypassing the lesson set by Muhammad and his followers in Makkah in order to move immediately to what should be a last resort.

Making a Hard Choice Harder

It is never easy to depart from the traditions of your society. Those you love and care for will often feel threatened and rejected, because our customs are so much a part of our communal identity. We expect strangers to question our ways because they come from outside our group experience. But when one of our own discards them, there must be something gravely wrong somewhere.

For nearly fourteen hundred years, Islam has contended with occidental culture for world dominance. To this day, the mention of no other religion so easily excites antipathy in the minds of Westerners. Although many Europeans and Americans can be quite objective and somewhat sympathetic toward other religions, very few are able to be so toward Islam or its believers. Many converts to the faith recall long periods of indecision and procrastination before joining the Muslim community due to the fear of being associated with a despised religion and people.

Above we considered what I feel are the three most prevalent western perceptions of Islam: Islam is an Arab, middle-eastern, or foreign religion incompatible with western culture; Islam demeans women; and Islam encourages violence and aggression. The three assumptions about Islam are not new to the West; they go back at least to the Middle Ages.[86] They may have been based on and meant different things to the West at different times, but they have remained fairly constant as overall perceptions. These

---

[86] Daniel, *Islam and the West.*

three notions are so firmly rooted in western culture that most sincere seek-ers of faith in God in Europe and America would never think of Islam as a religious option.

Almost all Muslims reject these characterizations of their faith. They argue that they are the result of centuries of distortions and misinformation propagated by western orientalists, litterateurs, politicians, and Christian missionaries. They also often blame the modern media, which they claim is under Zionist control.

This defense is oversimplified and unconvincing to anyone possessing some knowledge of past Islamic scholarship or modern Muslim society, for it fails to consider what Muslims may have done to encourage these per-ceptions. I have tried to argue that by idealizing past Muslim scholarly opinion and culturally influenced adaptations to and interpretations of Islam, Muslims may not only have contributed to the West's negative atti-tudes toward their faith, but, what is more important, they may have con-structed unnecessary burdens and obstacles to persons searching for God. An American Muslim leader recently remarked to me: "With all the bag-gage our community has added to this religion over the years, and with all the tensions and hardships that these accretions create for us today, it is a wonder that anyone in the West converts to Islam!" Yet they do so in ever greater numbers.

Islam is now the fastest growing religion in the West. It is also the fastest growing religion in history, for even though it is the youngest of the great world religions, it may now have the largest number of adherents. How can a religious community in such a state of culture shock and disar-ray continue to obtain converts? What is it about this faith that causes so many converts to remain deeply committed to it although the Muslim com-munity suffers from so much internal discord? Why do persons continue to join a community so different from and uncomfortable with the larger west-ern society to which they belong?

The Qur'an

I believe the modern West has experienced a tremendous loss of trust. Faith in government, traditional values, education, human rela-tionships, scriptures, religion, and in God has greatly diminished—for-feited it seems—in the struggle for material progress. This loss has left a great vacuum of meaning and purpose and has produced many indi-viduals who are not committed strongly to any system of thought and who are curious about and ready to listen to alternative perspectives. Of the many other religions and ideologies from which to choose, it seems that Islam has attracted much more than its statistical share of such persons. Perhaps this is due to the excessive attention the media gives to Islam, the recent arrival of large numbers of immigrants from Muslim societies, and the great increase in interaction between Western and Middle-Eastern countries these days. All of these factors have certainly aroused Western interest in Islam.

As mentioned earlier, converts give many reasons for choosing Islam and describe many diverse paths to this religion. Regardless of what initially spurred their interest or enticed them to finally make the choice to become Muslim, these proselytes almost always complain of the terrible frustration they endure as they struggle to adjust to their new religious community. The most important question we should be investigating concerning western converts to Islam is not how they came to Islam, but rather, why do so many of them remain committed? The answer obtained to the latter question is usually: the Qur'an.

Virtually all committed converts to Islam ascribe their faith to an unwavering conviction that the Qur'an, in its entirety, is no less than pure revelation from God. They may point to certain features of the Qur'an to support this belief, but, very often, these were learned after this conviction about the scripture already had developed. Typically, there is no easily definable or explicable aspect of the Qur'an that a convert could refer to as the cause of his or her faith in it. One very often discovers, after some probing, that this certainty is based on more than a convert's objective study of the Muslim scripture, but more so on his or her experience of it or, perhaps one should say, on his or her conversation with the Qur'an. Many converts, and indeed many Muslims, recall the wondrous sensation of being in communion with the divine word when reading the Qur'an. They recount occasions when the Qur'an seemed to respond to their emotional and psychological states or even to their reactions to certain of its passages, as if the scripture was being revealed to them personally, immediately, page by page, with each subsequent passage anticipating how the previous one would affect them. They found themselves slipping into and becoming immersed in a veritable dialogue with the scripture, a dialogue that occurs at the deepest, truest, and purest level of being, where a communication of attributes transpires and mercy, compassion, kindness, knowledge, love—divine and human, perfect and imperfect, infinite and finite, creating and created, of God and of man—embrace.

As many converts know, one does not have to be a Muslim to feel this intrinsic power of the Qur'an, for many of them chose Islam after and because of such moments. Also, many a non-Muslim scholar of Islam has reported it. The British scholar of Arabic, Arthur J. Arberry, recalled how the Qur'an supported him through a difficult time in his life. He stated that listening to the Qur'an chanted in Arabic was, for him, like listening to the beat of his own heart.[87] Fredrick Denny, a non-Muslim writer, recalls the "wonderfully disturbing experience" one sometimes has when reading the Qur'an, when the reader starts feeling "an uncanny, sometimes frightening presence." Instead of reading the Qur'an, the reader begins feeling the Qur'an is "reading" the reader![88]

Yet not every reading of the Qur'an leads to such an experience. Muslims believe that it requires a certain state of mind and spirit, of humility and sincerity, of willingness and readiness. They say that if the reader is aware of his own helplessness before God, if he is prepared to see himself for what he really is, if he is willing to discard the many false images he has made of and for himself, if he comes to know the reality of "there is no power nor might but in God,"[89] then he is ready, by the grace of God, to be transformed by this sacred scripture.

Each generation of Muslims has felt that the Qur'an was suited ideally to the mental outlook of their time. The articles and books that have appeared recently by western converts to Islam show that they are no exception. I cannot explain fully why past generations of Muslims felt this way, or why Muslims in other parts of the world currently have this perception, but I shall attempt to share a western convert's point of view.

As pointed out in the previous chapter, when a western reader first opens the Qur'an, he soon finds himself confronted, in a dramatic way, with one of the great questions that has caused so many in modern times to doubt the existence of God; for the Qur'an has the angelic hosts ask, "Why create this creature who will shed blood and spread corruption on earth?" (2:30). The Qur'an then begins an explanation, but it only provides enough of an answer to catch and hold the reader's attention. The reader will have to read on if he wishes to obtain more clues.

Having just read about Adam, whose story in the Qur'an differs in key respects from the parallel account in the Bible, the western reader

---

[87] *The Koran,* interpreted by Arthur J. Arberry (Oxford: Oxford University Press), introduction.

[88] Fredrick Denny, *Islam* (New York: Harper & Row Publishers, 1987), 88.

[89] A phrase frequently recited by Muslims.

wonders where, exactly, does Islam locate itself in relation to the Judeo–
Christian tradition? The Qur'an puts this into perspective, first with the
story of the Children of Israel (2:40-86) and then with a discussion of the
attitudes and beliefs of the People of the Book (Jews and Christians). This
is followed by an account of Abraham and Ishmael's building of the
Ka'bah that links Islam to the great Patriarch of all three religions (2:122-
41). Islam, the Qur'an informs us, is the restoration of the pure faith of
Abraham (2:142-67).

The reader naturally turns his attention to more practical matters: What
about the Muslim practices we hear so much about in the news: dietary
laws, fasting, *jihad*, the pilgrimage, the status of women in Islam? These
issues are taken up next (2:168-283). Interspersed throughout these exposi-
tions are reminders of the existence and oneness of God, of the many signs
of God's wisdom, mercy and power, and of man's desperate need to turn to
Him. The Qur'an will implant these essential truths in the reader's mind
continually and repeatedly as it works to penetrate the inner reaches of his
soul and reawaken him to the reality by which he lives and breathes.

The second *surah* ends with a prayer, which it teaches to the reader. It
reminds him that God only reveals His guidance not to burden man but to
aid him. It then instructs him to ask God to help him with his many difficulties and to turn to His infinite forgiveness, mercy, and protection. The
third *surah* opens with an answer to this plea: Our only real hope and refuge
is in

> God! There is no god but He,—the Living, the Self-
> Subsisting, the Eternal. It is He Who sent down to you, in
> truth, the Book, confirming what went before it. (3:1-6)

When the reader finishes *Surat al Baqarah* (the second *surah*), he has
already acquired a summary knowledge of Islam. In the remaining 113
*surah*s, the Qur'an will develop, reinforce, and elaborate further on the
themes introduced in *al Baqarah*. As mentioned in chapter one, the reader will find these themes interwoven throughout the text, for the Qur'an
does not let the reader consider them in isolation, but rather wants the
reader to see their interconnectedness. Nevertheless, each remaining *surah*
will emphasize, for the most part, one or two principle themes. The third
surah, *Ali 'Imran*, outlines the religious history of mankind, with special
reference to the People of the Book, and reminds Muslims of their duty to
fight tyranny and injustice. The fourth *surah*, *al Nisa'*, returns to the topic
of women's rights and family obligations. The fifth *surah, al Ma'idah,*

deals mainly with Judaism and Christianity and again emphasizes the corruption of the earlier religions of God, whose pure teachings are reclaimed and perfected with Islam.

As we move through the Qur'an, the *surah*s gradually shorten and their emphasis and style changes as well. In the middle *surah*s, we discover fewer rules and regulations, for the main emphasis has shifted to more parables and stories of past prophets, more frequent and more dramatic references to the many natural signs of God's wisdom and beneficence, and greater and greater stress on man's relationship and return to God. In addition, the literary style of the Qur'an, which can only be truly appreciated in Arabic, becomes ever more rhapsodic as we continue.

As we near the end of the Qur'an, the discourse focuses almost entirely on the reader and his relationship to God and on the organic relationship between one's deeds and one's state in the Hereafter. These *surah*s continually pound out these themes in short ecstatic bursts. Heaven and Hell, the Last Hour and the Last Judgment, the here and now and the hereafter, the obliteration of the universe and our return to Almighty God all converge to an apocalyptic climax.

The Qur'an has led the reader from his immediate and practical concerns, by means of a world of prophets, patriarchs, wonders and signs, to that ultimate moment when it will seem to him that there is only himself standing before his Lord and Creator. Many of those who make this journey experience something of the terror and the power of that meeting as they come to the end of the Qur'an. Self-doubt, fear, and pressure surround them as they near the choice that the Qur'an inevitably demands. Many fear society's backlash, question their own sanity, their ability to turn their lives around and submit to the requirements of Islam, or feel that it is too late for them—that they are far beyond the point where God could love them. Yet throughout the Qur'an, God assures the reader continually that he or she must never yield to this type of doubt and despair.

> And if my servants call on Me, tell them that I am near.
> That I heed the call of every caller. So let them with a will
> call unto me. And believe in Me, that they may walk in the
> right way. (2:186)

> "Never will I suffer to be lost the work of any of you, be
> he male or female. You are members one of another.
> Those who have left their homes, or were driven out there
> from, or suffered harm in My cause, or fought or were

slain—truly, I will blot out from them their iniquities, and admit them into gardens with rivers flowing underneath; A reward from the presence of God, and from His presence is the best of rewards. (3:195)

O My servants who have sinned against yourselves, never despair of the mercy of God: for God forgives all sins: for He is Oft-Forgiving, Most Merciful. (39:53)

You are not, by the grace of your Lord, mad or possessed. (68:2)

By the glorious morning light, and the night when it is still and dark, your Guardian-Lord has not forsaken you, nor is He displeased. And the promise of the here-after is greater than the promise of the present. And soon your Guardian Lord will give you (that with which) you will be well pleased. Did He not find you like an orphan and shelter you? And He found you lost and He guided you? And He found you in need and nur-tured you? (93:1-8)

Have We not expanded for you your breast? And removed from you your burden that did gall your back? And raise high your esteem? So, truly with every hardship there is relief. Truly, with every hardship there is relief. (94:1-6)

As the ultimate choice closes in on him, the Qur'an puts before the reader the words his soul so desperately wants and needs to say, com-manding him:

"Say, He is God, the One, the Eternally Sought by All!" (112:1)

"Say, I seek refuge in the Lord of every new day's dawn!" (113:1)

"Say, I seek refuge in the Lord of mankind!" (114:1)

It is as if God through the Qur'an is exhorting the reader: "Just say it and I will come to you; just say it and I will protect and comfort you; just turn to me and I will love you and your heart will finally know peace."

Many of us, after reading the Qur'an, stood paralyzed on the bridge of indecision, which stretches between faith and rejection, our material dreams and our hopes for the hereafter, our worldly desires and our spiritual needs. There were sleepless nights, seemingly endless pacings, haunting visions of our families' and friends' reactions, verses of the scripture that echoed in our minds, worries about our careers and our futures, and, worst of all, the emptiness of separation from the One who touched us and spoke to us through His revelation. Of those who knew this agony, some turned and fled, never to return. Yet there are also those who gave up resistance and ran with outstretched arms into the merciful embrace of their Lord, who surrendered themselves to their deepest needs and fell into an ocean of kindness and love.

Those who choose Islam soon discover that, for the rest of their lives, they will have to face the following question repeatedly: "How did you become a Muslim?" They will formulate various partial explanations at different times according to the context in which it is asked. However, all of us who made that decision know that even we cannot fully comprehend it, for the wisdom and workings of God are often subtle and unfathomable. Perhaps the simplest and truest statement we can offer is this: At one special moment of our lives—a moment that we could never have foreseen when we were younger—God, in His infinite knowledge and kindness, had mercy on us. Maybe He saw in us a need so great, a pain so deep, or an emptiness so vast. And maybe, He also saw in us a readiness. However He made it come to be, to Him we are eternally thankful. Truly, all praise and thanks belong to God.

5

CHAPTER 4

NOURISHING FAITH

Once the decision to accept Islam is made, the first thing almost every convert wants to know is, what do I do now? This is because conversion seeks fulfillment; it needs a way or a program to perpetuate the experience of self-surrender. The traditions of the Prophet report many a new Muslim asking Muhammad what deeds Islam requires of them. Very often he would begin by telling them that Islam is built upon five pillars: the *shahadah* (the witnessing of faith), salah (ritual prayer), *sawm* (fasting) during the Arabic lunar month of Ramadan, zakah (the annual charity tax), and *hajj* (the annual pilgrimage).[90] It is through these *five pillars of Islam* that the proselyte begins to build his faith. They present his first test of commitment and they are at the center of Islam's system of moral and spiritual growth. This chapter shares a few of this author's personal impressions and experiences of the five pillars. Each ritual will be discussed individually, but first let me make a few general comments.

Together, the five pillars of Islam touch many areas of a believer's earthly existence: his spirituality, ethics, personal hygiene, social relations, sexual relations, politics, finances, time management, eating habits, dress, travel plans and many others as well. In this way they remind and help the Muslim to direct all of his efforts towards God and to make the totality of his life on earth an act of worship. They also strengthen the believer's character, for they require considerable determination and self-restraint, and the Muslim must repeatedly and periodically interrupt his worldly pursuits to perform them.

Time plays a key role in Islam's rituals. Voluntary acts of worship are strongly encouraged and may be offered for the most part whenever one wishes, but the five pillars are obligatory and must be performed at specified times. Those who practice the pillars steadfastly and correctly soon dis-

---

[90] From the collections of al Bukhari and Muslim. See, *An Nawawi's Forty Hadith*, 34.

cover that they come to regulate their lives. They become an inner clock by which the believer sets and organizes his life. Like the different hands on a stop watch, each ritual is associated with a different measure of earthly duration.

The *shahadah*, which takes only seconds to pronounce, is in one sense Islam's briefest ritual. For those who wish to convert to Islam, its recital, witnessed by two Muslims, is required in order to join the Muslim community officially.[91] Muslims must also recite quietly the *shahadah* while in the sitting posture during ritual prayer. While these may be the only times the statement of the *shahadah* is compulsory, the *shahadah* is really a permanent requirement, for the instant someone genuinely rejects it, that person is outside the pale of Islam. In this sense, then, the *shahadah* is a continuous ritual, a moment-by-moment commitment to the oneness of God and the prophethood of Muhammad.

The salah (ritual prayer) is mandatory for Muslims five times daily: before sunrise (the *fajr* prayer), around noon (the *zuhr* prayer), in the afternoon (the *'asr* prayer), at sunset (the *maghrib* prayer), and before sleeping (the *'isha'* prayer). The time needed to perform the ritual prayer is rather short—as little as a few minutes—so that the compulsory Islamic prayers are just long enough and frequent enough to keep the believer focused throughout the day on the real purpose of life, without imposing too great an interruption of his necessary worldly pursuits.

The fast of Ramadan takes place during the ninth lunar month of the Islamic calendar. For this entire month, Muslims deny themselves food, drink, and sex between sunrise and sunset and also make special efforts to engage themselves in extra acts of worship. While it would be much too difficult to fast the whole year through, the fast of Ramadan signifies to Muslims that they should dedicate each month of their earthly lives to serving God.

Zakah is an annual charity-tax that follows specific rates that are applied to one's accumulated wealth. By paying zakah, believers aspire to purify the previous year's worldly gains. The *hajj* is the annual pilgrimage to Makkah, which Muslims are required to make once in a lifetime if they have the means to do so. For the faithful, to make the pilgrimage is one of their greatest goals in life, a chance to journey to the sanctuary toward which they have always prayed and to glorify God with their Muslim brothers and sisters from every corner of the earth.

---

[91] A Muslim relative will recite the *shahadah* for an infant at birth.

Thus through these five pillars, Muslims consecrate their time on earth: with the *shahadah* they commit to God their every moment; with salah, their days; with the fast of Ramadan, their months; with the payment of zakah, their years; and with the pilgrimage to Makkah, their lifetimes.

Although time has such an important place in these rituals, the five pillars, in several ways, also reach beyond time. For one thing, they persistently remind Muslims that they are moving, moment by moment, closer to their last days on earth and then to the next life, to a very different order of creation, where earthly time will seem to them strange and illusory.[92] The rituals, both in form and content, help to keep the worshiper alert to this. Indeed, many Qur'anic verses and the traditional invocations that Muslims recite during the rituals recall the themes of the afterlife and our return to God. In addition, many of the postures Muslims assume, hardships they endure, and ceremonies they perform in the rituals also parallel descriptions from the Qur'an and the sayings of Muhammad of the Day of Judgment. In this way, the rituals become for Muslims both a preparation and a kind of rehearsal for that Day, a vehicle by which the worshiper is allowed to almost experience in advance that decisive meeting with his Lord.

The Islamic rituals traverse the past as well by bringing the believer back to the days of the Prophet and his Companions. Muslims have always been extremely meticulous about performing the five pillars exactly as Muhammad instructed his followers to perform them. Therefore, the ritual of each disciple of Muhammad is the same as every other throughout history, which makes the five pillars of Islam a great leveler and unifier of the Muslim community that transcend time, place, race, and language.

Muslims realize that the rituals they practice were not introduced by Muhammad; rather, they date back to the very beginnings of humanity's worship of God. The Qur'an tells us that all of the prophets insisted on the oneness of God and that the divine guidance revealed through them must be heeded. They often established ritual prayer and enjoined upon their followers charity and fasting. Moreover, the Qur'an states that prophet Abraham first called for the *hajj* and, together with his son Ishmael, rebuilt the Ka'bah, the first house established on Earth for the worship of the one God. Therefore, when Muslims perform their rituals, they understand that they are not only practicing the religion taught by the Prophet Muhammad, but that they are returning to and restoring the pure and timeless religion revealed by God to all of his prophets: the religion of self-surrender to God—*Islam*.

---

[92] See the discussion on time and predestination on pages 70-73.

Self-surrender to God is what Islam is all about, and it is through these rituals that Muslims come to experience it most personally and directly. The five pillars of Islam are at the core of Muslim piety, as each worshipper brings into them all of his or her pains, efforts, and longings. The rituals form a nexus between a believer's relationships with his fellow man and his relationship with God, because his good deeds and his love of God are joined through them. Through the five pillars, Muslims have been able to know profoundly and intimately God's infinitely merciful power. This also helps explain why Muslims are so strict about preserving the original forms of their rituals, because they are convinced that the slightest modification inevitably would diminish their experience of the divine.

Calling to Faith

Of my three daughters, I have the clearest recollection of Fattin's birth. The fact that she is the youngest of my children, and hence the most recently born, has a lot to do with it. The experience I gained from my wife's two previous pregnancies definitely helped me to be more collected during her third. Even though her birth came rather unexpectedly—which, by the way, is typically Fattin—I was cool-headed enough this time to play my part correctly and to observe much of what was taking place around us in the delivery room. (During my first daughter's delivery, I almost fainted and my relatives had to take over the role I was supposed to have learned in prenatal classes.)

As we drove to Lawrence Memorial hospital that bright summer morning, my wife and I both felt that the mild contractions she had been having were a false alarm. We told her mother that we would probably be coming right back home. I joked to the doctor examining my wife that if the baby was coming today then she needed to hurry, because I had a class to teach in an hour.

"I think you might just make it," she informed me, "because your baby is coming now!"

Soon my wife's labor pains became extremely intense, and within forty-five minutes of our arrival at the hospital, Fattin was shouting her arrival into this world.

Fattin lay exhausted in her mother's arms while the doctor and nurses were finishing up. Then one of the nurses gently took her from my wife, wrapped her snugly in a blanket, and put a cap on her head that covered her ears. She then carried her over to me.

"Would you like to hold her?" she asked.

"Yes, of course," I answered.

It is amazing how you can already see so much personality in those tiny faces. The first time I gazed at Jameelah, I saw her brightness and inquisitiveness; with Sarah, I saw her gentleness and kindness. When I looked at Fattin's face, I could see so clearly her independence and fierce determination.

I walked a few steps with Fattin to a corner of the room so that we would not be in any one's way. I raised her in my arms very carefully and bent my head so that my lips were just touching her right ear. Then, like millions of Muslim fathers before me, I whispered to her,

Allahu Akbar (God is greater).
Allahu Akbar (God is greater).
Allahu Akbar (God is greater).
Allahu Akbar (God is greater).
Ashhadu an la ilaha illa Allah (I bear witness that there is no god but God).
Ashhadu an la ilaha illa Allah (I bear witness that there is no god but God).
Ashhadu anna Muhammadan rasulu Allah (I bear witness that Muhammad is the Messenger of God).
Ashhadu anna Muhammadan rasulu Allah (I bear witness that Muhammad is the Messenger of God).
Hayya 'alas salaah (Hasten to prayer).
Hayya 'alas salaah (Hasten to prayer).
Hayya 'alal falaah (Hasten to success).
Hayya 'alal falaah (Hasten to success).
Allahu Akbar (God is greater).
Allahu Akbar (God is greater).
La ilaha illa Allah (There is no god but God).

The pronouncement that I whispered in Fattin's ear that morning is the Islamic call to prayer, termed *adhan* in Arabic. They are among the first words spoken to every child born into a Muslim family.[93] When parents

---

[93] After reciting the *adhan* in the right ear of the newborn, the parent or relative will then recite the *iqamah*, the second call to prayer, in the child's left ear. The *iqamah* reads: *Allahu Akbar. Allahu Akbar. Ashhadu an la ilaha illa Allah. Ashhadu an la ilaha illa Allah. Ashhadu anna Muhammadan rasulu Allah. Ashhadu anna Muhammadan rasulu Allah. Hayya 'alas salaah. Hayya 'alal falaah. Qad qamat as salah. Qad qamat as salah. Allahu Akbar. Allahu Akbar. La ilaha illa Allah.*

make this summons to their infant, they do so with their fervent prayers that he or she will grow to be a righteous, God-conscious believer. It signifies a recalling of the child to his or her true nature, to the spirit which God breathed into him or her, and to that primordial bond to which every soul bore witness: "Am I not your Lord?" (7:172). While Muslim parents know that their son or daughter may make mistakes in life, that he or she may even come to neglect the requirements of faith at times, this *adhan* also signifies the parents' deepest hope that if this should happen, then their child will always come back to this first calling.

The *adhan* is typical of Islam in the way it uses the call to prayer to remind believers of Islam's broader objectives. Certainly, something like a bell or a horn could signal the times for the obligatory prayers; Islam chooses a method that offers the greatest possible meaning, for the *adhan* succinctly summarizes and interconnects Islam's attitudes toward God, the Prophet, worship, and life. For this reason, it seems appropriate that in this section and the next, we let the *adhan* introduce us to the first two pillars of Islam.

Bearing Witness

"Allahu Akbar! Allahu Akbar! Allahu Akbar! Allahu Akbar!"

Allahu Akbar! (God is Greater!) It is the supreme affirmation of Islam, the great axiom upon which all else depends. It qualifies all other statements about God and His creation and is the key Muslim perception of God. It is the reason for his or her worship, total trust in, and self-surrender to Him as well as the foundation of Muslim piety and spirituality.

God is greater than what or whom? The statement seems to beg the question. Its openendedness is at first perplexing. Why is it left incomplete? But as we insert various objects at the end of this assertion, we soon come to understand. The statement invites—indeed, it demands—our attempts at completing it. But all such efforts are ultimately futile, for God's infinite greatness cannot be encompassed by our comparisons. As the Qur'an itself says: "nothing can be compared to Him" (112:4).

We may ask: Is God greater than all creation? Is He greater in mercy, compassion, knowledge, wisdom, love, and justice than the most merciful, compassionate, wise, loving and just among His creatures? Is he greater than the greatest power we can imagine? *Allahu Akbar* repeatedly affirms that He is incomparably greater. He is greater than any likening we may use to complete this declaration, greater than anything and everything that we could ever conceive of, greater than the speculations of theologians or the assertions of dogmatists or the formulations of philosophers, and greater than human words could describe.

Allahu Akbar! This seemingly unfinished comparative is all-inclusive, for it allows for all our praises and glorification. Its openendedness invites us to imagine, but at the same time proclaims our inability to truly conceive of God's greatness. All other beings from the perspective of *Allahu Akbar* stand on the same level ground as infinitely inferior to God. Therefore, the second declaration of the *adhan*, which is also the first of the two testimonies of the *shahadah*, follows as a natural consequence of *Allahu Akbar*.

"Ashhadu an la ilaha illa Allah! Ashhadu an la ilaha illa Allah!" (I bear witness that there is no god but God!)

For how could it be otherwise? If God is infinitely greater, infinitely more merciful, infinitely more compassionate, infinitely more powerful, infinitely kinder, infinitely more just, infinitely nearer to us, infinitely more loving, infinitely wiser, infinitely more knowing, than how could there be and why should one seek, another god, another ultimate protector, another ultimate goal? Why should one seek other deities or intermediaries between oneself and God, or other persons, alive or dead, to whom to direct one's prayers? Are God's goodness and power somehow insufficient, that we should invent for Him partners? For Muslims, the answer to these questions is obvious: there is no *ilah* (deity) but God, and hence, worship is due to God alone.

The Islamic term for worship is *'ibadah*. It is derived from the same root as *'abd*, the Arabic word for "slave," and Muslims quite proudly refer to themselves as "slaves of Allah." At first, this seems like a rather severe description of the believer's relationship to God, for we normally think of a slave as someone exploited and debased. However, our initial discomfort with this term may reveal something about ourselves that is quite in tune with Islam's conception of worship.

We instinctively resent that a human being should choose to be the slave of another creation, whether it be to a tyrant, greed, drug addiction, power, or to his or her lust. Something within us rejects this as sick and humiliating. We feel how vulnerable such a person is—how very precarious his existence—because his happiness depends on masters who are themselves fickle and weak, perhaps even illusory. Even an atheist could appreciate the refusal to worship—in the sense of to enslave oneself to and to show complete obedience to—a being other than God.

Yet it seems that we all need to have faith in someone or something. A life without meaning or direction is wretched. Whether it be a political cause, a person, career, nation, a dream, an idea, money, power, prestige, family, fame, or revenge, it appears that we must have something for which to live and appreciate, for which to die. In short, I believe that it is human nature to venerate, that we are destined for servitude. Very often, however, the objects of our desires remain unattainable. But even when they are attainable, the reality cannot equal our expectations. They become, in the end, like mirages in a desert, nothing more than figments of our false imaginings (29:39).

As Muslims see it, life is a continual choice between masters, between those you create for yourself and the One who created you. When you make your own gods, you create your own oppression and debasement, but when you surrender yourself to the one God, you are shielded from the types of fears and insecurities that lead persons to idol worship.

In fact, from the point of view of Islam, all creatures, whether or not they are aware of it, are already slaves of God in the sense that they all serve His ultimate purposes and can accomplish only what He allows them to accomplish. God not only wants us to realize this truth, but to benefit as much as we can from it, by using the gifts and guidance He gives to us so that we may grow ever closer to Him. When we become true servants of God, we become servants of the divine attributes as well, of His Mercy, Love, Justice, and Truth. To worship a creation is, to the Muslim, utterly irrational and self-abasing, but to be the slave of God is a Muslim's highest honor and lifelong goal.

This is a goal that, at times, could be difficult to pursue. The Qur'an certainly does not paint a rosy picture of most of humanity in this regard. Misdirected worship, idolatry, comes all too easily to human beings, and thus the Qur'an refers to faith as an "uphill climb" (90:4-17). Islam (i.e., self surrender) requires hard work, self-discipline, determination, and, above all, following God's guidance. This brings us to the next statement of the *adhan,* the second and concluding statement of the *shahadah.*

Ashhadu anna Muhammadan rasulu Allah! Ashhadu anna Muhammadan rasulu Allah (I testify that Muhammad is the Messenger of God!)

The first testimony of the *shahadah*, that there is no god but God, is an independent statement of fact. It bears witness to a universal truth that applies to all of us, regardless of whether or not we acknowledge it. Before humanity came into being, before the creation of Earth, before the birth of the universe we live in, there was but one God—and there will never be another.

The second testimony of the *shahadah*, that Muhammad is the messenger of God, depends on the first. It too is a statement of a truth, but it is also a statement of commitment to the first and to the community of disciples of Muhammad. The first half of the *shahadah* declares the oneness of God; the second half informs us of God's great concern for man. The first proclaims God's incomparable being; the second tells us how to come to know Him. The first states the goal; the second shows the way. God willed to be known and, by His mercy, commissioned Muhammad to help guide us to Him.

From the moment someone joins the Muslim community, whether by birth or conversion, the *shahadah* will be an ever-present feature of that person's life. It will be chanted aloud during the call to prayer, invoked at the beginning of all major events, recited at least nine times a day during the five ritual prayers, exclaimed spontaneously by believers during moments of excitement or wonder, and sighed quietly by Muslims when they reflect on the greatness and glory of God. Moreover, it will become a statement of a lifestyle based on the Qur'an and the teachings of Prophet Muhammad. For Muslims, the Qur'an is God's word revealed, and the Prophet's *Sunnah* (literally, "way") is God's word most perfectly applied. When 'Aishah, Muhammad's wife, was asked about the Prophet's conduct during his life, she simply responded, "It was the Qur'an."[94] Her answer best expresses how Muslims view the relationship between their scripture and the Messenger of God.

The *shahadah* is where Muslim life begins, both literally and figuratively. It is the cornerstone upon which the community of believers rests and is their source of unity and strength. It is the boundary that protects them and the line of demarcation that must be crossed if one is to join them.

Like all converts, I will never forget my first *shahadah*. It was the single most difficult, yet liberating and powerful, moment of my life. Gradually, I came to better understand its many implications, but I especially came to see that it proclaims not only the oneness of God but also the

---

[94] Kazi, *Guidance from the Messenger*, preface.

unity and equality of humankind.[95] Of course, my discovery of this was in no way original. This egalitarian principle is so salient a theme in the teachings of Islam that it is impossible to miss. This is not to say that every Muslim would so readily articulate it, but rather, it is so clearly observable in the community's religious interactions and traditions. It is not at all surprising that this is one of the first things that struck Malcolm X on his pilgrimage to Makkah. He wrote,

> For the last week, I have been utterly speechless and spellbound by the graciousness I see displayed all around me by people of *all colors* . . . You may be shocked by these words coming from me. But on this pilgrimage, what I have seen, and experienced, has forced me to rearrange much of my thought patterns previously held, and to toss aside some of my previous conclusions . . . Perhaps if white Americans could accept the Oneness of God, then perhaps, too, they could accept in *reality* the Oneness of Man—and cease to measure and hinder and harm others in terms of their "differences" in color . . . Each hour in the Holy Land enables me to have greater spiritual insights into what is happening in America between black and white.[96]

I am not claiming here that Islam eradicates racial and color prejudices. That would be like claiming that Islam eradicates evil. Rather, I am asserting that Islam does not tolerate such prejudices and that when Muslims display them, they know full well that they are violating a fundamental precept of their faith and committing a serious wrong. Of all of the great world religions, I believe none has been more successful in fighting racial prejudice than Islam. I received a very personal and poignant demonstration of Islam's power in this regard several weeks after I became a Muslim.

It was at a lecture organized by the Muslim students of the University of San Francisco. The speaker that night was Abdul Aleem Musa, who at that time was the imam (leader) of Masjid al Nur in Oakland, California. He recounted his journey to Islam, which began with his joining the Nation of Islam in the sixties and his later transition to authentic Islam in

---

[95] See the discussion on pages 78–85.
[96] Haley, *The Autobiography of Malcolm X.*

the seventies. The African American Muslims that accompanied him from Oak-land showed by their reactions to his speech that their paths to Islam were very similar to his.

Physically, Abdul Aleem is a very imposing figure. He looks as if he could play tight end for the San Francisco Forty-Niners. He is extremely clever and intelligent, certainly not one to be taken lightly. On the way to the lecture, some of the students told me that Abdul Aleem had been a member of the Black Panthers long ago and that he was an ex-convict. I usually am suspicious of such rumors, but from his lecture I gathered that, at the very least, he had had a very tumultuous past. Nonetheless, the wisdom of his words and the serenity he now projected made me feel that he had discovered inner peace through his faith.

As I listened to Abdul Aleem, I kept recalling my teenage years and the terrible brutality of the race wars my neighborhood fought with young black men like him from the nearby slums. I pictured what a dangerous adversary he must have been—the type of enemy whom everyone would try their best not to notice when he entered your territory. I felt simultaneously inspired and intimidated, moved and yet confused. All my old reflexes and fears which I thought I had left far behind in Bridgeport, Connecticut, were now coming back to me.

The first question Abdul Aleem was asked when he had finished his speech came from one of the Arab students: "Do you feel that Islam has changed you; has it really changed your life?"

The question may have been entirely innocent, but it seemed to allude to his turbulent past. At least that is how I interpreted it and, apparently, so did Abdul Aleem.

"You don't know how many times I've been asked that," he sighed, shaking his head in near disbelief. "People just don't think that it can really happen, that you can turn your life around."

He was speaking slowly, measuring his words, working hard to contain his hurt pride. Then, in a low tone that betrayed mounting frustration, he stated, "People just can't believe in the power of Islam."

The audience tensed and held its breath, anticipating an eruption at any moment. Abdul Aleem's eyes scanned the room, as if he was looking for someone who might understand or some way to prove his point. Suddenly, I found his stare fixed on Grant, another white American convert sitting on my left, and me. The next thing I knew he was pointing right at the two of us.

Almost shouting he exclaimed: 'The very fact that you have white Americans like these, sitting here with black Americans like us, as brothers —BROTHERS!!!—when ten years ago we were killing each other in the streets, shows you how much Islam can change lives!'

It was as if he was reading my own thoughts. Grant and I are of the same generation as Abdul Aleem, and the look on Grant's face told me that he too could relate immediately to what Abdul Aleem said. After the program, Abdul Aleem walked over to the two of us and greeted us both with a warm smile and with what I have come to call an "Islamic triple hug." That was the start of an immensely important relationship for me. Abdul Aleem became a close friend and mentor and helped me to deal with the many pitfalls and roadblocks that threaten the sincerity of a newcomer to Islam.

When I met Abdul Aleem I was only a recent convert to Islam, and it takes time for Islam's many lessons to sink in. But on that evening, I learned much about Islam's egalitarianism. I would learn much more from Abdul Aleem in the months and years ahead.

Can Muslims be bigoted and prejudiced? Of course they can, and most are at various times and in various circumstances. Human beings generalize and prejudge based on experience. To a large degree, our survival depends on it. Sometimes we hurt others and ourselves when we misuse our intellectual abilities, but we can and should correct and learn from our mistakes. Time and time again I witnessed the corrective power that the *shahadah* has over Muslims. I have watched cultural, political, economic, and racial differences drive them apart and I have seen the *shahadah* bring them back together as brothers and sisters in faith. The next incident occurred about a year after my conversion.

Mosques and Islamic centers in Europe and America bring together a vast array of peoples from all over the Muslim world. Very often a masjid will contain many small cultural clusters with no one of them in the majority. This is especially true of the masjids run by Muslim student groups at western universities. Such a diverse assemblage of cultures will produce many differences of opinions, which can evolve quite easily into bitter arguments and community rifts.

Such a quarrel arose one night in the mosque at the University of San Francisco. I do not remember the precise cause of the fray; it had something to do with a pile of anti-Shiite tracts that someone left in the mosque. This happened at the height of the Iran–Iraq war, and a great deal of politico-religious propaganda was being disseminated by both sides of the conflict and by their allies. I recall vividly how explosive the scene became.

The Saudis raged against the Kuwaitis and Iranians, the Pakistani students allied themselves with the Saudis, the white Americans defended the Iranians, the African Americans were against the white Americans, the North African and Palestinian students seemed to be fighting each other and everyone else, the Malaysian students looked terrified. All sorts of bitter, malicious, racial and personal attacks flew back and forth.

'You Shiah are Kaffirs!'

'You Saudis worship your king!'

'What do Americans know about Islam?!'

'Pakistanis are nothing but the lackeys of the Saudis!'

'Our people were Muslims long before you white boys ever were!'

'You're proud of following Elijah Muhammad?!'

'Palestinians got what they deserved!'

Faces were red with rage. Shouts became threatening roars. The American students were clenching their fists and tensing their arms, readying themselves for a fight. This was definitely going to be the end of our community.

From over in the corner of the room a desperate cry rang out:

'La ilaha illa Allah! Muhamadan rasulu Allah!'

It was Ilyas, the always quiet, skinny, short student from Indonesia. He hardly ever spoke a word. The room quieted.

'What did he say?' Several persons asked each other.

Ilyas shouted again at the top of his lungs:

'La ilaha illa Allah! Muhamadan rasulu Allah!'

'Say it!' Ilyas yelled, 'Say it!'

Most of us murmured confusedly: 'La ilaha illa Allah—Muhamadan rasulu Allah?'

'What does he want?' Someone whispered.

'Say it like you mean it!' Ilyas screamed.

Maybe it was because he said it with so much authority or with so much passion, but for some reason we now felt the need to obey this normally meek and inconspicuous member of our mosque. Our voices rose in unison with Ilyas leading us:

'La ilaha illa Allah! Muhamadan rasulu Allah!'

You could feel the hate and anger dissipating. All eyes were fixed on Ilyas. The faces of the brothers looked mesmerized. Some of them showed sadness, some remorse, and others excitement. The whole company now needed Ilyas to lead them again.

'Again!' Ilyas bellowed. 'Again!'

This time we all rang out in one passionate, thundering cry:

'La ilaha illa Allah! Muhamadan rasulu Allah!'

Then again we cried out, following Ilyas's lead:

'La ilaha illa Allah! Muhamadan rasulu Allah!'

Ilyas stopped, froze there for a moment with tears in his eyes. He looked at us in the way a child looks at his parents when he wants them to stop fighting.

'That's what it is all about, brothers!' Ilyas pleaded, his voice cracking. 'That's what binds us!'

'Just look at us!' He shouted, stretching out his arms.

At that, the brothers began to slowly approach one another with looks of great embarrassment on their faces. What easily could have exploded into a spectacle of complete pandemonium, was now a scene of hand-shakes, brotherly hugs, and sincere apologies. The next day, the mosque was back to normal, and I never heard anyone discuss the argument again.

Experiencing Intimacy

And when we pray and put our nose to the ground, we feel a joy, a rest, a strength, that is outside this world and no words could ever describe. You have to experience it to know.

—Ghassan Zarrah, former imam of the masjid at USF[97]

Hayya 'alas salaah! Hayya 'alas salaah!
Hayya 'alal falaah! Hayya 'alal falaah!
(Hasten to prayer! Hasten to Success!)

On the day I converted to Islam, the imam of the masjid gave me a manual on how to perform salah, the Islamic prayer ritual.

'Take it easy,' the Muslim students urged me, 'Don't push yourself too hard!' 'It's better to take your time.' 'You know: slowly, slowly.'

I was surprised by their concern.

How hard could it be to pray? I wondered.

That night, ignoring their advice, I decided to start performing the five prayers at their appointed times. I sat for a long time on the couch in my

---

[97] A quote from *Struggling to Surrender*, 13.

small, dimly lit, living room, studying and rehearsing the prayer postures, the verses of the Qur'an that I needed to recite, and the supplications that I would have to make. Much of what I would be saying was in Arabic, so I had to memorize the Arabic transliterations and the English interpretations that the manual provided. I pored over the manual for a couple of hours before I felt confident enough to attempt my first prayer. It was close to midnight, so I decided to perform the 'isha' prayer.

I walked into the bathroom and placed the manual on the sink counter with it opened to the section describing how to perform wudu' (ritual ablution). Like a cook trying a recipe for the first time, I followed the step by step instructions slowly and meticulously . When I finished washing, I shut off the faucet and returned to the living room with water still dripping from various parts of my body, for the instructions stated that it is preferable not to dry oneself with a towel after wudu'.

Standing in the center of the room, I aimed myself in what I hoped was the direction of Makkah. I glanced back over my shoulder to make sure I had locked the door to my apartment. Finding that it was, I then looked straight ahead, straightened my stance, took a deep breath, raised my hands to the sides of my face with my palms opened and my thumbs touching my ear lobes, and then, in a hushed voice, I pronounced, 'Allahu Akbar.'

I hoped no one heard me. I felt a little bit anxious. I couldn't rid myself of the feeling that someone might be spying on me. Then I suddenly realized that I had left open the curtains of the living room window. What if a neighbor should look in and see me? I thought.

I stopped what I was doing and went to the window. I glanced around outside to make sure no one was there. To my relief, the back yard was empty. I then carefully pulled the curtains closed and returned to the middle of the room.

Once again, I approximated the direction of Makkah, stood straight, raised my hands to where my thumbs were touching my ear lobes, and whispered, 'Allahu Akbar.'

In a barely audible tone, I slowly and clumsily recited the first surah of the Qur'an and another short surah in Arabic, although I doubt that my pronunciation that night would have been intelligible to an Arab. I then quietly said another, 'Allahu Akbar,' and bowed with my back perpendicular to my legs and with my hands grasping my knees. I had never bowed to anyone before and I felt embarrassed. I was glad that I was alone. While still in the bowing position, I repeated several times the phrase, 'Subhana-rabbi-l 'Azeem', which means, Glory to my Lord the Great.

I then stood up and recited, 'Sami'a Allahu liman hamidah' (God hears those who praise Him), and then, 'Rabbana wa laka-l hamd' (Our Lord and to you belongs all praise).

I felt my heart pounding and anxiety mounting as I meekly called out another 'Allahu Akbar'. I had arrived at the moment when I had to perform a sajdah, a prostration. Petrified, I stared at the area of the floor in front of me, where I was supposed to be down on all fours with my face to the ground.

I couldn't do it! I could not get myself to lower myself to the floor, to humble myself with my nose to the ground, like a slave groveling before his master. It was as if my legs had braces on them that would not let me bend. I felt too ashamed and humiliated. I could imagine the snickers and cackles of friends and acquaintances watching me make a fool of myself. I envisioned how ridiculous and pitiable I would look. 'Poor Jeff,' I could hear them saying, 'he really went Arab crazy in San Francisco, didn't he!'

Please! Please help me do this! I prayed.

I took a deep breath and then forced myself to the floor. Now on my hands and knees, I hesitated for a brief moment, and then I pushed my face to the carpet. Ridding my mind of all other thoughts, I mechanically pronounced three times,' Subhana rabbi-l a'la (Glory to my Lord the highest!).

'Allahu Akbar,' I called and sat back on my heels. I kept my mind blank, refusing to allow any distractions to enter it. 'Allahu Akbar,' I pronounced and put my face again to the carpet.

With my nose touching the ground I called out mechanically, 'Subhana rabbi-l a'la, Subhana rabbi-l a'la, Subhana rabbi-l a'la.' I was determined to finish this, no matter what.

'Allahu Akbar.' I called and lifted myself from the floor and stood up straight. Three cycles to go, I told myself.

I had to wrestle with my emotions and pride the rest of the prayer, but it did get easier with each cycle. I was even almost calm during the last prostration. While in the final sitting posture, I recited the tashashhud and then ended the prayer by calling, 'Assalamu 'alaikum wa rahmatullah' with my head turned to the right, and again, 'Assalamu 'alaikum wa rahmatullah,' with my head turned to the left.

Spent, I remained on the floor and reviewed the battle I had just been through. I felt embarrassed that I had to struggle so hard to get through the prayer. With my head lowered in shame I prayed: please forgive me my arrogance and stupidity. I have come from very far and I have so very far to go.

At that moment, I experienced something that I had never felt before and which is therefore difficult for me to put into words. A wave of what I can only describe as coldness swept through me, which seemed to radiate from some point within my chest. It was rather intense, and initially I was startled; I remember shuddering. However, it was much more than a physical sensation, for it affected my emotions as well in a strange way. It was as if mercy had taken on an objective form and was now penetrating and enveloping me. I cannot say exactly why, but I began to cry. Tears began to run down my face, and I found myself weeping uncontrollably. The harder I cried, the more I felt the embrace of a powerful kindness and compassion. I was not crying out of guilt—although I probably should have—or shame or joy; it was as if a dam had been unblocked and a great reservoir of fear and anger within me was being released. As I write these words, I can not help wondering if God's forgiveness involves much more than His absolution of our sins, if His forgiveness is not also curative and assuaging?

I remained on my knees, crouched to the floor with my head in my hands, sobbing, for some time. When I finally stopped crying, I was completely exhausted. The experience I had just had was for me too unfamiliar and overwhelming to try to rationalize at that moment, and I thought that it was definitely too strange to tell anyone about right away.[98] I did realize this much, however: I needed God and prayer desperately.

Before getting up from my knees, I made one last supplication:

Oh God, if I ever gravitate towards disbelief again, then please, kill me first—rid me of this life. It is hard enough living with my imperfections and weaknesses, but I cannot live another day denying You.

"Hasten to (*salaah*) prayer—Hasten to (*falaah*) success!" the *adhan* urges. If our main purpose in life is to grow ever nearer to God, then toward this end prayer is indeed essential. For Muslims, salah is one of the most important ways to pursue and experience this goal. It is a Muslim's spiritual compass by which he repeatedly checks his progress and direction in life, and it is his lifeline to paradise in the hereafter. Through the experience of salah, a Muslim tries to stay alert to the fluctuations of his

---

[98] In the months ahead, however, I had several, what for me were, intense spiritual experiences during *salah*, and I slowly became aware through conversations with other Muslims that mine were not at all abnormal or unusual.

faith. A Muslim will ask himself: Am I becoming lazy about my prayers, lately?; Am I rushing through them, without feeling any benefit?; Are my experiences of prayer weaker or stronger than they used to be?; Do I feel closer or farther from God in my prayers these days? Although each of the five pillars helps a Muslim gauge his growth in faith, the salah is the principle day to day measure of a believer's submission to God.

To perform the Islamic ritual prayer five times every day at the appointed times requires a considerable commitment to Islam. A single salah (ritual prayer) is not very taxing, but just to rise out of bed before dawn, every day of the year, workday or holiday, for the rest of one's life, to make the *fajr* prayer on time already demands great determination. All of Islam's rituals test and challenge a Muslim's will-power and self-control in various ways and, in so doing, help to build these qualities in him. The *shahadah* tests a person's allegiances; the fast of Ramadan tests his control of his physical needs; the zakah tests his ability to discipline his material desires; and the pilgrimage to Makkah in some ways tests all three. The salah may not be as emotionally demanding as one's first *shahadah*, or as physically or materially demanding as the other three pillars of Islam, but the ritual prayer, more than any of the other rituals, tests constancy and per-severance. I have known many Muslims who fast every Ramadan, who pay zakah every year, and who have made the *hajj*, yet who are unable to remain constant in their prayers.

Most of us are capable of great moments of virtue or religiosity and can rise to the occasion on rare occasions. However, too many of us are inca-pable of being even moderately virtuous or religious consistently. In terms of our spiritual and moral growth, we are too often like the person who sud-denly decides he will get in shape one weekend by going out and running a marathon. But to really become physically fit, he needs to begin and fol-low a regular program of exercise. The Qur'an repeatedly exhorts the believer to develop *sabr*, the Arabic word that connotes patience, persever-ance, and fortitude—qualities that are essential to spiritual development. Very often these exhortations are combined with exhortations to establish regular salah, as the two obviously complement each other.

Yet the rewards of salah far outweigh the demands. A Muslim student once informed me that the power of salah is indescribable. He said, "When we pray and put our nose to the ground, we feel a joy, a rest, a strength, that is outside this world and no words could ever describe. You have to expe-rience it to know." The day he told me this was the day I became a Muslim, and it was not long before I began to understand what he meant.

There are moments during salah—moments of truth—of true honesty, sincerity, and humility—when a Muslim perceives the omnipresence of God's most merciful and compassionate light. These are not moments that can be anticipated, for they almost always come unexpectedly. But when they do come, he or she feels the caress of the most tender and most overpowering kindness. It is an utterly humbling experience, because a Muslim knows it is too infinitely beautiful to be deserved. It is a tremendously intoxicating experience, for with your hands, feet, and face placed firmly on the ground, you feel as if you are suddenly lifted into heaven and you could breath its air, smell its soil, and feel its gentle breezes. It feels as if you are about to be raised off the ground and placed in the arms of the most benevolent and affectionate love. These moments of divine intimacy create in the worshipper an overpowering longing to be near to God, and the hereafter becomes the focus of his living and striving.

This helps us understand why devout Muslims are so zealous about their prayers, why they would seemingly prefer death to missing one of them. Thus they can be seen at airports or on sidewalks, in city parks or public buildings, alone or in congregation, standing, bowing, sitting and prostrating, paying no attention to the activity around them, seemingly in their own world. This is because they have come to need salah so desperately; it has become their main source of spiritual sustenance and their most personal and powerful means of relating to God. A devout Muslim cannot risk missing a salah, for he knows that his spiritual center, what people refer to symbolically as one's heart, is real and that it grows in its ability to receive and experience the divine with the continual and steadfast performance of the ritual prayer. This is a conviction born of experience. A Muslim comes to know firsthand that his spirituality and spiritual receptivity increase with and depend on the persistent exercise of prayer.

As stated earlier, a Muslim also knows that his growth is tied to his deeds and his relationship with others, a fact that is reinforced by the form of the congregational prayer. Muslims pray in tight formation, shoulder to shoulder, foot to foot, as they stand, bow, sit, and make the prostrations in unison. The visual beauty and gracefulness of Muslims in prayer depend on the unity of movement of the congregation.

A Muslim student once informed me that he could not understand why the Prophet ordered his Companions to pray in such close contact with each other, when they should be focusing all of their attention on God. I told him that perhaps he had confirmed with his question an important theme of

Islam: Even in our most intense worship, we should not forget that our relationship to God is tied to our relationships with others.

There is a well known saying of the Prophet in which he insists that a Muslim should not leave a gap between himself and his neighbor during the prayer, otherwise they will leave an opening for Satan. Another Muslim student told me how silly that sounded. So I asked him if he had ever prayed next to someone whom he felt was purposely trying to keep his distance and how that made him feel. He responded that he had known that experience and it made him suspicious of the motives of the person next to him. 'Exactly!' I told him, 'You see, a door to temptation was opened.'

As time passed, I grew more and more to appreciate the student Imam's statement that the beauty of the experience of salah cannot be truly described. Its beauty seems to have no upper bound, and it increases over time with the steadfast performance of the five daily prayers. As it does so, the believer comes to see with ever greater clarity just how much is at stake in this life—how much there is to gain and how great and terrible the potential loss. A pious Muslim parent certainly can understand the urgency behind prophet Abraham's prayer: "O my Lord! make me one who establishes regular salah and also among my descendants Our Lord!" (16:40).

My daughter, Jameelah, once asked me just after we finished the noon prayer together: "Daddy, why do we pray?"

Her question caught me off guard. I didn't expect it from an eight year old. I knew of course the most obvious answer—that as Muslims we are obligated to—but I did not want to waste the opportunity to share with her the experience and benefits of salah. Nevertheless, as I tried to put together a reply in my mind, I bought a little time by beginning with, 'We pray because God wants us to!'

'But why, daddy, what does praying do?' she asked.

'It is hard to explain to a young person, honey. Someday, if you do the five prayers every day, I'm sure you'll understand, but I'll do my best to answer your question'

'You see, sweetheart. God is the source of all the love, mercy, kindness, and wisdom—of all the beauty—that we experience and feel. Like the sun is the source of the light we see in the daytime, God is the source of all of these and much more. Thus, the love I feel for you, your sisters, and mommy is given to me by God. We know that God is kind and merciful by all the things He has given us in this life. But when we pray, we can feel God's love, kindness, and mercy in a very special way, in the most powerful way.

For example, you know that mommy and I love you by the way we take care of you. But when we hug you and kiss you, you can really feel how much we love you. In a similar way, we know that God loves and is kind to us by the way He takes care of us. But when we pray, we can feel His love in a very real and special way.'

'Does praying make you a better daddy?' She asked me.

'I hope so and I would like to think so, because once you are touched by God's love and kindness in the prayer, it is so beautiful and powerful, that you need to share it with those around you, especially your family. Sometimes, after a hard day at work, I feel so exhausted that I just want to be alone. But if I feel God's kindness and mercy in the prayer, I look at my family and remember what a great gift you are to me, and all the love and happiness I get from being your daddy and mommy's husband. I'm not saying that I am the perfect father, but I believe I would not be as good a father without the prayers. Am I making any sense at all?'

'I kind of understand what you mean,' Jameelah answered.

Then she hugged me and said, 'And I love you, Daddy!'

'I love you too, sweetie pie. I love you too.'

Ramadan

> O you who believe! Fasting is prescribed to you as it was prescribed to those before you, that you may learn God-consciousness. (2:183)

"Dr. Lang! Congratulations!" A beaming, middle-eastern student called to me, as I stood by the math department post boxes checking the morning mail.

"And you too!" I called back to him while he hurried down the hall toward his class.

"What was that for?" A colleague asked me, looking up from his letters.

"That student is a Muslim," I explained. *"He just congratulated me on the start of Ramadan, our month of fasting."*

"He congratulated you on having to suffer a month of hunger?" He said with a laugh. *"I could understand him congratulating you at the end of the month, but not at the beginning."*

"We have a different perspective," I told him, *"we view the fast of Ramadan as a great opportunity for personal and spiritual growth."*

"I thought it was an act of penance," said another professor who was listening in on our conversation.

"No, not really. We believe that God is very forgiving and that we are especially receptive to His forgiveness during the month of fasting. But we think of the fast of Ramadan more as a spiritual benefit—a chance to review and reorient our lives and to grow closer to God. Muslims look forward to Ramadan with great anticipation and optimism."

"That may be," he remarked, *"but I know for sure that I could never survive an entire month of fasting!"*

Each day during the Arabic lunar month of Ramadan, Muslims abstain from food, drink, and sex between sunrise and sunset. They must also restrain their temper and avoid backbiting. One obvious objective of this month-long fast is to teach the believer self-control and to prepare him for the challenges that life may offer. Non-Muslims often mistakenly assume that the aim of the fast is self-mortification—to weaken the body so as to free the soul—as is the case in some other religious traditions. The fact that Muslims are encouraged to replenish themselves between sunset and dawn, and not to fast if they are ill or traveling, shows that the fast is intended to cause discomfort but not any physical debilitation.[99]

Most non-Muslims view the fast of Ramadan as Islam's severest ritual. When I describe this pillar of Islam to non-Muslim friends, I often get reactions like, "How can you do that to yourself?" or, "I could never do that!" I must admit that I held similar feelings before becoming a Muslim. In addition, when I was considering converting to Islam, I had very serious doubts as to whether I would be able to observe the fast completely and correctly. However, my first Ramadan, which occurred during the summer, turned out not to be as difficult as I imagined. Within a day or two, my body adjusted to the changes in eating and drinking habits and I was fine as long as I followed the well-known instructions on fasting contained in the traditions of the Prophet. By the end of Ramadan, I had gained a new confidence in myself. I found that I had greater endurance than I thought I had and that with some patience, determination, and God's help, a seemingly very difficult task could become quite achievable.

Islam definitely encourages such a positive attitude; it is one of the Qur'an's major themes, and the rituals seem to be designed to strengthen this conviction. Perhaps this is one of the principle reasons why Islam

---

[99] Nursing mothers and menstruating women are also not supposed to fast. If a Muslim is unable to fast part of Ramadan, at a later time he or she can make up for the missed days either by fasting the same number of days missed or by performing certain prescribed acts of charity.

discourages severe asceticism, because so few of us are capable of it. Although Islamic rituals challenge the believer, they are not so difficult so as to habituate him or her to failure. Thus we have the statement of Prophet Muhammad that the best act of worship in the eyes of God is the one that is practiced consistently.[100]

Each of the pillars of Islam promotes community solidarity, although this may not be at first obvious with the fast of Ramadan. Yet with the possible exception of the *hajj*, there is no other time of the year when fraternal feeling among Muslims is so strong and so evident. During this month, mosques throughout the Islamic world are packed with worshippers throughout the night, charitable work and donations increase dramatically in the community, and Muslims make special efforts to visit friends and family, especially those whom they have not seen in some time. Muslims consider it a great blessing to share *iftar* (the meal taken just after sunset) with others. A Muslim household will hardly ever break the fast alone during Ramadan, but will invite friends and neighbors, including non-Muslims, to join them for *iftar*. In the West, communal feeling among Muslims is also heightened during Ramadan, because their lifestyle becomes even more distinguished from the non-Muslim majority.

Ramadan is a very spiritual time for Muslims, who often refer to it as the *Month of Peace* and the *Month of Mercy*. It is the month in which the revelation of the Qur'an to Prophet Muhammad began (2:185), the revelation that brought and still brings God's serenity and security to so many Muslims. Muslims believe that they are especially receptive to God's boundless grace and forgiveness during this period. The experience of fasting, together with the many voluntary acts of worship they perform, helps them to better focus on their relationships with God. Of the five pillars of Islam, the fast of Ramadan is perhaps the most personal expression of self-surrender to God; we can observe a Muslim performing the other four pillars, but, in addition to himself, only God knows if he is staying with the fast. Due to this, the fast is not something a person can perform to be seen and respected by others. We can tell people that we are fasting, but they have no practical way of verifying it. The Prophet explained it best when he stated that God says, "The fast is for Me [alone]."[101]

---

[100] An-Nawawi's *Riyadh-Us-Saleheen*, trans. by S. M. N. Abbasi, 1:95-106.

[101] *Sahih al Bukhari*, trans. by Muhammad Muhsin Khan (Dar Al Arabia): Vol. 3, *The Book of Fasting*, p. 65.

Ramadan is also the month of sharing God's mercy with others, a time of community healing and renewal. Many broken friendships are restored and hatchets are buried during this month. One Muslim friend told me: "If hurt feelings between Muslims can not be mended during Ramadan, then there is no hope of them ever being mended."

The ritual fast especially should increase empathy among Muslims for the poor and deprived, because for an entire month the faithful must do without even some of the simplest daytime pleasures. Yet, even while fasting, it is sometimes all too easy to forget our responsibilities as God's vicegerents.

One Ramadan, I was so preoccupied with problems at work that I began to feel somewhat sorry for myself and irritated that I had to fast during such a trying episode in my life. On a particularly hard day, while I was just starting *iftar*, a news flash came on TV describing the mass starvation gripping Ethiopia and Somalia. I still remember the face of one starving Somali father as he helplessly watched his naked infant son, whose stomach was severely bloated, tossing in agony in the dirt. The father, who had already lost the rest of his family, sat on the ground by his child, waiting, patiently and pathetically, for the relief that death would soon bring his little boy, while I sat watching from my couch, eating a sumptuous meal. The child, who seemed not yet resigned to death, screamed furiously and defiantly, as if at the obvious injustice of it all, at the callous and cruel neglect of people like me who did not want to be disturbed but only entertained by the television.

I had known of this tragedy in Somalia and Ethiopia for months, but I had done nothing—not even allowed myself to care. The statement of Prophet Muhammad, that when you see an injustice, you should change it with your hands, and if you cannot do that, then you should change it with your tongue, and if you are still unable to do that, then at least you should change it in your heart, and this last alternative is the lowest level of faith,[102] tore into me while I stared, with a plate of food before me, at the television screen. I had fasted for almost an entire month and never once considered the much greater suffering that others were enduring right before my eyes. It was as if God had chosen that moment to put me in my place, to show me all the things I had, and how thankless I was being.

---

[102] From Sahih Muslim. See *An-Nawawi's Forty Hadith*, trans. by Ibrahim and Johnson-Davies, 110.

When Ramadan ends, Muslims hold a three day celebration, called *eid* in Arabic. It is a very joyful holiday, a festival of gift giving and family get-togethers. It compares to the Christmas celebration in the West. It is also a time when Muslims feel especially grateful to God, because the experience of fasting reminds them of the many gifts God has given them. Every Muslim has had the experience of getting ready to take a drink or a bite of food during the *eid* when they suddenly are seized by the alarming impulse to rid themselves of the snack they are about to enjoy. A fraction of a second later, they breath a sigh of relief as they realize that their minds momentarily had slipped back into the fasting mode it had gotten so used to and that it is now all right to indulge their thirst or hunger. It may seem strange, but Muslims will say how utterly wonderful these occurrences are, because, for a brief moment, that drink or morsel of food seems like one of life's great pleasures, as enjoyable as any luxury this Earth may offer. As they delight in that moment, they are filled with feelings of thanksgiving to God, for they know that His mercy and bounty are truly great.

Zakah and Spiritual Cleansing

> Every Muslim, male or female, who, at the end of the year, is in possession of approximately fifteen dollars or more, in cash or articles of trade, must give zakah at the minimum rate of two and one-half percent.[103]

The collection of this tax is administered by the state, and it is incumbent on all liquid, visible, movable, and immovable properties belonging to Muslims. Three principles govern its levying.

> First, no zakah is due on property intended for consumption, such as houses, gardens, clothing and furniture. Jewelry of gold, silver and precious gems is excepted because it may serve as a channel for hoarding wealth, which Islam condemns. Taxable property is that which is intended for production, whether industrial, agricultural, or commercial. Second, zakah is not an indiscriminate tax on all properties. Assessment of zakah must take into consideration the net income produced by the property in question. In a year of a losing operation, no zakah is levied on the property concerned. Third, a reasonable

---

[103] Hammudah Abdalati, *Islam in Focus* (Indianapolis: American Trust, 1975), 96.

amount necessary for the owner and his dependents' sub-
sistence must be deducted from the assessment.[104]

Islamic Law elaborates many more technicalities concerning the
payment of zakah, but already it can be seen that the classical description does not take into consideration the vast majority of today's
Muslims, who are citizens of secular states. While most believers living
under secular governments wish to observe this important pillar of
Islam, there are no generally agreed upon standards for determining precisely who must pay zakah, exactly how much should be paid, and to
whom it should be given. In the seventh century C.E., a person who
owned no property intended for production was probably not someone of
means; today many people own no such property and yet have substantial incomes. How much zakah should such individuals pay? Various
formulas for calculating one's zakatable wealth have been suggested
recently but I know of none that is widely applied. (I recall that The
Islamic Society of North America ISNA, published one in 1995 based on
one's federal income tax calculation.) Certain Islamic organizations in
the United States and Canada, like ISNA, the Islamic Circle of North
America (ICNA) and others, have recommended that zakah payments be
sent to them, but it seems that most Muslims living in the United States
simply pay what they think they should owe to their Islamic centers or
directly to the poor in their local communities.

When to pay zakah is another problem. Traditionally, payment is
made annually, usually at the end of Ramadan. Muslims who receive a
weekly or monthly salary often find it difficult to put aside and save what
they estimate they should contribute from their paychecks. Typically, they
find that the money they save to pay zakah eventually gets spent. I know
quite a few Muslim Americans who avoid this problem by contributing a
fixed amount, usually at least 2.5 percent, of each paycheck to a Muslim
charitable organization. In this way, they pay zakah in advance (weekly or
monthly), depending on when they receive their salaries.

Many non-Muslims view this ritual as mundane and prosaic, as the
least spiritual of the five pillars of Islam, for it appears to remove the charity involved in giving if it is compulsory and subject to many computational
technicalities. To many outside the faith, it seems to have about the same
spiritual content as preparing an income tax return.

---

[104] Isma'il R. Al Faruqi, *Islam*, (Beltsville, MD: amana publications, 1995), 24–27.

Even the most objective study of another culture can produce only limited understanding of its perceptions. Membership in a culture is often needed in order to appreciate many of its points of view. The next best source of understanding, which is a distant second, is the personal reports of its members. The Muslim experience of zakah is far-removed from the characterizations listed in the preceding paragraph. For them, the facts that the payment of zakah is obligatory and, under ideal circumstances, levied by the state does not detract from its spirituality or humaneness. A line between law and religion has never been drawn by Muslim religious scholars; classical and modern Shari'ah texts discuss not only civil law but also Islamic rituals, family relations, proper hygiene, and many other matters that western culture considers outside the purview of law. It should also be kept in mind that Muslims feel obligated, both religiously and legally, to perform all of the *five pillars* of Islam. From the Muslim viewpoint, laws must be in conformity with God's will. Hence, a perceived legal obligation becomes a duty owed to God and a moral obligation (and *vice versa*).

Muslims recognize that not everyone will benefit equally from observing the rituals, for there are always those who will lack sincerity while doing so. The benefit of any ritual, and for that matter of doing any good deed, corresponds to the intention with which it is done. If an act is done out of a sincere love of God and concern for others, then the highest spiritual reward may be gained; if it is done to gain the respect of others or to avoid condemnation, then that much (and little else) will probably be obtained by the doer. A statement of the Prophet summarizes this concept:

> "Your deeds will be judged according to your intentions, and unto every person is due what he intended. Therefore, whoever migrates (joins the Muslim community) for the sake of this world or to get married, his migration is [accounted] for that which he migrated.[105]

The five pillars represent the minimum ritual requirements that Islam imposes on its believers. Supererogatory worship, termed *nawaafil* (plural of *nafilah*) in Arabic, is, however, strongly encouraged. Many observant Muslims recite the *shahadah*, perform salah, fast, give in charity, and make pilgrimage to Makkah much more often than the five pillars require. Although by paying zakah a Muslim fulfills a ritual obligation, his or her

---

[105] *Sahih al Bukhari: The Early Years*, translated and explained by M. Asad, 3.

charitable obligations may be much greater. The Qur'an imposes a high moral standard in this regard on the believers:

> They ask you how much they should spend [in charity];
> Say: "Whatever is beyond your needs." Thus does God
> make clear to you His signs so that you may consider
> [their bearings] on this life and the hereafter. (2:219-20).

There are many sayings of the Prophet in the same vein. On one occasion, he is reported to have startled his Companions by telling them that believers were obliged to perform as many acts of charity each day as there were bones in their bodies. When the poorer ones mentioned that they did not have the financial means to meet this obligation, he insisted on it nonetheless and informed them that a smile, an act of kindness, and a helping hand are all acts of charity.[106] He is also said to have told his followers that no one can call himself a believer while he eats his fill and his neighbor goes hungry.[107]

That Islam includes the annual payment of zakah in its ritual pillars is a reflection of the duty it imposes on believers to act as God's emissaries (*khalifah*) on earth. The year-long effort to set aside a fixed portion of one's earnings to give to the poor should serve as a constant reminder to a Muslim of this office that he or she has accepted and of his or her greater charitable obligations.

The importance Islam assigns to zakah is also indicative of the emphasis it places on charity in our spiritual development. There are two qualities that hasten a person's spiritual growth more than any others and two that impede it more than any others: benevolence and humility, and arrogance and greed, respectively. Both humility and charity, as well as their above-mentioned opposites, correlate with our expectations of others. Humility relates to what we expect from others, and charity relates to what we believe others should expect from us. The Muslim ideal is to have low expectations with regard to the first and to accept the high expectations of others with regard to the second.

The effects of benevolence and acts of humility on a believer's spirituality are usually not immediately discernible. There is often a delayed reaction, like when a person takes an antibiotic for an infection.

---

[106] *An-Nawawi's Riyadh-Us-Saleheen*, trans. by S. M. N. Abbasi, Dar Al Arabia, Beirut, 1:85-95.

[107] Asad, *The Road to Mecca*, 297.

For example, he or she starts to notice that his or her prayers begin to increase in beauty and power and that the moments of divine intimacy both inside and outside the rituals seem stronger and more frequent. He or she comes to feel a type of freedom or lightness of spirit, as if his or her soul has been cleansed. A great sense of peace and security comes over such individuals, material possessions become less and less important, and their need to help and give to others grows. The Arabic word zakah is an apt description of this experience, for it is derived from the Arabic verb *zakaa*, the two primary meanings of which are "to purify" and "to grow."

Of course philanthropy can sometimes work against humility, as it is easy to slip into self-admiration and become self-congratulatory. This is why Islam discourages testimonials and making a show of one's charitable deeds. According to Islam, the best acts of charity are those done in secret. If that is not possible, at least one should refuse praise (Qur'an 2:261-74). When a Muslim gives something as charity, he or she should do so with the profound sense of obligation that the office of God's *khalifah* imposes. A story my wife told me typifies this attitude.

My wife's grandfather was one of those austere and fiercely independent self-made men that the Arabian Peninsula was once famous for, especially before it became a kingdom. He was known by everyone from the Najd to the Hijaz and was greatly feared and respected—not only because of his esteemed lineage or the wealth he had accumulated (both of which wield great influence in Arabia), but much more so because of his strong and unyielding character. Of course he had his faults, but there was one thing you could always count on when it came to Abdul Qadir: when he gave you his word he kept it, regardless of the consequences.

The day he died of a heart attack, the members of his large family felt as if the earth had given out beneath them. Although his three wives, many children, and grandchildren were well provided for materially, there was no replacing the feelings of security and protection that his mere presence provided them. Their mourning of his passing was long and hard.

Several weeks after his death, poor families began showing up at the door of his home. Widows, disabled men, and orphans, all told the same story: Abdul Qadir had been providing them with free housing and a regular allowance all these years. When he did not appear for his usual

*monthly visit, they became concerned for his and their welfare and so
came to his home.*

*Abdul Qadir was remembered by many as a hard but good man, but
almost no one knew that he took care of so many impoverished families. I
feel sure he would have preferred that it remain that way, and I hope someday he will forgive me for disclosing this. May Allah, the Kind and
Merciful, reward him and grant him peace.*

Pilgrimage

> "*Mon ami*, do you think the hadj begins in Makkah? No,
> no. It starts the moment you decide to go."[108]

In 1991, several months after the end of the Gulf War, I took a leave
of absence from the University of Kansas to teach at the University of
Petroleum and Minerals (UPM) in Dhahran, Saudi Arabia. As the Saudi
Airlines 747 that would carry us to Jeddah rose above the runway at
JFK, I felt like an emigrant on my way to a new homeland. I was tired
of life in America; tired of being a stranger (by choice, of course) in my
own land; and tired of living in a country where my religion was
despised, or at best, grudgingly tolerated, and where my wife was often
harassed and threatened because of her middle-eastern dress and looks.
I was also relieved for my three young daughters, who would have
faced many difficult choices between their religion and the surrounding
culture if we had remained in America. I thought of how it would have
been to their material and social disadvantage to practice Islam in my
country and how much easier it would be for them to grow up in a
Muslim land.

I also reflected on how I would finally complete my own *hijrah*—my
personal flight to religious freedom. It was an emigration that I had begun
emotionally and intellectually eight years earlier in a small mosque in San
Francisco. On that day when I said my first *shahadah*, I consciously for-
sook my culture and committed myself to an outlook that defied the American mainstream. I mentally alienated myself from people who I believed
could never comprehend the choice I had made and the life I now lived. As
we soared into the starlit sky, I was filled with feelings of hope, excitement,
defiance, and deliverance.

---

[108] A quotation from Michael Wolfe, *The Hadj: A Pilgrimage to Mecca* (Seeker and
Warburg, 1994).

At last! I told myself. At last! To the land of the Prophet!

As optimistic as I was, I did not expect to find Utopia there. Eight years in the Muslim community of America showed me that although there were many differences between Americans and Muslims from the Middle East, neither had a clear advantage in virtue. Each community has its vices and its virtues, and I could not see how one was definitely superior to the other in conduct or morals. Unlike many American converts, I was not drawn to Islam by the example set by Muslim friends. My only Muslim contacts for many years were drug users, adulterers, and gamblers. I am not judging them, for we were birds of a feather and they played an indirect but important role in my coming to Islam. However, I certainly did not see them as particularly high-minded persons. I had also spent the eight years since my conversion observing how petty, jealous, slanderous, and unjust so-called religious Muslims could be toward one another and how they could prostitute their religion for worldly gain. I may have been happy to be leaving the United States behind, but I entertained no romantic visions of emigrating to a nobler Middle Eastern society.

My quest was not for the perfect society, but rather for peace and for a place where my religion and practice of it were respected. I wanted to live among fellow Muslims and to observe with my friends, neighbors, and co-workers the Friday prayer, the fast of Ramadan, and the Islamic holidays. I wanted to know in my everyday life the comfort and security I had found in our tiny Islamic center in Lawrence, Kansas—although we are as human as anyone else, we Muslims are committed to the same goal and source of guidance, and when we relate sincerely to each other on the level of faith, a wonderful communion occurs. This fellowship of purpose is impossible for us to experience outside our community, and this realization weighed heavily in my decision to make my *hijrah* to Saudi Arabia.

Nevertheless, a year later, I was on another Saudi Airlines plane on my way back to the United States. Exhausted and burdened with a terrible sense of failure, I returned to my position at the University of Kansas. My dreams of finding a religious refuge for my family and making a contribution to Muslim society by teaching Saudi students died and shriveled in Dhahran. Since my wife was very happy in her homeland and my young children were slowly adjusting to the new environment, I have only myself to blame; I was the sole member of my family who could not adapt. In spite of my strong sentiments about having made a personal *hijrah*—of having forsaken western culture to become a Muslim—I returned to the

United States having learned that for me, at least, there was no escape from being an American.

It is true that I was involved in some unfortunate incidents during my brief tenure at UPM, but I prefer not to defend myself by lambasting Saudi society. The culture to which I could not adapt is not mine and not for me, as a foreigner, to change. I will offer only one excuse, because I believe it was my primary motivation for returning to the United States: for reasons I do not fully comprehend, I felt I was spiritually suffocating in Saudi Arabia. In the land that saw the birth of the mission of Prophet Muhammad, that contains the two holiest cities of Islam and the Ka'bah toward which I pray, a land dominated by Muslims and home to a culture imbued with religion, I felt hopelessly spiritually stagnated. In Saudi Arabia, Islam ceased to be a force for personal change, and my faith was soon drained of its vitality. Not that the country was deficient in good and religious people—on the contrary, I met many sincere and devout Muslims there—but to me the religious movements in the kingdom were directed toward an idealized past that I could never be a part of and were based on an interpretation of Islam in which I was quickly losing confidence.

This is what I mean when I say that there was no escape from being an American. My whole approach to religion—my way of investigating and studying it and the kinds of religious issues and questions that are important to me—is influenced strongly by my cultural background and very often is discomforting to Muslims from traditional cultures. I never realized it before I went to the kingdom, but my conversion to Islam and my living as a Muslim in the United States are in some ways very American. What brought me to Islam, the kind of search I conducted and the struggles I fought within myself and against my upbringing, are not unusual in America.

Many Americans have changed religions or broken away from family traditions, for the country itself was built upon uprooted lives that had to adapt quickly to radical change. Americans have a certain admiration for the individualist, the underdog, and the maverick who defies convention and blazes his or her own trail. But I believe it would be almost impossible for a young Saudi Arabian to confront his or her society's values and traditions as directly as I did. Indeed, the message I frequently received from my Saudi friends was that the critical approach I once took toward religion was fine—as long as it led me to Islam. Now that I was a Muslim, however, I should learn to accept things as they are and to rely on the knowledge and sound judgment of Muslim religious scholars. A few times I was told that the questions I ask and methods of investigation I employ are dangerous, for they could lead to innovation and heresy. I have also heard this from Muslims in America, but I believe that the American Muslim community allows much greater intellectual freedom and diversity than the one I found in Saudi Arabia. I am not insisting that these traits make the American Islamic community a better living environment, but I know that I desperately missed that freedom during my stay in Dhahran.

My year in Saudi Arabia became more and more of a spiritual prison sentence. As the second semester began, I was counting how many days were left until my departure. Yet as unhappy as I was, I always consoled myself that my journey to the Arabian peninsula could never be a total failure. After all, it provided me with a chance of a lifetime: a chance to make the *hajj* and to accomplish the fifth pillar of Islam. However, as the year progressed, I became so worn out and eager to return to the United States, that even this opportunity's consolatory effect began to diminish. When I first came to Saudi Arabia, I could think of almost nothing but the pilgrimage; by the time the month of *hajj* arrived, my initial ebullience had deflated to a very sober, dutiful attitude toward performing this ritual.

I performed the pilgrimage with a faculty group from UPM. It was the year after the Gulf War, and the number of pilgrims was extremely large— over two million—so large that thousands were refused admittance (due to overcrowding) at Mount Arafat on the Day of Standing and so unable to complete one of the essential rites. Modern transportation and technology have helped to make the journey less arduous and less physically hazardous then it once was, but it has also contributed to a dramatic increase in the number of pilgrims each year. With so many people packed into so tiny an area, the pilgrimage still presents a significant health risk and physical discomfort.

I came down with a bad case of influenza a few days before we left for Makkah *al Mukarramah* (Makkah the Blessed). Unfortunately, it grew worse during the *hajj*. It was July, a time when the peninsula is normally very hot. To make conditions a little worse, the Hijaz was in the grip of a severe heat wave. Veteran pilgrims in our group kept informing us that this was the most difficult *hajj* they had ever experienced, the crowds were usually not so large, the delays in getting from one place to another never so long (it would take us many hours just to travel several miles by bus), and the heat was normally not so intense. One traveler told me that the hardness of the conditions was a sign of God's mercy: He was granting Muslims an opportunity to shed the many sins accumulated during the Gulf War.

Before entering Makkah, pilgrims must remove their normal clothes and ornaments, perform a purifying ablution, and declare to God their intention to perform the pilgrimage. Each pilgrim puts on two pieces of unsewn white linen or cotton: one piece covers the body from the waist down, and the other from the waste up (the head is left bare). For the next few days, until the Day of Sacrifice, pilgrims must not shave, cut their hair, clip their fingernails, or wear anything that might differentiate them from other pilgrims. In this way, all pilgrims are equal in appearance, which is symbolic of the fact that all individuals are equal before God.

When we arrived in Makkah, we went immediately to the Holy Mosque, which is located in the heart of the city. It was evening, and the the mosque's lavish lighting made it glow like a gigantic lamp illuminating the city. Its courtyard is uncovered, and the sky above it this night made a beautiful star-studded canopy. I was hoping to get close to the Ka'bah, which is located in the center of the courtyard, but crowd of tens of thousands of pilgrims made it impossible for me to do so. I went over to one of the two recently constructed tiers that contain walkways situated above the courtyard's outer rim and designed to accommodate overflow crowds wishing to circumambulate the Ka'bah. There was no room on the second tier, and barely any on the third.

I thought that from the third tier I should be able to get a great view of the Ka'bah. However, I did not want to fight my way through the dense crowd to get to the inner wall of the walkway. I then discovered a small ledge from which I could get an excellent view. I gazed wonderstruck at the scene below—a huge vortex drawing humanity in to the Ka'bah, a massive whirlpool of people from every corner of the earth, above which rose a steady drone of supplications in a multitude of languages. There were thousands and thousands of white-clad pilgrims circumambulating the Ka'bah and petitioning and glorifying God. It reminded me of the descriptions in the Qur'an and the prophetic traditions of the angels going around God's throne on the Day of Judgment. I felt an overwhelming need to go back to the main floor so that I could enter that current of humanity and experience firsthand its power and pull. I made my way down one of the staircases to ground level and squeezed through the crowd until I reached the courtyard's outer rim.

I quickly slipped into a tiny space that momentarily opened in the outer edge of the mass of pilgrims. Squeezed from all sides, I stood as straight I could, trying to make myself as narrow as possible. A strong push from behind sent me surging forward with the crowd. Then the throng shifted to the left, and I was propelled along with it. The more I tried to secure my footing, the more I was pushed and turned about. I quickly realized that the best thing to do was to relax and let the motion of the multitude carry me.

All pilgrims hope to touch the Black Stone, which is lodged in one of the walls of the Ka'bah. There are many stories and traditions associated with it. For example, it is reported that the Prophet would kiss it upon finishing *tawaf* (walking around the Ka'bah seven times). As I circled the Ka'bah, I found that I, like everyone else, was moving ever-closer to it along a decreasing spiral. I was being pulled nearer and nearer to an irresistible singularity. I was only one tiny molecule in an ocean of humanity and, although we were traveling different paths, we were all drawn to the same great power. On the seventh circuit, I had come within only a few feet of the Ka'bah. As I approached the Black Stone, I slipped forward and was able to touch it with my left hand. As I bent to kiss it, I was bumped hard in my head by someone to my left and knocked away.

"Let him!" someone shouted in Arabic, "Let him!"

A handful of pilgrims held back the crowd for a second. I quickly touched my lips to the Black Stone and was then pushed away.

I prayed two *rak'ahs* (cycles) of prayer far behind the station of Abraham and then picked my way through the throng until I reached Safa and Marwah, two hillocks about a mile apart and within the mosque. Pilgrims are supposed to cover the distance between the hills seven times at a trotting pace, but that was impossible on this night, since the conditions were more crammed here than in the courtyard. Many times the multitude surrounding me came to a dead stop, unable to advance, and a few times we were forced backward. At one point, I dropped my prayer booklet and, as a reflex, bent down to retrieve it. I felt a great push from the crowd, and a man standing next to me grabbed me by the arm just as I started to lose my balance. He forced me back up.

In English he said: "Forget it. You could easily end up trampled to death."

He was right of course, and I thanked him.

It was extremely hot and damp in that mass of human beings. People were sweating profusely, and the smell of body odor hung in the air. I saw a few people panicking and crying, but most were very sedate. Holding yourself up against the constant press of the crowd could be quite fatiguing, but I personally found the tightness of our conditions the most trying part of the pilgrimage rites. I am somewhat claustrophobic and a few times became anxious and faint, but I held on and was all right.

I saw many tender scenes as I inched my way through the seven circuits between the two hills: children carried on their father's shoulders, parents and grandparents supported by their children, spouses locked arm in arm, all fulfilling the same dream. There were a few frustrated and angry faces in the crowd, but most of the expressions around me were peaceful and happy. I reflected on how if this were any other place on earth in which such a large mass of people were this tightly packed, there would certainly be many violent outbreaks. Yet during the eight days I spent in the *haram* (the area encompassing Makkah, the plain of Arafat, and other pilgrimage sites), I did not see a single physical altercation.

I had made 'umrah (the minor pilgrimage, which consists of walking around the Ka'bah seven times and trotting between Safa and Marwah seven times) many times before, and the longest it took me to finish was forty-five minutes. On this night, it took me over two hours to complete the rites. When I got back to our bus, I had to wait a little over an hour for the rest of our group to finish. Then we discovered that one of the older ladies in our group was missing; it took us another hour to find her. By the time we reached our campsite in Mina, it was almost 3:00 A.M.

We used the next day to rest, since the pilgrimage proper would not begin until the following day.[109] After breakfast, I decided to go for a walk and look around.

Our campsite was located several hundred yards from the three pillars of stone that symbolize Satan and at which pilgrims throw pebbles on the Day of Sacrifice. Nearly the entire tiny valley of Mina, which is surrounded by steep, rocky cliffs, is paved with asphalt. Above the three pillars is a wide, concrete bridge about a half-mile long. The bridge has three holes in it, approximately ten feet in radius, through which the pillars rise. This gives pilgrims the option to stone the pillars from either ground level or from on top of the bridge, which reduces congestion on the Day of Sacrifice.

The first thing that struck me as I stepped into the main thoroughfare was the thousands of pilgrims camped underneath the bridge. These were clearly the poorest group of pilgrims, those who came with little more than a change of clothes. They had no tents, no running water, no refrigeration

---

[109] Our group performed what is known as *hajj al tammatu*, which consists of performing *'umrah* (the lesser pilgrimage) and then *hajj* (the major pilgrimage).

for the food they carried, no air-conditioning, and access to only a few public toilets with very long lines of users. Some had blankets or sleeping bags, but many slept on cardboard or on the bare asphalt. At least they had plenty of shade from the searing rays of the sun.

The next class of pilgrims were those camped in tents. Their conditions varied, but most seemed to have it only slightly better than those who settled under the bridge. Their tents were everywhere, taking up every inch of available ground. They covered the roadside, the cliff tops, and even the small ledges jutting out from the cliffs. I thought it would probably be cooler under the bridge, but of course tents afford more privacy.

Some groups of pilgrims are fortunate enough to stay in hangers constructed specifically for the pilgrimage and used only at that time. The word is that UPM always rents one of the best. This was easy to believe, for our hanger had wall-to-wall carpeting, toilets, sinks with mirrors, showers, ceiling fans, air conditioning and a large kitchen containing several ovens and a big barbecue. I heard that the rent for the hanger—it accommodated approximately one hundred of us—was more than one hundred thousand dollars for the eight days we stayed in Mina.

A few pilgrims stay in hotels. I only noticed two rather small ones in Mina and a number of very luxurious hotels in Makkah. Certainly this would be the most comfortable way to spend the pilgrimage, but only a relative handful of pilgrims can afford it.

When I returned from my stroll, I looked around for a pay-phone to call my family, who were staying with relatives in Jeddah. While I was waiting in line, I overheard some young men speaking about me in Arabic.

"Maybe he's German," one of them said.

"No," said another, "he's definitely American."

"Ask him," said a third.

"I'm American," I responded in English, and they all smiled.

It turns out that one of them, who was from Dubai, spoke English. "Can I ask you something?" He said politely.

"Go ahead," I told him, although I knew what it would be.

With a big and excited grin he asked: "How did you become a Muslim?"

I began to tell him my story and he acted as translator for my steadily growing audience. They were laughing and sighing and nodding their approval. Some of the eyes that were fixed on me were swimming in tears. It took me about twenty minutes to finish, and then I fielded questions through my translator for another half hour. I finally reached the front of the phone queue and dialed my wife. When I finished the phone call, I turned to the assembly and waved good-bye.

"*As-salaamu-alaikum!*" I called out to them, feeling like a dignitary. "*Wa alaikum salaam!*" they shouted back.

I then hurried off to my campsite with a few of my listeners running to catch up with me to get my address and phone number.

The same scene occurred repeatedly during the next several days. It seemed that no matter where I was or what I was doing, a group of curious pilgrims would approach me with the same two questions: "Are you American?" and "How did you become Muslim?"

I do not know what made them assume that I must be American rather than European, but something about my manner or appearance clued them in.

At first, I rather enjoyed the instant celebrity. I would crack little jokes and be quite animated as I told the story of my conversion to Islam. I seldom had so responsive an audience. But in no time at all I began to feel like an exhibit in a museum and got tired of repeating the same stale tale over and over again. There was nothing special or heroic about my becoming a Muslim. I began to wonder if it was not my white Anglo-Saxon American-ness that made my story so inspirational to my listeners. I started to long for anonymity and privacy. Of course, in so crowded a place the latter is probably too much to hope for, but it felt like I was under constant examination. It was not long before I only wanted to sit quietly somewhere without having to pretend to be asleep so that others would leave me alone.

I think if I had not become so ill so quickly, I would have enjoyed my prominence a little longer. However, by dinner time that night I was very sick with a high fever and pounding headache that stayed with me and grew progressively worse almost for the entire *hajj*. I was burning up one moment and shaking from chills the next. Each morning I awoke in a pool of sweat, despite the fact that the air conditioning kept our hanger very cool. I was so nauseous that I ate hardly any of the appetizing and plenti-ful food that we were so often served. Nevertheless, I never entertained the thought of quitting the pilgrimage. As far as I knew, this might be my only chance; I was determined to complete it no matter what.

Early the next day, we set out by bus for Makkah in order to begin the formal rites of *hajj*. We reached the holy mosque that afternoon and again performed *tawaf* (circumambulating the Ka'bah seven times) and *sa'y* (has-tening between the hills of Safa and Marwah seven times). Not only was the masjid even more crowded than it had been two nights before, but it was much hotter outside. The wail of ambulances running back and forth with the heat-exhausted to one of the local hospitals was nearly constant. The sun's rays baked the marble flooring of the Holy Mosque's courtyard to such a high temperature that the bottom of my feet became badly blistered. Apparently, most pilgrims had much tougher soles than I, for their feet did not appear to bother them. Perhaps this was because they were more accustomed to going barefoot than I was.

After a light snack, we were off to Arafat. We pulled into traffic and moved along slowly but steadily for about a mile. Then we came to a full stop, and our bus remained where it was for a couple of hours. Many in our entourage started getting nervous, for we had to make Arafat before sunset or our pilgrimage would not be valid.

If we had stayed in line, we probably would never have gotten to Arafat on time, but our driver was very experienced and knew the back roads of the *haram* well. After turning the bus around, he drove against the flow of traffic a short distance on the shoulder of the highway and then turned on to an empty two-lane service road. For the next hour or so, he drove us through a maze of vacant dessert roads. Amazingly, he got us to Arafat shortly after noon.

This day, the heat wave we had been under reached its peak. There was no air conditioning at Arafat, and my fever was still on the rise. I had never felt so hot at any other time in my life. Too weak and nauseous to sit or stand, I spent most of the time before *'asr* lying on my back on my sleeping bag.

I awoke around three in the afternoon. Kneeling, I lifted my sleeping bag so that the large puddle of water that had accumulated on it could run off. Glancing around, I noticed that everyone around me was now either sitting or standing, facing the Ka'bah with their hands raised and making quiet and earnest supplications. A Bangladeshi janitor from UPM, who understood neither English nor Arabic and who had hardly uttered a sound the entire trip, was sobbing mournfully behind me. It was an eerie scene; I felt as if I had suddenly awakened into a great and terrible human crisis.

The Day of Arafat is also called the Day of Standing; because from the noon to the sunset salah, pilgrims will stand for long periods and make private prayers to their Lord. From about three o'clock until just before sunset, I stood with around two million Muslims on that scorched and dusty plain, petitioning and thanking God. During this time, I completely forgot the terrible heat, my illness, and the difficult year I had been through; I could only think of the Day of Judgment, which this phase of the pilgrimage ritual made seem quite near.

Just after the sunset prayer, we boarded the buses to go to Muzdalifah, a small gravel-covered plane on which we would spend the night during our return trip to Mina. A fire that had broken out in a large, densely packed campground along the road to Muzdalifah stalled traffic for several hours, so that we did not get there until two in the morning.

We had to be careful not to step on anyone as we walked about Muzdalifah's stony surface in search of a place where we could sleep. As far as the eye could see, the ground was blanketed by sleeping pilgrims; I was reminded of pictures I had seen of the 1972 Woodstock festival at night. It was obvious that we would not find a space large enough to accommodate more than a few of our group at a time. I finally saw a small space of bare ground where one of my traveling companions and I could fit our sleeping bags.

The pebbles beneath my bag pinched my back as I lay staring at the stars. I thought about how I never took to camping while growing up in the city and that I could never fall asleep in such a place with no tent to cover me and with people snoring loudly all around me. That was the last thought I had that night. The next thing I knew, someone's hand was on my shoulder, shaking me. I had slept so deeply I had forgotten where I was. For a few seconds, I thought I was at my mom's house in Connecticut and that I had to get up for school.

"Brother, wake up, it's *fajr*," a young man from our group told me.

I was still groggy while standing for the morning prayer. I felt as if I had slept for days.

To our surprise, it did not take us too long to reach Mina. After dropping off my sleeping bag at our campsite, I immediately went to throw at the three pillars the pebbles I had collected at Muzdalifah. The air in Mina was gay with celebration. A myriad of bright bold colors filled the streets. For the last few days everyone had been in pilgrim clothes, but now Mina looked like a huge international fair with pilgrims proudly arrayed in their native clothing. People were beaming big, happy smiles, children were playing and darting about, and crowds were gathered around the many street vendors selling cheaply priced religious momentos of the pilgrimage. Others flocked to the many government trucks where free water, ice, milk, and food were being distributed as gifts to pilgrims by the Custodian of the Two Holy Mosques.[110] Others gaped at

---

[110] A title used by the King of Saudi Arabia.

the crippled beggars scattered all over the streets and pleading for charity while presenting their deformities as grotesque exhibits.

In all the commotion, I could not make out the pillars, so I simply headed for the largest mob of people underneath the bridge. The first pillar was surrounded by a large swarm of pilgrims that began about twenty-five feet from the pillar.

"Allahu Akbar!" They shouted as they fired pebbles at their target.

I wanted to get closer to the pillar to have a better shot at it, for my eyesight is not that good and I was afraid I might hit someone inadvertently. I made my way through the crowd until I reached the circular wall surrounding the pillar. A deluge of pebbles, tossed by pilgrims who chose to perform the stoning while standing on the bridge, rained down from above like sand in an hour glass and formed a large, growing conical pile of stones at the base of the pillar. At the same time, hundreds of pebbles thrown by pilgrims at ground level were whizzing by my head. I felt a few mild stings in my back where I was hit by pebbles, so I ducked down a little when I tossed mine.

Most of the pilgrims around me were calmly performing this rite, but a few were extremely agitated. Even though the pillars only represent Satan and throwing stones at them symbolizes the pilgrims' resolution to resist temptation, some pilgrims behaved as if the pillars were the Devil himself. They furiously fired their pebbles as they angrily cursed the columns of stone. Some of them threw shoes, sticks, and other objects at these targets of their revenge.

"Curse you! You made me lose my wife!" One enraged man screamed in Arabic.

When I finished the stoning, I had only one major rite left to perform: the sacrifice of a sheep or goat. In times past, pilgrims used to either bring their sacrifices with them or buy them in Mina, where they would slaughter them themselves, keep a little of the meat for their own consumption, and give the rest to the poor. As the number of pilgrims grew, the traditional way of sacrifice became less and less practical and sanitary. Hundreds of tons of meat rotted in the sun until it could be plowed underground, as there were many more sacrifices being performed than there were poor people in the *haram* to feed.

Today, a few pilgrims still make the sacrifice in Mina in the traditional way, but most simply pay to have a sacrifice performed on their behalf in a nearby slaughtering facility. The meat is then frozen and shipped to various Muslim charities throughout the world. I stepped up to the window of a booth where such payments are made, and the clerk asked what type of animal I wanted to sacrifice and to what Muslim country I wanted it sent. I answered him, he quoted a price, I paid him the amount, he handed me a voucher on which was written the information I had given him, and with that I was done with the essential parts of the pilgrimage.

When I returned to camp, I trimmed my hair, shaved, took a hot shower, and then put on a pair of pants, a T-shirt, and a pair of sneakers. What a luxury it was to be wearing my usual clothes again!

We spent the next few days in Mina, celebrating *Eid al Adha* (the feast of sacrifice), mainly resting, relaxing, and listening to talks by Muslim scholars that were arranged by the leaders of our group. A frequent topic of discussion in the question-and-answer periods after the lectures was the roles of men and women in Islam. I found the Saudi Arabian perspective on this issue fascinating and extremely conservative.

When I got tired of staying in the camp, I would step outside to stretch my legs. I noticed that as time progressed, Mina became increasingly filthy. The Saudi government hires extra janitorial crews to keep the *haram* clean during the pilgrimage. Those assigned to the Holy Mosque did a superb job—each time we visited the Ka'bah the Masjid al Haram was immaculate—but those assigned to Mina were clearly undermanned. Hour by hour the garbage continued to pile up in the streets. If the refuse had consisted only of paper products, bottles, and cans, it would not have been so bad, but food, raw meat, and human waste were among the things dumped in the road. In the evening, Mina was so jammed with pilgrims that they could not always see or chose where they walked, which meant that the waste matter would get trampled, pressed, and kneaded together throughout the night. The next day, the sun would cook the feculent mixture, producing a terrible stench that hung over the valley. One member of our group quipped that the government should hire the people who run Disney World to organize the pilgrimage, since they handle as many as two million visitors a day and still keep the park clean and orderly. Another member retorted that the pilgrimage is not supposed to be a picnic, which led a third to reply that that does not mean it should be so unclean either, especially since Islam puts so much emphasis on hygiene and cleanliness.

All told, we spent eight days in the *haram* during the pilgrimage, including the day we arrived in and the day we departed from Mina. Most of us decided to make the traditional farewell visit to the Ka'bah the day before departure, since we were intending to leave for Jeddah early next morning.

About mid-morning, I, together with three more members of our group, left for Makkah. I got separated from the others in the commotion at the bus stop, so I ended up going alone.

I was feeling slightly better this morning, although I was physically exhausted from a week of battling the worst attack of flu I had ever had. I made the seven rounds around the Ka'bah and performed the rite of *sa'y* at a very slow pace. A few minutes after I finished, the call to prayer was announced. Right after the prayer, an announcement rang over the loud-speaker asking those present to stand for salah *al janazah*, the funeral prayer; most probably a pilgrim had died in the last twenty-four hours. With the completion of that funeral prayer, another announcement asked the worshippers to stand for yet another funeral prayer. This continued until we had prayed a total of four consecutive funeral prayers.

The funeral prayer is different from the daily salah, for there is no bowing or prostration. The congregation remains quietly standing throughout, like soldiers bidding farewell to a fallen comrade. There is also no *adhan* to announce the funeral prayer. Some Muslim scholars say that the first *adhan* whispered in a Muslim child's ear at birth is an announcement of his or her funeral prayer, since death must be expected at any time from the moment of birth and often comes suddenly and unexpectedly. Of course, this interpretation does not account for the case of a convert to Islam, but I have heard it said that when a nonbeliever converts to Islam, angels announce the *adhan* for him or her in heaven. When the fourth funeral prayer ended, I slowly made my way through the crowded mosque to King Abd al Aziz gate. I walked over to the street corner where the busses to Mina stopped and sat down by the curb.

Although I was now technically done with the pilgrimage, I had an uneasy feeling that I had left something undone or that something was missing. I knew I had performed each rite meticulously and with due solemnity, but I still felt somehow frustrated and unfulfilled.

My thoughts then shifted to the idea of returning to America. I thought of how I could not wait to be on board the plane that would bring me home again. I joked to myself that I would get out and kiss the runway when we landed in JFK. I recalled what a terrible year it had been and how it would all be over in just a few weeks. I imagined how great it would be to be around my fellow Americans again, to be among people whom I understood and who understood me, to watch American TV, to go to American restaurants, to have a picnic in an American park, to go to an American library or bookstore, to see my parents and brothers and their families again!

A bus pulled up to the curb.

"To Mina?" I asked the driver.

He nodded his head.

I paid the driver ten riyals and then scanned the bus for a place where I could sit by myself undisturbed. It seemed like I had been asked about my citizenship and conversion to Islam a couple of hundred times in the last week, and I was ready to punch out the next inquirer. To my relief, the last three rows of seats were completely empty. I avoided making eye contact with anyone as I walked down the aisle. Choosing the middle seat in the last row, I sat down, stretched out my body, crossed my legs with one ankle over the other, folded my arms, leaned my head back, shut my eyes, and hoped that no one would bother me.

As the bus pulled away from the curb, I opened my eyes slightly to make sure that I had excited no one's curiosity. Sure enough, a man in the second row on the left in the aisle seat was staring and smiling right at me. Please stay where you are! I thought to myself. Then I closed my eyes completely and turned my head to the right.

A few seconds later, I felt someone take the seat to my left.

"Excuse me, but could I ask you something?" He said in a very polite and apologetic tone.

I slowly turned my head straight while keeping my eyes shut.

"Go ahead," I said with a deep sigh.

"Are you American?" he asked, sounding astonished.

"Yes." I sighed wearily, knowing what to expect next.

He then leaned a little closer to me and asked, almost in a whisper, "Can you tell me how you became a Muslim?"

During the last seven days, my answer to that question became progressively shorter each time it was put to me. The first time, it took me about a half hour to tell my story but by now I had reduced it to a half-minute blurb. Without altering my posture nor opening my eyes, I gave him the following dry summary: I was born a Christian. I became an atheist at eighteen because of certain rational objections I had to the idea of God. I remained an atheist for the next ten years. I read an interpretation of the Qur'an when I was twenty eight. Not only did I find in the Qur'an coherent replies to my objections but I came to believe in God again through reading it. And so, I became a Muslim.

When I finished my synopsis, I peeked to my left to see if he was put off by my curt reply to his question. To my surprise, I saw tears running down the man's cheeks. And was I ever embarrassed!

At that moment, I asked God to forgive me for being so insensitive and arrogant and begged Him to help me to become more like this humble brother of mine, whose strong love of faith could move him to tears so easily and who could still perceive the mercy and greatness of God in such an uninspired story. I sat up straight and turned towards him.

"What's your name and where are you from?" I asked.

"My name is Ahmed and I'm from Bangladesh," he answered with a smile, as he wiped away his tears.

"It is a pleasure to meet you, Ahmed. My name is Jeffrey. I'm from the state of Kansas in the U.S."

After we exchanged a little more information about ourselves, Ahmed suddenly asked joyously, "Wasn't this a wonderful *hajj*, brother Jeffrey?"

I offered no response.

"Remember on the day we arrived," he continued, "how all around you could hear the pilgrims calling, '*Labbayka Allahumma Labbayk! Labbayka Allahumma Labbayk!*'[111] Do you know what "*labbayk*" means in my country?" he asked.

"I'm sorry to say that I know almost nothing about Bangladesh," I replied.

He looked at me very intensely and said: "In my country, when a teacher calls on a student in class, the student will at once stand at attention and call out '*Labbayk, teacher, Labbayk!*' as if to say: 'I am ready, teacher—I am at your service!' This is the way we Muslims are supposed to be towards Allah—this is the way the prophets were. Like when Allah ordered Prophet Ibrahim, *alayhi salaam*, to call for the *hajj*, there was almost no one else in Makkah with him at that time—at most his family and a few shepherds may have been in the area. If that were you or me, we almost certainly would have hesitated and said, 'Why make a call to the *hajj* when there is no one around to hear it?' But Prophet Ibrahim's faith and trust in Allah were so great that he did not wait for a single moment. Instead, he stood up in that empty place and immediately called the *adhan*! O, brother Jeffrey, if only Prophet Ibrahim, *alayhi salaam*, could see the millions of worshippers here today responding to that call, if

---

[111] In English, this roughly translates as, "I am at your service, Oh God! Oh God, I am at your service!"

only he could see the two of us—you from America and me from Bangladesh—sitting here together—as brothers—on a bus back to Mina!"

It was now my turn to feel a rush of emotion. I felt so ashamed of myself. I felt like crying—and I almost did—but I successfully fought the impulse.

I knew now what my pilgrimage lacked: it was deficient of any feelings of unity, brotherhood, and love that Islam enjoins upon its followers.

As a result of a few unfortunate incidents in which I was involved during the past year and a little bit of culture shock, I had allowed myself to slip into cultural chauvinism and racism. I let myself feel superior to and distant from the Muslims all around me, so that in the end, even my pilgrimage became a private ritual (it is supposed to be just the opposite). It was Ahmed's words of inspiration that showed me the error of my ways. I now knew that I could have gained so much from this year in the Middle East and so much from this pilgrimage, but once again I had let pride get in the way. I felt as if I needed to make the *hajj* all over again, for one of its most essential ingredients—love for my fellow Muslims— had been absent from my performance.

A few minutes later, our bus stopped where I had to get off.

"I'm lucky to have met you, Ahmed," I told him while shaking his hand, "and may Allah bless you! *Assalamu alaykum*, brother Ahmed!"

"*Wa alaykum salaam*, brother Jeffrey!" he said with a big smile.

CHAPTER 5

THE BEST OF COMMUNITIES

There is no monasticism in Islam. A Muslim's submission to God carries with it obligations towards humanity. The office of God's *khalifah* (vicegerent) on Earth, which Islam assigns the believer, requires community involvement. "You are the best of peoples evolved for mankind, for you enjoin what is right and oppose what is wrong" Qur'an 3:10 informs Muslims. From the standpoint of Islam, faith is never solely a personal and spiritual matter; it must be applied and tested in society. The Qur'an and the Prophet's teachings supply Muslims with guidance, the five pillars provide spiritual support, and society furnishes testing, learning, and growing environments.

Obviously, the society in which we live strongly influences our religious development. Most of us acquire our outlook on religion in the following natural order, corresponding to our discovery of society: we inherit our parents religious beliefs, modify and develop them further through contact with the faith community into which we were born, and then challenge and test them as we meet those who follow a different religion (or denomination). Religious conversion to some extent involves reversing this normal sequence: through encounters with people of other faiths, a person comes to believe in a religion different from the one in which he or she was born into and brought up in, enters a new faith community, and very often later marries and raises children within it.

This reverse path could be much more difficult than the common one, for it is somewhat like swimming upstream. In *Struggling to Surrender*[112] and in chapter three of this book, I discussed problems that many western converts have with regard to some of the behavior and traditions of the *ummah* (Muslim community) and the difficulties they often have in trying to identify those Muslim beliefs and practices that are essential to Islam. In

---

[112] Lang, *Struggling to Surrender*, chapters 3-5.

this chapter, I will discuss some spiritual and emotional challenges that may face a new Muslim who is seeking to join the Muslim community. In the next chapter, I briefly look at the future of Muslims in America.

A Wild Bunch

"What is it with American converts to Islam?" a Muslim immigrant to America asked me. "They are too extreme! They are either the staunchest and loudest conservatives in the community or else they have nothing to do with the community at all! And frequently they bounce back and forth between the two! Can't we attract any normal, moderate Americans to Islam?"

His question hurt me deeply for several reasons. First, he did not exclude me from his criticism, and so I assumed he felt the same way about me. Second, so many close friends of mine seemed to fit his observation. Third, I must confess that what he said did in reality apply to me—at times I was one of the most radically conservative members of the mosque I attended, and other times I isolated myself from the community for months. His statement awoke many painful memories, so many and so hurtful that I could not handle his question right then. I shook my head and told him I was not sure why American Muslims might seem that way to him.

I had a hard time deciding how best to write about the emotional, psychological, and spiritual turmoil that some converts to Islam go through as they try to adapt to their new community. I first considered writing as an objective observer, but how can one evaluate or describe another person's psychology and spirituality with any accuracy? Two persons may outwardly act the same but be motivated and affected inwardly in very different ways. Also, it would be nearly impossible for me to detach myself from something that I had experienced so profoundly. I thought about attempting an abstract, analytical approach, but faith experiences are too personal for that. Such an attempt reminds me of classical Muslim philosophers who tried to reduce faith in God to a series of syllogisms.

I finally decided to simply recall as best I could my own early involvement in the American Muslim community. After my first book appeared, many American converts informed me that their paths to the faith bore many similarities to mine and that it helped them to know that others went through some of the same difficulties. I hope that this chapter will perform a similar service to converts. I also hope that it will be useful to the many Muslims who were born into their religion and who are trying hard to assist and understand their new brothers and sisters in faith from America. I must caution the reader, however, not to assume that just because an American convert appears to be extremely zealous or conservative that he or she must be on the verge of a crisis of faith, for there are many persons who are passionately conservative by nature.

The Greater *Jihad*

After leading his troops back from a battle in which there were heavy casualties on both sides, a Muslim military commander turned toward his men and called out, "We go now from the lesser *jihad* to the greater *jihad*." When they asked if a more difficult military assignment were intended, he explained that by the greater *jihad* he had meant the *"jihad an nafs"* (the struggle within oneself).[113]

For a long time after my conversion to Islam, I considered my greatest and most difficult *jihad* to be the struggle I fought within myself on the day I became a Muslim. On that day, I had to confront, combat, and overcome a multitude of fears and excuses before I was able to make my first *shahadah*. The better part of that battle went very badly for me, and I came close to fleeing the fight several times. But by the grace of God, I was finally able to obtain victory in surrender to Him.

As hard as that decision to become a Muslim was for me, I no longer see it as my greatest *jihad*. When I fought to make my first testimony of faith, my enemy was conspicuous and its weapons and tactics were obvious. I was aware that I was in a fight, that I needed God's help to win it, and that to succeed, I only had to turn to Him. The hardest fights, however, are those in which the opponent is elusive or concealed, when you are not sure when or how it will come at you, or whether it has not already penetrated your lines. I would discover soon after becoming a Muslim that the latter is more often than not the case with temptation, and that the more you grow in faith, the more subtle, seductive, and destructive are the traps that lure you.

My conversion to Islam may have been a sudden impulse on my part, but it was definitely not a courageous act. I believe that I became a Muslim because that was what God willed, for, under normal circumstances, I would never have made such a radical decision—one that was bound to make my life in America more difficult both materially and socially. Yet for a brief moment, just when it felt as if the weight of the world was

---

[113] This statement is often attributed to the Prophet on the authority of Ibrahim ibn Aylah, but the *isnad* of this tradition has been judged weak by Muslim experts.

against me, when my head was spinning with a thousand reasons why I should avoid making the choice, when I had decided to turn tail and run, my mind suddenly cleared, my nerves calmed, and I was able to consider the matter rationally. It was at precisely that instant that to become a Muslim seemed the only logical thing to do.

One of the many things that deterred me for a long time from choosing Islam, even after I had become convinced of its calling, was that I considered myself unfit to be a Muslim. Over the years, I had accumulated so many sins and vices that I felt it would be impossible for me even to come close to living up to Islam's requirements. When I finally stated the *shahadah,* I committed myself to it in spite of my awareness of my own corruption. I reasoned that it is better to live and die acknowledging the truth—even if I might fall short of meeting its demands—then to live and die in silence or denial of it. When I embraced Islam, I knew I was probably the most wretched of all Muslims. However, I promised myself I would do the best I could to practice the faith.

It may seem strange, but I had some of the most intense spiritual moments of my life during those first few weeks after my conversion. It seemed that the weaker and lower I perceived myself to be, the more beautiful and moving would be my experiences of salah. The more I admitted my need for God's mercy and forgiveness, the more I felt them in my heart. In spite of all the weaknesses I had still to overcome, I felt the most tender and loving kindness when I turned to the only One Who really knew me.

I had never really known love before becoming a Muslim. I had always felt it too risky to trust anyone—even myself. As an atheist, I had come to believe that "love" was nothing more than a euphemism for a particular form of human insecurity and selfishness. I had given up on love a long time ago and now wanted never to know it, either as a giver or a recipient. I just wanted to live my life as comfortably as possible until I died and became long-forgotten soil underneath an unmarked grave. But as I read the Qur'an and prayed the Islamic prayers, a door to my heart was unsealed and I was immersed in an overwhelming tenderness. Love became more permanent and real than the earth beneath my feet; its power restored me and made it so that even I could feel love. I ask the reader to keep this in mind throughout the rest of this chapter. Know that it was deep, inner pain and emptiness that led me to Islam, and the irresistible love of God that kept me there. During those first several weeks as a Muslim, I received so much more than I ever could have imagined. I came to Islam with very modest expectations—I was happy enough to have found faith in a sensible religion—but I never expected to be touched by such intoxicating mercy. I never knew that one could experience so tender and warm an embrace.

This love, this relationship with God, should have remained my only real goal; it should have stayed the focus of all of my religious endeavors. The love of God should have been sufficient for me; it should have made me secure, strong and independent. But I somehow allowed myself to get distracted and so strayed from the penitent and humble slave I had been when I was still a new Muslim.

Big News

The day after my conversion, I began attending all five prayers at the University of San Francisco mosque. As I was a faculty staff member, it was easy for me while at work to attend the three middle prayers. In addition, since it was a short drive from my apartment to campus, I also had no problem getting to the two remaining prayers.

Much to my chagrin, my conversion to Islam was instantly big news on campus. I would have preferred that only those few Muslims who attended the prayers regularly know of it, but within a day or two it became the talk of the university. I suppose I should have expected as much; after all, the conversion of a faculty member of a well-known Catholic university is at least somewhat noteworthy.

Right from the start, I felt like an oddity as an American Muslim. The congregation in the mosque, except for me, consisted of foreign, undergraduate, male students, who kept staring at me in shock and wonder. During the sermons of the Friday congregational prayer, which were always delivered in Arabic, faces would keep turning in my direction. I found out later that this was because my conversion was the main topic of the *khutbah* (Friday prayer sermon) for several consecutive Fridays. Muslim students, male and female, frequently would stop me on campus to congratulate me or to ask me if I had really become a Muslim.

At the same time, many of my colleagues began to look at me worriedly. Some took the time to ask me if I was all right or if I was having trouble adjusting to life in San Francisco. A few professors seemed put off by my conversion, and a few others told me that what I did was very courageous. Very little of this made sense to me, for as nearly as I could tell, I was much the same person I had been only a couple of weeks earlier. I felt that everyone around me was definitely overreacting.

It was not long before I realized that the mosque was divided into several factions that were vying for control. These groups were connected to such international organizations as the Jama'at Tabligh (based in India and Pakistan), the Salafi movement (based in the Arabian Peninsula), and the Ikhwan al Muslimun (originated in Egypt). At times, I also felt as if they were vying for control of me. I was always being taken to the side and warned not to get too close to "those other brothers." Each group informed me that the others were straying from true Islam. Back then, I almost never had to cook for myself, because practically every night some member of the mosque would invite me to dinner (during which I would be questioned and corrected about things other Muslims were telling me). I soon got the impression that even though Islam severely condemns rumor-mongering and backbiting, Muslims were habitual gossips; it appeared to be a community preoccupation.

During the first few weeks after my conversion, I kept my feelings about the choice I had made to myself. I could sense that many members of the community were curious—some were clearly suspicious[114]—but belief in God—not to mention Islam—was all so new to me that I needed time to reflect on the implications of what I had done. I really needed time to simply get my feet back on the ground, because everything seemed to have happened and to be now happening so fast.

Instant Angel

One night—I believe it was a Friday—some of the brothers asked me if I would like to go with them to a lecture being held that evening in Davis, California. I really did not want to, but I knew I could not refuse without disappointing them greatly. They were extremely pleased when I finally agreed to go.

The program began with dinner, which we ate with our fingers while sitting on the floor. I was quickly getting used to many foreign customs, but I never quite got the hang of eating rice with my fingers. While everyone else had finished their plates and had started desert, I had only managed to eat a few mouthfuls of my dinner. Nevertheless, dinning in this way was a new and fun experience.

After dinner, the president of the UC Davis Muslim Student Association announced over the loudspeaker that the lecture was about to

---

[114] Some members of the mosque later confessed that they had thought I was from the CIA. Several others asked me point blank if I became a Muslim in order to get married to a Muslim woman.

begin. We rearranged ourselves on the floor in rows facing the microphone. After a brief supplication, a reading from the Qur'an, and a number of announcements, the president told the audience that tonight's speaker was going to be none other than me. At first I thought I must have misheard him, but when I glanced around, I saw that everyone was looking and smiling at me. I sat there stunned and embarrassed. I had not the slightest inkling that I was going to be asked to give a speech that night.

I turned towards my good friend Rosli, a student from Malaysia who was sitting beside me, and pleaded: "I can't! I don't know what to say!"

"It will be O. K.," he nodded, "I will pray for you."

I looked at the president of the MSA.

"Please, I can't!" I begged him.

He smiled reassuringly and said calmly, "Please, come to the microphone."

The president briefly introduced me to the audience, which consisted of about three hundred Middle-Eastern young men, and told them that I was going to tell the story of how I became a Muslim. I began with an awkward apology. I said I had not prepared anything and that I was not sure exactly what led me to Islam, but that since they had come to hear an account of my conversion, I would do my best to recall some of the things that I felt may have played a role in that decision. The story I told them is essentially the first chapter of *Struggling to Surrender*.[115] Throughout my speech, I was very nervous and the audience was extremely hushed. When I finally finished, there arose from the audience several emotional and thunderous choruses of *"Allahu Akbar!"* (God is Greatest!). The president then asked the audience if there were any questions, and I remember being asked several times about how Muslims should present their religion to non-Muslim Americans. I advised that Muslims should try not to be pushy, for that will immediately turn most Americans off, and that they should be kind and compassionate towards non-Muslims, because that is the first thing an American will look for in a person who claims to be religious. The president then closed the meeting with a few words of encouragement, followed by a supplication.

I will never forget the reception I then received: the entire audience converged on me with greetings, hugs, handshakes, and kisses on my cheeks. Tears were flowing down faces all around me. A few brothers were close to sobbing. Everywhere I looked, hands were outstretched towards me; many brothers simply wanted to touch me for a moment or pat me on

---

[115] Lang, *Struggling to Surrender*, chapter 1.

the back. I was told how great I was, how much better a believer I was than the Muslims from foreign lands, how inspirational I was, how sinless I now was, how much God must have loved me! It took me over an hour to reach the door of the mosque, which could not have been more than forty feet from the microphone. By the time I got to the parking lot, the pockets of my pants were bulging with scraps of paper on which were written the addresses and phone numbers of members of the audience.

Some brothers whom I had not met before offered to drive me home to San Francisco. They talked excitedly about Islam and my conversion on the way. I mentioned to them that the reaction of the audience was very emotional.

"Brother Jeffrey, if you only knew what it means to them to see an American convert to Islam!" the brother next to me exclaimed. "The idea that a young, white, blonde-haired, blue-eyed American would become a Muslim is like a miracle to them! So many of them would cut their hands to be you! Oh, I wish I could take you to my country and put you on television! To the people back home, seeing you would be like watching an angel coming down from the clouds!"

"Why?" I asked him. "What does being an American have to do with it?"

The brother who was driving answered me, "Back home everyone worships America. There are Muslims who don't know a single *ayah* of Qur'an, who can sing all of Michael Jackson's songs! They can tell you more about the Dallas Cowboys than about Islam. When they see you—a white American—practicing Islam, it shocks and humiliates them. They start thinking: If this white *Amreekee* can love and follow Islam, then what is wrong with us?!"

The Champion

I am not sure why, but before I gave the lecture in Davis, celebrity was never very important to me. At times I may have hoped that certain persons liked me, but I never worked hard to obtain people's admiration or friendship. I was always fairly confident and independent, unconcerned with obtaining the approval of my peers. And yet, the response I got from the audience in Davis aroused in me a weakness to which I thought I was immune. While I told my story, I was the same ashamed and repentant sinner who had thrown himself desperately on the mercy of God only a few weeks earlier; by the time I finally crossed the prayer room and reached the door to the parking lot, I was inebriated with the veneration of that assembly and delirious with self-admiration.

I suppose I could offer the excuse that this sudden surge of vanity occurred during a period when I was acutely vulnerable. I certainly felt on the defensive among my own people, as I was constantly forced to explain and defend my conversion to friends and family. Before becoming a Muslim, I had always known the respect of others—perhaps this is why I had never felt the need to work for it—but now it seemed that everyone I knew and loved was doubting me. I also felt out of place and under scrutiny in the Muslim community. Moreover, I sensed strongly that most brothers in the mosque questioned whether I would remain a believer for very long. They would take on such a patronizing tone when speaking to me, as if I had not previously studied Islam or was totally immoral before becoming a Muslim. They also seemed to assume that "American" and "Muslim" are two mutually exclusive attributes and that I would never be able to completely purge myself of the first; hence, I would never be able to fully become the second. In a sense, I felt that I did not quite fit in anywhere anymore.

The night in Davis changed everything. I gave one speech and was instantly a hero among the Muslims. How I loved the adoration! I could not get enough of it, and apparently they could not get enough of me—at least at first. I was asked to make speeches at virtually every Muslim gathering to which I was invited. At first, I would simply repeat the story of my conversion, but after a while I began to prepare and memorize other speeches, which, when called upon, I would pretend to deliver off the cuff.

The various groups vying for control of the USF mosque now made an even greater effort to recruit me, and I felt it necessary to join one of the factions. First, I tried the Jama'at Tabligh, as I was initially very impressed with their strong mystical leanings, but I soon became tired of their somewhat ascetic practices. I briefly considered aligning myself with the Muslim Student Association, which was founded in America by student members of the Ikhwan al Muslimun, but I could not relate to their strong focus on Middle-Eastern politics. I finally fell in with the brothers from the Arabian peninsula, who seemed mostly to be Salafis.

As I went from one group to the next, I began to display an extremely bad habit: When brothers would deprecate members of other groups in our mosque, I would join in their derogation. Not only had I no excuse for doing this, since I had been a Muslim for too short a time to be passing judgment on other believers—not to mention the fact that Islam prohibits this behavior—but the brothers whom I maligned behind their backs were the same ones who only recently had invited me to their homes and showed me the utmost kindness. After a while, however, even I could not stand my own hypocrisy, and eventually I was able to resist the urge to demean other members of our mosque behind their backs.

Yet I still needed to strike at someone, for how can you remain a hero without a cause or a fight? I am not saying that back then I consciously schemed in this way, but as I see it now, I think I was motivated by such a subconscious impulse. It was not enough for me to merely be accepted as a Muslim by the Muslims—I wanted them to look up to me. Naturally, I became a passionate denouncer of everything American and a staunch defender of Middle-Eastern culture. In speeches, I would magnify my country's vileness and repeat and embellish the many Western—usually Jewish—conspiracy theories I found to be so popular among Muslims.

I also became increasingly conservative in my approach to Islam. There is a certain guaranteed respect that comes with religious rigidity; when you are radically conservative, other believers may question your thinking but never your religiosity or commitment. Publicly, I upheld the literal interpretation and application of all statements in the Qur'an and *hadith* collections and refused to consider any historical or situational contexts. But no matter how hard I tried to convince others and myself of this approach, I was never totally comfortable with it. I became a vociferous advocate for traditional Muslim gender roles. In particular, I championed the seclusion of women in our community and their exclusion from positions of community leadership. I tried desperately to grow an "Islamic" beard, but apparently my genetic background does not produce much facial hair; the most I could grow was a five o'clock shadow interspersed with several bald spots. I would decry constantly the lack of faith and the impotence of "us" modern Muslims, whom I described as too weak to live up to the demands of our religion. Although I never stated it, I did not at that time consider myself one of the feckless Muslim majority.

I also began to attack my parent's religion with a vengeance. I studied all of the arguments currently used by Muslims against Christianity and watched every Muslim–Christian debate video on which I could get my hands. In interfaith dialogues, I would repeat the same arguments against Christianity almost word for word. The material I drew upon was hardly new; classical Muslim polemicists had made the same arguments as modern ones, only the classical scholars' research was more thorough and scholarly. Christian thought, however, has changed greatly over the last several centuries, and many arguments used by modern Muslims are outmoded or apply only to certain extremists sects within Christianity. Actually, I was well aware of this when I participated in the dialogues, but I found that the majority of the Christian laity were as ignorant of the evolution of Christian scholarly thought as were the Muslims. Thus, to the unknowledgeable, my Christian opponents would appear to be on the defensive and evasive as I attacked various positions that they probably never held. My strategy was deceitful, albeit it did earn me a certain popularity with my coreligionists.

Poison

Altogether, I lived in San Francisco for five years after my conversion. The first three were marked by steady progress in the direction of radical conservatism and intolerance of those points of view that differed from mine. The fourth year was one of disillusionment, when I seriously questioned the course I had been following. The fifth year began a time of recovery, a period when I sought to reconcile my true self with my faith. I believe that several key incidents and factors, which I will discuss below, affected this turn around.

As stated earlier, I promised myself that I would never participate again in my faith community's gossip. However, there was one group of Muslims who were excluded from our community and who were absolutely loathed by the brothers with whom I kept company. Members of the USF mosque, which had been established and run by Sunni Muslim students, made it clear that the local Shi'ah Muslims were quite unwelcome in the mosque. In fact, the two communities barely got along at all. Most Sunni brothers strongly disapproved of the Shi'ah, but those from the Arabian peninsula utterly despised them. The Iran–Iraq war was well underway, and a large amount of anti-Shi'ah literature was coming to the mosques of America from the Gulf states, who, at that time, supported Sadaam Hussein. (Shi'ah Islam is the predominant school of Islam in Iran.) These writings were obviously more propaganda than serious scholarship, but I studied them nonetheless and used the information they provided to denounce vehemently Shi'ah Islam whenever the opportunity presented itself.

One night while giving a lecture in the mosque on the dangers of Shi'ah Islam, I ended my diatribe by describing that school of Islam as "the greatest current threat to Islam" and "a virulent poison in the body of the Muslim *ummah*." As I was leaving the mosque later that evening, a Middle-Eastern student politely requested to speak privately with me for a moment. He told me that he was from Iran and that, although he had grown up in a Shi'ah family, he had become a Sunni Muslim several years ago. He said that the speech I made hurt him deeply, because he could not stop thinking about his mother and father as I delineated all the ills and dangers to Islam posed by Shi'ah Islam. He said that even though he had lived in a predominantly Shi'ah society almost his entire life, he had never heard of most of what I had stated that the Shi'ah believe and practice. In a horrified voice he exclaimed, "You made my parents sound like enemies of Islam! Where, in God's name, did you get your information?!"

I was immediately seized by feelings of remorse, for I knew I had gathered my "facts" in a hasty and irresponsible way and that what the Iranian brother said was probably true. Toward the end of our conversation, I begged him to forgive me, promised that I would research Shi'ah Islam more thoroughly and objectively, and that I would correct publicly any false statements I might have made. It was not long before I discovered that my lecture that evening was full of misinformation, misinterpretation, and exaggeration. To this day, I still hear many of the same false claims I had made in my lecture and try to correct them whenever I do.

This conversation with the Iranian student did much more than make me improve my research methods; it frightened me. It was the first time I was confronted personally by a target of one of my verbal assaults. When I ridiculed the backboneless Muslims in our community, I never singled out anyone by name; when I attacked Christians in dialogues, they never responded so personally; but this time, with the Iranian, I could see and feel the harmfulness of my behavior. I began to deeply doubt my own religiosity and sincerity and to question my actions and motives. I wondered how I had come to be so angry and why I felt such a strong desire to deprecate others. I asked myself what had happened to me since I first converted to Islam? I entered this religion in peace, yet now I only showed severity and narrow-mindedness. I thought: Whom am I really fighting and why?

A few months after the incident with the Iranian student, something happened in our community that brought my discomfort to a critical point.

Abandoned

Not long after I converted to Islam, Grant, a white American about my age, also became a Muslim. I was thrilled to see Grant join our community, for until then I had met only two American Muslims of European descent. However, they both lived far from San Francisco. Grant and I hit it off right from the start and became very close friends. During much of the time we spent together, we would discuss our experiences of and feelings about Islam and would support each other through the many adjustments that come with entering the Muslim community. It was great to be able to talk to someone of the same generation and cultural background. I thanked God over and over again for guiding Grant to Islam, for his friendship was, for me, a valuable gift.

Sometime during my fourth year in San Francisco, Grant stopped attending the prayers at the mosque, including the Friday prayers. I called him many times to find out if he was alright, but never got an answer. I thought perhaps he had left town for a while, but he had never mentioned any future travel plans. I stopped by his apartment a number of times with some of the brothers from the mosque who were also worried about Grant, but no one answered when we rang the door bell.

One evening, several weeks after Grant's disappearance, I decided to go to his house alone. I waited a few minutes after knocking on his door, but, as usual, no one answered. As I was walking back to my car, I heard a door open behind me. I turned around and there was Grant, standing half hidden behind his partially opened front door.

"Grant! Wow! It's really good to see you! Where have you been? Are you OK? I've been trying to get in touch with you for weeks! Thank God your OK!"

I was not giving Grant a chance to respond as I hurried back toward him. My jubilance, however, quickly deflated, because the cheerless expression on his face told me that he was not glad to see me at all. When I reached his door, I asked him soberly, trying my best not to sound hurt: "What's wrong, Grant? What's going on?"

He halfheartedly invited me in, and we sat in chairs on opposite sides of his small, dark, sparsely furnished living room. I started by telling him how worried I had been about him, how I thought he must have been very sick or in some terrible accident. He told me that he should have called me, but that he did not know how I would react to what he was about to say. He then began a slow, dispassionate explanation of his recent absence from the Muslim community.

He said he had entered and left many religions over the years, that he tried on more faiths than pairs of socks. He stated that he had searched not only for a set of beliefs with which he could agree, but for a community that lived and represented those beliefs as well. He said he was originally attracted to Islam by what he first saw in some Muslims he had met, but in time had discovered that the Islamic community fell far short of the noble ideals which it preached and that the defects in its character far overshadowed its virtues. He said he had finally found the faith community he had always been looking for, one that truly translated their religious beliefs into mutual respect and love; he had become a Buddhist.

I was stunned. I sat there silently, struggling to come up with an effective response. I could only think of how much I would have preferred that my fears about Grant having had a serious accident or illness were true.

Grant then drove the dagger a little deeper into my wound: "Jeff, I know that you just recently married a Muslim woman and that now you have a kind of vested interest in Islam, but I think you would really enjoy meeting these Buddhist friends of mine. They gave me this small book that describes the main beliefs of Buddhism—you can have it if you like!"

I took the book from Grant and leafed through it, staring down blankly at its pages. Unable to raise my gaze to look at Grant, I shook my head and told him, "Grant, unlike you, I did not try on Islam like a pair of socks; I really and truly surrendered to what I perceived to be the truth. I did not even *want* to be a Muslim or to belong to a religious community. For goodness sake, Grant, I was an *atheist* before becoming a Muslim! Whether or not the Muslims are good or bad people had no bearing at all on my choice to convert, or for that matter, on my decision to stay in this religion!"

"Then why *did* you convert?" he asked, sounding bewildered.

"Because of the Qur'an!" I blurted impatiently, as if he should have already known. "Because of the Qur'an!"

Grant was sensitive and intelligent, but I could see from the vacant look he gave me that my reply blew right past him. I thought I should elaborate on my answer.

"Grant, I read the Qur'an—fought and struggled with it—argued with it—and finally capitulated to it. I surrendered to the one God, whom I came to know and trust through reading it. I cannot simply walk away from all that."

"I didn't read very much of the Qur'an," Grant admitted.

Turning Point

I did not go right home after I left Grant's flat. I was still in shock and needed some time to think. I parked my car on Geary Street, about ten blocks from my apartment, and got out and started walking in the opposite direction. Trudging along, I thought about how Grant's news could not have come at a worse time, for although I had not told him, I was going through my own crisis of faith. I was drowning in confusion and self-doubt, which, under normal circumstances, I would have discussed with Grant. Since becoming a Muslim, I had reached an all-time spiritual low. I felt distant from God, isolated, and lost. My performance of the rituals had become spiritually lifeless. In my prayers, I begged God to touch me the way he did when I had been a new Muslim—to love me with the love I had experienced back then—back when I was a lowly, mistake-prone, bungling newcomer to Islam. I kept interrogating myself as I walked along: Was I not performing each of the five prayers every day in the mosque? Was I not practicing the pillars of the faith steadfastly? Was I not serving God through my involvement in the community? Did all the speeches I gave on Islam amount to nothing in His sight?

I could not figure out where I had gone wrong. Worst of all, I felt I had no where to turn. Discussing my faith crisis with Grant was now out of the question, the brothers in the mosque would certainly never understand, and I did not want to disappoint my wife, who had so much admiration for and confidence in me. All the while, Grant's words kept echoing in my mind: "Then why did you become a Muslim?"

I had not thought about my motivations for embracing Islam in some time, and yet I did not have to reflect on his question. My answer to him was simply a reflex that he provoked.

"It was the Qur'an!"

I came to a stop. Staring down at the sidewalk, I focused on my response to Grant. It was as if a great light had suddenly illuminated my mind: "It was the Qur'an!"

I thought about how I had lost touch with this answer, and I started to remind myself of various aspects of my conversion. I recalled how I was not in the market for a religion when I first became interested in Islam; I was initially only curious about Muslim beliefs. I remembered that I did not become a Muslim to find the comfort and support of a faith community, or to someday obtain a wife and a family. I reminded myself how the Qur'an first captured my mind and then guided me to the knowledge I needed and the love of God; how it was to His infinite love and forgiveness that I surrendered; how my conversion was nothing but an acquiescence to a truth; how I had given myself over—heart, body, and soul and with all my failings—to an invincible power that I had tried to withstand for a while but was finally unable to resist.

I started walking again, briskly, with my head bowed in concentration, as answers began coming to me in flashes. I realized I had strayed far from my original motives for embracing Islam: I had been serving myself more than anyone else with all my community involvement; I had become more concerned with obtaining the respect of the Muslim community than with my relationship with God; I had hurt others with my uncompromising severity in order to win the admiration of my coreligionists; I had acquired what I had always disliked most in religious types back when I was an atheist—hypocrisy and base conformism to prevailing sentiment; I had erected a false image of myself and tried to brainwash myself into believing in it; I had become like one of those half-crazed evangelists—a ranting and raving, fire and brimstone heaving, Muslim version of Elmer Gantry.

I turned around and headed back to my car. I knew now what I had to do: I had to return to my original purpose for becoming a Muslim; I had to give up making speeches; I had to learn to be myself again; I needed to be more honest and open with others and myself; I had to voice concerns when I had them, or, at the very least, I had to stop supporting ideas about which I had doubts or questions. Most of all, I needed to beg God for His forgiveness and guidance.

Fresh Start

When I arrived home, I had a long talk with my wife. I told her about everything I had been through and apologized for keeping her in the dark so long. When she asked me why I had not shared my feelings with her sooner, I explained that, until recently, I was unable to make sense of them. I also confessed that I had not wanted to disappoint her. She replied that it was foolish of me to think that way and that I had greatly underestimated her love for me.

I needed some time to be alone, away from the community pressures that I had handled so poorly. I went into a state of semi-retreat and went to the mosque only for the Friday prayers, since its attendance is mandatory. I performed the other prayers at home or in my office at school. As expected, many Muslim students at the university were greatly disappointed in my sudden change of behavior, but as painful as it was for me to let them down, it was at the same time liberating not to be a hero anymore.

The ways and mercy of God are at times very difficult to understand. Although I would never recommend to another Muslim that he or she adopt a policy of self-isolation from the community, strangely enough, I did begin to feel spiritually alive again. My retreat lasted a few months, and I would have prolonged it a little longer if I had not become active in the mosque once again through my dealings with several new American converts who entered our community that Spring semester.

All but one of the converts were young women, and I became drawn into their campaign to be allowed to attend the five daily prayers in the mosque. The textual sources of Islam assure women this right, but, over the centuries, various Muslim cultures have made the mosque an uncomfortable place for them in which to pray. Actually, many Muslim men in our community were quite sympathetic with the lady converts, but a few very loud and conservative Muslim students fought hard to keep the new female believers out of the mosque. One of them went so far as to threaten that if he found any ladies at the prayers, he would throw them out bodily. The female converts soon became tired of being at the center of what was fast becoming an extremely heated and divisive controversy and thus quit trying to attend the mosque. The community returned to normal. To the best of my knowledge, not one of these women is a Muslim today.

Toward the end of this dispute over the female converts, I met the male newcomer to Islam. Out of respect for his privacy, which I believe he may prefer to guard, I will refer to him as "Khalid," rather than use his birth name or the Arabic name he used temporarily.

I was thirty-three when I met Khalid, and he was in his mid-twenties. What I remember best about him was his likable personality and his great enthusiasm for Islam. He was bright, witty, cheerful, gentle, humble, and kind. He seemed to always have a smile on his face or a kind and encouraging word. He was very happy about his new faith and worked tirelessly for it. He was involved in all of the mosque's charitable activities and was always helping organize community get-togethers and programs.

Khalid was married to a devout Catholic, and they had a ten-year-old daughter and a two-year-old son. His conversion caused some tension in his marriage, and he asked me if I would be willing to talk to his wife about Islam. I warned him that I was unwilling to pressure her in any way, but he assured me that was not his intention; he only wanted her to have a better understanding of Islam, so as to alleviate some of her anxiety about his conversion. I agreed to his request, and this led to several get-togethers between our two families.

About two months after I first met Khalid, his daughter became a Muslim, followed by his wife a few weeks later. Their entry into Islam breathed fresh life into our community, for Khalid's family instantly became one of the most active and innovative in the USF mosque. Around this time, my own family and I began making preparations to move to Lawrence, Kansas, as I had accepted a position at the university there. My wife and I lamented how much we would miss our new friends.

As the weeks passed, I became increasingly troubled that Khalid might be falling into some of the same traps from which I was now fighting to free myself. A few incidents made me feel that he may have been imposing unnecessary and burdensome practices upon himself and his family members out of a desire to become more religious.

I recall one afternoon when Khalid's daughter came with him to the mosque. After the prayer, while we all sat in a circle on the floor, a brother asked her what her name was. She kept silent and cringed slightly, and then looked to her father beseechingly, as if seeking a reprieve. The room quieted as the rest of those present turned curious, reassuring smiles toward Khalid's daughter. The brother gently repeated his question to her. Once more she directed an uncomfortable glance towards her dad.

"Answer him," Khalid anxiously urged her, trying to coax her with his eyes.

His daughter sighed deeply, paused a few more seconds, tightened her lips, took another deep breath, and then slowly and painstakingly uttered a timid and awkward: "Aaaa-ishshsh-aaaa?"

Relieved, Khalid smiled at her while nodding his approval.

A little later I asked Khalid about the incident, and he informed me that he was considering having the names of his family members legally changed to Arabic ones. I told him I did not think that was a religious requirement. I reminded him of Bilal and Salman al Farsi and that the Prophet only advocated changing one's name when his or her present name was offensive to Islam. I pointed out that his own birth name, which meant "a gift from God," was hardly offensive to Islamic principles. I also mentioned that in the *hadith* collections there are sayings that discourage Muslims from hiding their family backgrounds.

Khalid argued that the Muslim community would be much more comfortable with Arabic names. I agreed with him and said that as long as that was his motivation, then his choice might be a good one, as far as he and perhaps his wife were concerned. But I pointed out that he might reconsider changing his ten-year-old daughter's name, for a such a sudden change may be much more difficult to handle for a young girl who is just beginning to develop her self-image. I asked him to imagine the reactions of her friends at school. Khalid finally just smiled and assured me that he knew his own daughter and that she would be just fine.

Khalid also instituted the separation of the sexes in his home. One evening when he invited my family and a few other families from the mosque to his flat for dinner, he surprised me by ushering me into a room reserved for the men, and my wife and daughters into a separate room for the women. (We had been to Khalid's home many times before and had always sat together as families) I was even more startled, however, when he brought our two families back together in the living room after the other guests departed. When I informed him of my perplexity, he explained that he had assumed his other guests, who were from the Middle-East, would have been uncomfortable if we had all dined together.

I was definitely perturbed. I complained that as eminent a scholar as Imam Malik saw nothing wrong with families dining together in mixed company and that there are many authenticated reports in the *hadith* compilations where Muslim men and women interacted in the presence of the Prophet. I protested that the seclusion of females is primarily a cultural tradition that could do much more damage than good in the American Muslim community. Although I thought it nice that he wanted to make his Middle-Eastern guests feel comfortable, I asked him why he did not consider the comfort of his American guests as well and, furthermore, whether or not our brothers and sisters from the Middle East felt a similar need to accommodate *our* culture when we go to their homes? I also remarked that we American converts are becoming like religious schizophrenics, displaying one personality in front of the Muslim community and another when we are outside it. With the last statement I had gone too far, for Khalid was visibly insulted. We parted that night on bad terms and our relationship was never quite the same.

Khalid also started getting and accepting invitations to lecture on Islam, and this, of course, only increased my apprehension. Sincerity is indispensable to one's spiritual growth, and it is put to its severest tests in front of audiences. In my eyes, my recent downfall was triggered by my public preaching. I would not encourage any Muslim to take up public speaking on Islam, but I would especially urge a new convert to avoid the podium.

On the other hand, when I thought about Khalid's situation more objectively, I realized that I was probably overreacting and may have been projecting my own recent bitter experience onto his. That Khalid had become rather conservative in his approach to the religion did not necessarily mean he was heading for a crisis; I knew several very conservative American converts who were extremely happy and well adjusted. The few cultural practices that he and his family had adopted, which I felt Islam does not require, were really no cause for alarm. Some of them, such as the separation of the sexes, did deter licentiousness (its ostensible purpose). In any case, many people in the melting pot of America absorb various foreign customs. I also had to admit that Khalid's speeches on Islam were much more moderate than mine had been. His personality was much gentler and more balanced than mine, and I could never imagine him using the pulpit in a destructive way.

I finally decided to never bother Khalid again with my apprehension. Unfortunately, during my last several weeks in San Francisco, I could never get myself to apologize to him for interfering in his family life. I feel bad about that to this day.

To Kansas

Grant helped me load the moving van the day before I left for Kansas. He was the last person I said good-bye to in San Francisco. Despite his apostasy from Islam, we had remained good friends.

Even though he was no longer a Muslim, I continued to find his unusual perspective on religion extremely thought-provoking. Our conversations had helped me to explore deeper and to strengthen my faith in Islam. I feel it quite ironic that Grant's defection from Islam was a catalyst for my own spiritual revivification, but as the Qur'an so frequently reminds us, God guides as He chooses.

Grant's attempt at Buddhism turned out to be short-lived, lasting only a few months. The day I departed San Francisco, he belonged to no official religion, although he still believed very much in God.

Vanished

Ever since my graduate student days at Purdue University, I had wanted to live in the Midwest. Although I instantly took to Kansas, my heart was for some time, as the song says, still in San Francisco. It seemed that at least every other week my wife and I were in touch with friends from the USF Muslim community.

I had given Grant my new address and phone number the day he helped me move, but for some reason he never wrote or called. I tried calling him a number of times, but found that he had mysteriously and unexpectedly left his flat. I asked the brothers in San Francisco to try to locate him, but no one heard from or saw him again. He simply disappeared.

During the Spring semester following my departure from California, the USF mosque, which was located in a small room in the basement of St. Ignatius Church, was closed by the university. The Jesuits, who had lent the Muslim students the room so they could perform their five daily prayers there, needed the space for storage. It was in that little room that I had made my first *shahadah* and had performed almost all of my ritual prayers during the next five years. I thank God that it had been there for me when I needed it.

During the school year following our arrival in Kansas, Khalid's daughter began wearing full *hijab* (the traditional dress of Muslim women) to public school. The abuse she received from her schoolmates was apparently too much for her; she lost much weight and had to be hospitalized for a while. Khalid then moved his family close to one of the Bay Area's Islamic centers and enrolled Aishah in the Islamic school run by the center. A short time later, Khalid was elected to the center's board of directors. Several months passed, and then Khalid took Aishah out of the Islamic school and re-enrolled her in public school, which she now attended in typical American dress. He then resigned from the board of directors of the Islamic center, and he and his family relocated again, this time leaving no forwarding address or phone number with anyone in the Muslim community.

After much detective work, my wife somehow obtained Khalid's new phone number. She spoke to his wife, who informed her that the rest of her family had left Islam and that she had become very confused about the religion. She also mentioned that they were getting ready to move to somewhere in the southern United States. That is the last we heard from them.

No Regrets

I felt bad for Khalid, but his apostasy did not affect me as Grant's had. I have seen many Americans enter and later leave Islam; about half of the converts I have met over the years eventually left the faith. I think Grant's apostasy was so disturbing to me because of our close friendship and because my faith had reached such a critical point at that time.

My experience of faith in Kansas has been much more serene than it was in San Francisco. The local Muslim community has received me warmly and seems to accept me as I am. I do not do much public speaking any more—at most one or two talks per year—and when I do lecture on Islam, I prefer small audiences, because I have learned that I do not handle the temptations of fame at all well.

I bear no ill-will toward the San Francisco Muslim community. I blame no one but myself for the tumultuous years I had there. The Muslims at USF were of course not perfect, but they were very good and dedicated believers and were extremely kind and generous toward me. The only mistake they made with respect to me was that they had too much admiration for and confidence in me.

I also have few regrets concerning San Francisco. The pain and inner turmoil I experienced during that phase were very valuable to me. I believe they caused me to learn a great deal about myself and about serving God. I see that part of my life as a necessarily difficult period of growing and learning. As I wrote earlier in this book, I came to Islam from the farthest corner of the spiritual spectrum, and so had to expect that there would be much to learn and suffer on my way to self-surrender to God. I hope that those whom I may have hurt or misled back then while I was swinging between radicalism and conservatism took what I did and said with a grain of salt. I also hope they can find it within themselves to forgive me.

CHAPTER 6

THE ROAD AHEAD

I have accompanied the reader about as far as I can on this journey to Islam in America. The future lies ahead, and only God knows what is in store for American Islam. Nevertheless, I feel certain that the road forward for Muslims in America will have many sharp turns and difficult climbs. I urge those who hope to keep on this journey to prepare themselves as best they can for the coming challenges.

It is not at all clear that Islam will grow into a significant indigenous social and spiritual force in North America during the next century. The approximately five million believers currently residing in the United States and Canada and the several thousand mosques scattered about the two countries are hopeful signs, but it is conceivable that the practicing Muslim American population could dwindle, especially if it ceases to be augmented by immigration. It is even possible that the many mosques in America might someday be converted to other uses, surviving as vestiges of a generation of Muslim Americans whose descendants were swept into the American mainstream. History has known such examples.

I believe that for Islam to prevail in North America, three things are necessary: (1) a substantial fraction of the present generation of American children of Muslim descent must emerge as adults who are strongly committed to Islam; (2) the Muslim community must remain united and not fracture into sects; and (3) the American Muslim community needs to produce its own religious scholars who can respond effectively to the unprecedented questions and problems that are bound to arise. These points are very briefly discussed in this last chapter.

Newcomers

The North American Muslim community is very young, both in terms of the distribution of its members' ages and in terms of its noticeable presence here. Three decades ago it was negligible; today, Muslims are about two percent of the North American population.

Anyone who attends a Friday prayer service or an Islamic conference in the United States or Canada cannot help noticing the scarcity of Muslim senior citizens in attendance. The fraction of Muslims over age sixty in the community is extremely small. This helps to explain why the leadership of such national Islamic organizations as ISNA, ICNA, and the Islamic Assembly of North America (IANA) is made up of men and women mostly in their forties and early fifties instead of older, more experienced persons.

The sudden rise of Islam in America sprang from two campaigns for equality that fermented during the 1960s: the fight for civil rights by African Americans in the United States and the struggle in the Middle East to achieve economic and technological parity with the West.

African American Muslims

In the United States, the name of Martin Luther King, Jr., has come to symbolize the Civil Rights era. The most recollected images from this period are of Reverend King leading dignified, well-dressed, well-behaved, spiritual singing, black freedom marchers through the streets of southern state capitals, while indignant white crackers and police in riot gear, holding back high-strung German shepherds, look on, waiting for the slightest instigation to unleash their anger.

Yet in those turbulent times, not all African–American men and women shared the Reverend King's dream of a harmoniously integrated America. A few African–American leaders believed in the futility of Dr. King's vision and were convinced that it was against the very nature of the white man to treat other races justly. Elijah Muhammad, founder of the Nation of Islam, was one of the most important proponents of this view-point. Though he died in 1975, his teachings and the religion he built around them are winning converts from the African–American community to this day and are still strongly influencing America's perception of Islam.

The Nation of Islam, under the leadership of Elijah Muhammad, offered African–Americans a radical religious interpretation of world history that pitted black man, as the true elect of God, against white man, as the devil himself. The Nation also provided its members with a religious discipline that promoted self-respect and self-realization. Yet except for a few superficial borrowings from Muslim customs, there was little in Elijah Muhammad's teachings or the Nation's religious practices that was based on Islam; there was much that was opposed to it. The Bible was and has remained the principle scripture of the Nation. Minister Louis Farrakan, the Nation's current leader, quotes from the Bible much more frequently and with much greater confidence than he does from the Qur'an and often makes assertions (that the Qur'an rejects) based on the Bible or the teachings of Elijah Muhammad.

A short time after Elijah Muhammad died, the Nation of Islam split into two factions: one led by his son, Warithdeen Muhammad, and another led by his chief spokesman, Minister Louis Farakhan. Muhammad led his followers to orthodox Islam, and their religious beliefs are now in line with those of Muslims worldwide. Minister Farakhan's group, which has retained the title "The Nation of Islam," adheres to the teachings of Elijah Muhammad, a decision that causes Muslim scholars to doubt their orthodoxy. The overwhelming majority of the approximately one million African–Americans who today call themselves Muslims are followers of W. D. Muhammad. It should be noted, however, that most of the leadership of the current African–American Muslim community was at one time members of the Nation. Thus, in this way, The Nation of Islam paved the way for the emergence of orthodox Islam in Black America.

Immigrant Muslims

Governments of Muslim countries, out of a desire to become technologically independent of the West, began in the 1960s to send large numbers of their young people to European and American universities. Many of these students returned to their countries imbued with notions of democracy and human rights. Many also went back to their homelands more committed to Islam than when they first began their education in the West. Both types of students posed a threat to the politically repressive regimes that funded their western education, which may account partially for the marked decline in recent years of Muslim foreign student enrollment at western universities.

A large number of the western-educated Muslims managed to immigrate to the United States and Canada. Together with their families, these immigrants account for about three-fourths of the North American Muslim community and have led the way in providing Islamic education and establishing mosques and Islamic schools in America. Their numerical dominance of the American Muslim community has assured that, for the present and the immediate future, the way American Muslims practice and understand Islam will be very similar to the way it is understood and practiced in the Middle East and the Indian subcontinent.

An Ignored Community

Even at this point in time, most Americans remain unaware of the sizeable Muslim community in North America. In part, this may be a result of how rapidly the Muslim community of North America has grown in the last thirty years. Also, the American population may have not had sufficient time to meet this new subculture. The fact that most Americans are uninformed about the religions practiced in other parts of the world may also help explain the public's unawareness of the arrival of Islam.

Another important reason why Americans tend to disregard Islam as an indigenous religion is that the Islamic communities of Canada and the United States exist on the fringes of these societies; even though there has been a steady trickle of non-African–American converts to Islam, African–American converts and foreign-born Muslims account for the vast majority of Muslims in America today. Even though this number has now surpassed the number of Jews, Americans continue to view Islam as a religion practiced by foreigners and/or African–Americans.

Devout American Muslims would like to see a change in the current public perception of Islam as a religion alien to America, for as long as this view prevails, it will be all the more difficult for their children to grow up as Muslims in America. Islam's perceived foreignness may cause some of these children to feel the need to distance themselves from the Muslim community or to downplay the role that religion plays in their lives. In addition, Muslims feel obligated to share their religious viewpoint, a task that would be greatly facilitated if Islam were to become an acknowledged and contributing part of American culture.

Unfortunately, the senior generation of American Muslims can only do so much to alter the public's image of Islam, for the simple reason that their physical appearance so strongly reinforces it. Time is also running out for this generation of Muslim Americans, as their children are fast approaching the age at which they should take up the baton and carry the faith forward. For better or for worse, and whether or not they are adequately prepared, the establishment of Islam in America depends much more on the next generation of American Muslims than it does on their predecessors.

The Larger Society

A middle-aged, African–American woman asked me an interesting question during a program I participated in at an Islamic conference a couple of years ago. After remarking that Islam is part of the Muslim immigrants' cultural background and that it came to Black America through the Civil Rights struggle of the 1960s and 1970s, she asked me if I thought it really possible that many white Americans would embrace the religion without some similar social impetus. Both of these groups, she said, were and are drawn to Islam in part because it answers certain social needs: immigrants are returning to their religious and cultural roots, and African–American Muslims are choosing Islam as an alternative to the religion and culture forced upon their ancestors.[116] What social incentive, she asked, is there for European–Americans to consider Islam as a religious option?

I responded that for most of the American public, no such incentive presently exists. Generally, Americans—and I am not referring here to only white Americans—are quite proud of the culture they live in and are disinclined to join what is widely perceived as a counterculture movement. The average non-Muslim American may not only be unimpressed by the observation that Islam seems to require a certain distinctive culture, but more than likely, this will be viewed as problematic.

Nevertheless, I do believe that Islam has the potential to attract many Americans who have no strong social motivation to look into it. Religions have to do, first and foremost, with human spiritual needs, and they thrive or perish according to their ability to fulfill them. Since the time of the Prophet, Islam has nourished these needs for billions of persons of every race, color, and culture; it seems to have lost little of its original appeal, as it is now gaining more converts around the world than any other faith. Islam's vitality, as stated earlier, comes primarily from the Qur'an, and I feel that there is nothing special about men and women of the West that they cannot be reached by its call.

Muslims complain that the western media is doing all it can to prevent the true message of their faith from reaching the public and that this is the biggest reason why so many Americans are not inclined toward Islam. While it is true that many individuals in the western press continue to demonize Islam, I also feel that Muslims themselves may be interfering with its call in another and perhaps more detrimental way.

Many years ago when I began to investigate Islam, one of the first things that impressed me about Muslims was how familiar they were with

---

[116] It should be noted here that many African–Americans have Muslim ancestry. Thus by accepting Islam, some may indeed be returning to their African religious origins.

their religious texts, especially the Qur'an and the various compilations of the prophetic traditions, and how frequently they would refer to these sources when explaining their beliefs and practices. I noticed they cited their sacred texts in conversations much more often than believers in other religions. It was not long, however, before I realized that all too often my Muslim friends were equating revelation with their explanations of it. This is often hard to avoid, and Muslims are no exception in this respect,[117] but the average believer in other faiths tends not to do this so often, mostly because he or she is usually not as familiar with the relevant scriptures.

Persons seeking guidance from scripture are forced to interpret it. Although there are many revealed statements that all believers will understand in more or less the same way, this is not always the case. If a scripture is supposed to be a source of guidance for all of humanity, then we must expect that many of its statements will have different, appropriate meanings for believers of different times, places, and circumstances.

The problem with confusing revelation with our interpretations of it is that the latter, even when justifiable, restricts and limits the divine communication to our level of human understanding. As a result, we may be placing an obstruction between the revelation and those who trust that our explanation of it is accurate and correct.

On a visit to the Middle East, I met a pious young Muslim who informed me that the Qur'an forbids Muslim women to drive cars. When I pushed him to explain how he arrived at that, he began by quoting several Qur'anic verses that exhort Muslims to obey the Prophet. He then went on to quote several *hadiths* that he felt argued against women being allowed to drive. Since I did not accept his interpretation of the *hadiths* he used, he saw he had no chance of convincing me. As it turned out, the young man did not mean by his original claim that the Qur'an contains an explicit prohibition against allowing women to drive automobiles; what he meant was that he could provide an argument for such a prohibition based on certain verses of the Qur'an, certain traditions of the Prophet, and his interpretations of these. If I had not some knowledge of Islam, I might have accepted his claim.

I admit that the case I just recalled is an extreme one. This is precisely why I used it, because practically all Muslims would likewise disagree with

---

[117] For example, the Christian dogma of the Trinity is a theological conception and hence a theory based in part on the New Testament. However, many Christians claim that Jesus stated it explicitly in the Gospels.

the young man's comment. I have also been told that the Qur'an and say-ings of Muhammad command female seclusion, forbid women to vote in political elections, order the execution of apostates from Islam, and con-done the conquest of non-Muslim lands. I have discovered that many Muslims would agree with some or all of these statements, and yet I am convinced that each statement is an interpretation and not an explicit, revealed commandment.

Muslims should be extremely cautious before insisting that their responses to revelation are the only proper ones. I strongly urge Muslims to be very precise about the sources of their statements when they share their religious perspective with non-Muslims. They should be as accurate as pos-sible concerning the bases of their assertions about Islam. In addition, they should be sure to point out that they are citing a verse from the Qur'an, a *hadith*, a judgment of a scholar, something they heard somewhere, or are merely stating their personal opinion. It may take a little extra effort to describe these sources and the authority they carry with Muslims, but this is essential knowledge if one is to convey an accurate picture of Islam. Moreover, it may help listeners remain above secondary or controversial issues and allow them to acquire a better and more comprehensive under-standing of the message of Islam.

Between Worlds

A freshman came to my office this past summer for advising. His face looked very Middle-eastern, but he dressed, sounded, and acted like a typ-ical American teenager. His registration form stated that his name was Darik, so I wondered if he was of Arabic descent. I was wearing a T-shirt that had the Arabic alphabet on its front, and when Darik saw it, he imme-diately asked me with a big, gleaming smile, "Do you speak Arabic?"

"Marhabah, Darik! Kayf haalik?" I answered him.

"I'm sorry, I don't know any Arabic," he appologized. "My father is from Egypt, but I never learned his language."

"Is your Dad a Muslim?" I asked him.

"Yes, but he's not religious and I know almost nothing about his reli-gion. I think all religions are pretty much the same."

As director of math placement at the university, I briefly interview sev-eral hundred incoming freshmen each year during our Summer orientation sessions. Only a handful of these new students have Muslim American par-ents. When I inform them that they might be interested to know that there

is a mosque on campus, I almost always find that they, like Darik, have little or no interest in Islam or, for that matter, in any religion.

By *first-generation American Muslims*, I mean either American converts to Islam or Muslim immigrants to America. I will refer to their children as the *second generation*. I do not refer to their children as *second-
generation Muslims*, for the simple reason that I have discovered that
many of these young people do not believe in Islam. Not long ago, the
vice-president of ISNA told me that the one statistic he keeps hearing
from experts in his organization is that only approximately 10 percent of
the second generation become committed to Islam. We should not conclude from this that the other 90 percent abandons the faith; the fact is that
most who turn out not to believe in it had little or no exposure to Islam
when they were growing up.

Over the years, I have learned that the majority of first-generation
American Muslims regularly ignore Islam's ritual requirements, make hardly any effort to educate their families about Islam, and have practically no
contact with their local mosque or Islamic center. This, I believe, is the
biggest contributing factor to the widespread disbelief in Islam among the
second generation. In America, children of Muslim parents are given plenty of arguments against Islam from the surrounding society, while their
own families provide them with very few counterarguments.

Unlike the second generation, almost all first-generation Muslims I
have met are indeed Muslims, in that they profess to believe in Islam even
if they do not practice it or routinely violate its ordinances. I have received
several typical explanations from these Muslims for their lack of contact
with the mosque: it is out of touch with their needs and lives, its leadership
is too conservative or traditional, Muslims who go to the mosque do not get
along with each other, its leadership is autocratic, and there is not enough
time to go to the mosque.

So far, it appears that the leadership of Muslim America has no set
strategy for recruiting first-generation Muslims and those second-generation Muslims who have little or no contact with the mosque. Their focus
seems to be on providing spiritual and intellectual support for already committed and active Muslims and their families. Due to limitations in
resources and personnel, this is probably the most practical thing to do right
now. The prevailing feeling among devout American Muslims is that if
they do not concentrate on teaching themselves how to preserve, defend,
and bear witness to their faith in the secular West, there may soon be no
practicing Muslims in America.

For the previous two decades, devout Muslims in America have concentrated primarily on taking the message of Islam to the general population. With great enthusiasm, they pursued the conversion of America. With debates and dialogues, they tried to prove to American audiences the deficiencies of Christianity and the superiority of Islam. To their dismay, Muslims came to realize that most Americans were simply not interested. The only Americans who did seem to care were the minority of fundamentalist Christians who seized the opportunity to proselytize their own beliefs. Muslims did not understand that most Americans have become numb to religious questions and that their greatest adversary was not Christianity, but rather, the deep-seated and pervasive apathy of people who had lost confidence in almost everything. America had come to doubt its legal system, its institutions, its leaders, and religion. America had come to distrust beliefs and convictions and had resigned itself to a kind of nihilism, or what the political sociologist Frank Furedi describes as a relativist noncommittal liberalism.[118] Not only were Americans uninterested in what Muslims had to say, but they were uncomfortable with the way Muslims were saying it. Religion, most Americans believe, should be a private matter, not something to propagate, and certainly not a proper subject for debate.

In the twentieth century's last decade, the attention of devout Muslims has shifted toward their own children, for it is nearing the time when second-generation believers should take on leading roles in the American Muslim community. These parents are gravely concerned for the religious future of their children and are doing all they can to prepare their sons and daughters to live in America as practicing Muslims. There is cause for optimism, because just as nonpracticing first-generation Muslims tend to have agnostic or disbelieving children, sons and daughters of practicing Muslim parents usually adhere to Islam. However, as mentioned in the introduction, the intellectual and social fabric of American society can exert considerable pressure on even religious Muslim children to compromise their faith. I know of a fair number of cases of devout Muslim parents whose children have left Islam.[119]

Muslims who struggle to bring up their children in the faith must contend with exactly the same force they met when they attempted to take the

---

[118] "The Panic About Islam: An Interview with Professor Frank Furedi," *Iqra Magazine* (April 1996): 13 ff.

[119] Only a few weeks ago, I received a letter from a heartbroken father whose son had become an atheist.

message of Islam to non-Muslim America during the two previous decades: Their children are almost continuously taught outside the home not to believe and trust in anyone or anything, to be morally and religiously apathetic, and to accept that all systems of belief are equally valid and, hence, equally flawed.

Children who come from religious Muslim families are caught between very different worlds: that of their home and that of the larger society. They may be Muslims, but their experience is very different from their parents. Unlike their mothers and fathers, they are not immigrants, converts, or children of the Civil Rights struggle. Their situation is much more ambiguous. Their causes, goals, and identities are not defined so clearly. Unlike immigrants, America is the only culture they really know. Unlike converts, Islam was chosen for them as a religion. They may face discrimination and prejudice, but it is very different from what African–Americans faced in the past. The way they think about, discuss, and explore issues is identifiably American. Their religion does influence their morals and ethics, but these are also influenced by the mores of American society. My oldest daughter is only ten, and yet she has already become deeply concerned about the treatment of women in the Muslim community and the subject of religious tolerance in Islam.

Children of devout Muslim parents will often shock their parents by their "American" ways of thought and expression. A devout Muslim father recently complained to me that his daughter dresses, looks, and acts like a normal Muslim girl, but every now and then she will say or do things that are very American—things that a Muslim child from the Middle East would never dare do or say. When I asked him for an example, he mentioned that she asked questions about God that are considered *haram* (forbidden) back in Egypt.

I have discovered at the Muslim youth camps and conferences in which I have participated that the religious issues and questions that are important to Muslim American young people are much the same as those raised by non-Muslim Americans interested in Islam. The questions they ask are almost exclusively of two types: those that pertain to the separation of culture from religion—especially when it comes to gender roles—and those that relate to theodicy, the branch of theology that studies divine justice. One reason why these subjects are so important to young American Muslims is that they must frequently defend Islam on these grounds to non-Muslim friends and acquaintances. Yet I think that this is not the chief motive behind their concern, for the fact is that these issues are currently of extreme interest to Americans in general, and as Americans—we must not lose sight of the fact that this is what these young Muslim men and women are—these topics are of vital importance to them.

Second-generation Muslims are faced with a very difficult task. Naturally, they are seeking to harmonize their Americanness and their religion, striving to be good Muslims while being good citizens. This endeavor is made harder by the fact that many Muslims and non-Muslims in America see this as impossible. Many participants in Muslim youth conferences tell me that they are often torn between their society and their faith, and that they are forced to live with many perceived irreconcilable differences. Quite a few have admitted to me that they have begun to become confused about or to have doubts about their religion.

It is a true that there are conflicts between the teachings of Islam and modern American mores and that Muslims can (and should) try to influence these mores by sharing their moral and ethical perspective with the larger society. But first-generation Muslims must be alert to the possibility that they may be placing unnecessary stumbling blocks before their children, thereby making it very difficult for them to thrive, both spiritually and vocationally, in America.

I believe that Muslim parents should present Islam to their children in much the same way as I have suggested that they should present it to non-Muslims: They should do their best to separate the essentials of Islam from the nonessential historical and cultural adaptations and interpretations and should try to communicate it in the language of rational thought. If Muslim parents find themselves unequal to this task, then they should search out those who can do this successfully, for this would be a great help to their children who want to live as practicing Muslims in America. In addition, it could help them communicate the message of Islam to others.

No group of Muslims in America is currently in a better social position to inform the larger public about Islam than the second-generation believers. Americans often have difficulties sympathizing with immigrants because of their foreign cultural backgrounds. Also, "immigrant" Islam will likely be seen as part of the person's previous culture—something that is either better off discarded or modified over time.

Americans are often intimidated by converts, since conversion seems like a radical and almost unnatural thing. Since a convert chose a perceived alien religion, he or she is frequently asked, or feels it necessary, to explain and sometimes defend that choice. As a result, conversations about religion between converts and non-Muslim Americans are frequently tense.

However, the Islam and the Americanness of second-generation Muslims is likely to be viewed as very normal and natural, for these young people were born into both of these. I find that my daughters' friends and teachers feel much more comfortable asking my children about their religious beliefs than they do my wife, who is Middle-Eastern, or me, a convert to Islam. I have also noticed that my children are less defensive in discussions with friends about Islam. Many Muslim parents have told me that the same is true of their children.

Second-generation Muslims could become the breakthrough generation—the communication bridge between the universal Muslim community and American society. They already understand and can communicate effectively with fellow Americans; yet the crucial element that may be missing is a coherent, rational, and cogent perception by these young people of what the message of Islam is. Muslim parents can help their children discover such a perception, but it will require great patience and courage on their part. Patience is needed, since discovery and growth is seldom a smooth and steady climb; courage is needed to allow their children the room to develop their own understanding of Islam.

The Rope of Allah

> And hold fast, all of you together, to the rope of Allah, and
> do not separate. (Qur'an 3:103)

Every now and then I am asked by moderate or liberal American Muslims to join or help organize a "new" Muslim community in America—one with its own mosques and approach to Islam. The underlying motive is usually frustration with the current, conservative leadership of the American Islamic community. The hope is to effect a more authentic and practical implementation of Islam in America, one unburdened of obsolete foreign cultural accretions, more in tune with the thinking and experiences of "most" Muslims in America, and one that welcomes the full participation of Muslim women.

Even though I share some of this frustration, I am very uncomfortable with such invitations (they seem to be increasing as of late). I would not be at all surprised if someday soon there are "orthodox" and "reformed" mosques in North America. There is a real threat that in the near future, the Muslim community in America will split into conservative and progressive sects. If this happens, both conservative and moderate Muslims will be equally to blame, for both groups are infected with intolerance.

Muslims in the United States and Canada applaud the level of freedom of expression in these countries and complain how difficult and often dangerous it is to speak out in modern Muslim countries. The freedom to speak carries with it the obligation to let others be heard. The right to express one's own opinion is easy to embrace, but the principle of free speech hinges more heavily on respecting and protecting everyone's freedom to do so. As a community, the Muslims of North America have been slow to grasp the latter half of this formulation, even though the principles of *shura* (mutual consultation) and *ijma'* (consensus) are recognized in Islamic law as two fundamental elements of Muslim communal decision making.

The existence of diverse viewpoints in the Islamic community could be of benefit to Muslims, for contending outlooks tend to check and balance each another. Such diversity helps the community keep to a middle course and prevents it from racing toward extremes. It forces individuals to consider alternative perspectives, which has a tempering effect. It insures slow and cautious transition, which could be frustrating for advocates for change but which may be for the general good of Muslims. It also offers non-Muslims who are interested in Islam a single, unified, moderate religious community, a community that allows a wide range of intellectual vision.

The institutionalization of viewpoints into distinct religious factions can only be to the overall detriment of Muslims. It promotes extremism, narrow-mindedness, and further division; saps the community of energy and resources as contending sects compete to win converts from one another; and presents to non-Muslims a complicated and confusing image of Islam—of a religion with many contradictory versions. For potential converts, they now have the added issue of which Islam to join.

If Muslims really hope to better themselves and their fellow believers, I strongly recommend that they get involved in their local mosques and Islamic centers and make sure to make their viewpoints known during community meetings. They should also be ready to listen to and consider carefully opinions contrary to their own. Most importantly, Muslims must learn to defer to the majority viewpoint. This does not mean that a Muslim must stop advancing an opinion when the majority disagrees with it, but he or she should abide by the decisions reached by consensus unless and until they are changed.

Is There a Scholar in the House?

When speaking to non-Muslims, Muslim lecturers will often emphasize that there is no clergy in Islam. This is a reflection of the Islamic principle that each of us is ultimately accountable for his or her deeds and that no one but God can unburden us of moral responsibility. Only God can judge another person saved, forgiven, or enlightened.

For Muslims, there is no ecclesiastical authority that can decide personal, moral and spiritual dilemmas. When such questions arise, a Muslim is encouraged to search the textual sources of Islam and to seek the advice of fellow believers respected for their knowledge of the faith. But in the end, and after much prayer and soul-searching, a believer accepts responsibility for his or her resolution of a personal problem and, thereafter, trusts in and relies upon the wisdom, forgiveness, and mercy of God. Within this system, the best one Muslim could offer another Muslim who is faced with a moral predicament is sound, knowledgeable counsel and his or her prayers.

In most faiths, religious scholars are not involved in the many day-to-day problems of believers. Their studies are usually too advanced and abstract for digestion by nonspecialists. In Islam, the common problems of Muslims are and always have been the focus of most scholarly investigation. The research of a Muslim religious scholar is much more practical than theoretical and is usually accessible to his or her coreligionists. A Muslim scholar feels that the main purpose of learning is to be able to better advise fellow believers on how to live properly. Although Muslim scholars have no official ceremonial or ritualistic duties, they serve as counselors to the faithful in much the same way that clergy do in other faiths.

The Muslims of North America are in need of religious scholars who can help them deal with the many new problems they are facing. In particular, there is an urgent need for scholars who can help young Muslims discover how to be true to their faith in America and who can help the Islamic community to remain unified. Unfortunately, there are currently very few Muslim scholars qualified to assist them. Throughout the Islamic world, there are many specialists in the various classical Islamic sciences, but not many of them live in North America. The latter qualification is most important; to give sound advice to American Muslims, a scholar must fully appreciate the special circumstances in which they live.

The issues raised by young believers and those that are disuniting the American Islamic community revolve around the vast legacy of Muslim scholarship that has come down to us. In order to address these issues responsibly and convincingly, scholars must possess a comprehensive knowledge of Islamic history and the evolution of Islamic thought. In addition, they must be prepared to scrutinize critically the works of some of the most influential and respected Muslim scholars of the past. I am not sure that the world Islamic community, or even the American Islamic community, would be able to tolerate such self-examination just yet.

For the past century, Islam has been the target of a seemingly continuous barrage of criticism from the West, much of which has been nothing more than malicious, bigoted carping. Muslims in North America meet with misconceptions and misinformation about their beliefs almost daily and are forced to repeat, again and again, the usual counterarguments. Muslims have gotten so used to defending their faith against false and slanderous accusations (often presented as objective scholarship), that they react defensively to virtually any critical study of Islam, from whatever source. They tend to see another Muslim's criticism of the scholarly or cultural tradition as a concession to the disbelievers—a kind of defection to the enemy. In such an intellectual milieu, it is very difficult for a Muslim scholar to challenge long-established, prevailing viewpoints.

Perhaps this is why the same themes are rehashed each year at American Islamic conferences: How to establish an Islamic lifestyle in America, the need for American Muslim unity, *da'wah* (Muslim witness to non-Muslims) strategies, the rights of women in Islam, how to respond to the western media's misrepresentation of Islam, Islam vs. terrorism. I do not mean to trivialize these topics, for I obviously regard them as important. Rather, I wish to point out that the repetition of them, year after year, indicates that the community has not been able to address them satisfactorily and move forward. The Muslim community in America is stuck in the "newcomer" or "outsider" phase, unable to adapt to the new environment and unable to find in traditional Islamic thought viable solutions to many of its current problems.

The first step American Muslims can take toward creating an intellectual climate in the community that fosters original, critical research is to follow the recommendation I made earlier in this chapter: American Muslims need to become more open-minded and trusting of each other. As every convert to Islam discovers, today's Muslims are very suspicious of one another, exceedingly prone to spread rumors and gossip, and extremely quick to declare each other guilty of heresy. An American convert once remarked to me that backbiting and spreading rumors about one another seems to be the favorite entertainment of Muslims. Such widespread, impetuous backbiting and rumor-mongering create a climate of intimidation that thwarts free speech and critical inquiry. It also causes those who think about such issues to refrain from airing viewpoints that challenge popular feeling and encourages scholars to keep away from sensitive or controversial topics—the very topics that need to be discussed.

In other faiths, the existence of a clerical order helps to curtail such behaviors among the lay people, who feel that it is not their place to pronounce religious judgments on other believers. In Islam, it is first and foremost up to each believer to suppress these malicious impulses. Since the Qur'an and Sayings of the Prophet rank rumor-mongering and backbiting among the greatest of sins, it is a wonder that this behavior is so prevalent among Muslims. Consider the following small sample of well-known admonitions from the Qur'an and Sayings of the Prophet quoted by Yusuf al Qaradawi:[120]

> God does not like the public utterance of hurtful speech, except by one who has been wronged; and God is ever Hearing, Knowing (4:148)

> Those who love that scandal should circulate respecting those who believe, for them is a grievous chastisement in this world and the hereafter. And God knows, while you do not know. (24:19)

> O you who believe, avoid most of suspicion; for truly suspicion in some cases is sin; and do not spy nor allow some of you to backbite others. Would any of you like to eat the flesh of his dead brother? You would abhor it! So keep your duty to God, surely God is Oft-returning, Merciful. (49:12)

> The one who spreads gossip which he has overheard will not enter the garden. (*Sahih al Bukhari* and *Sahih Muslim*)

> Avoid suspicion, for airing suspicion is the most lying form of speech. (*Sahih al Bukhari*)

> Do not be envious of each other, nor backbite nor hate one another, but be brethren in the service of God. (*Sahih al Bukhari*)

---

[120] Yusuf al Qaradawi, *The Lawful and the Prohibited in Islam*, trans. by K. El-Helbawy, M. M. Siddiqui, and S. Shukry (Indianapolis: American Trust Publications), 307-22.

> He who listens surreptitiously to peoples' conversations against their wishes will have molten lead poured into their ears on the Day of Resurrection. (*Sahih al Bukhari* and *Sahih Muslim*)

It is not conceivable that the American Muslim community—or for that matter, any society—will someday entirely rid itself of intolerance, rumor-mongering and back-biting; but certainly societies, like individuals, can always improve themselves with regard to these socially destructive vices. Right now, these vices seem more common among Muslims than among most other religious communities in America. Reform, however, may be close at hand.

The so-called liberal sector of North American society, which presently dominates the media, the entertainment industry, and the education establishment, is intensely promoting the ideas of tolerance, freedom of expression and inquiry, and the acceptance of social and cultural diversity. Since American liberals tend to be more bigoted in their attitudes toward Islam than moderates or conservatives, Muslims doubt that their well-being figures into the liberal agenda. Nevertheless, the leadership of the American Muslim community generally has supported these ideas, since many Muslims in America believe that they are (or have been) victims of discrimination and bigotry. One can say that Muslims are calling on the rest of America to live up to its proclaimed ideals—a kind of "put your money where your mouth is" strategy.

Also, some Muslim apologists and proselytizers have attempted to demonstrate that many of the freedoms esteemed by the West, such as freedom of speech and religious tolerance, were established for the first time in history by Islam more than fourteen centuries ago during the rule of Prophet Muhammad. They also point out that, until recently, Islamic civilization offered greater religious and intellectual freedom than Christian lands.

Both of these trends indicate that the American Islamic community has come to appreciate and employ the concepts of tolerance and free expression in its dialogue with the larger society. But so far, American Muslims have been slow to embrace these notions with regard to community life. Many Muslims in America complain that their mosques, Islamic centers, and community organizations remind them of the totalitarian systems of the Middle East, where you simply are not allowed to challenge authority. I expect, however, that the American Islamic community is soon to enter a new era of openness; it cannot continue to embrace tolerance, free inquiry and free speech, in general, without these ideals influencing the behavior of Muslims with respect to each other. In addition, the next generation of American Muslims, who will eventually lead the community, should be very comfortable with these notions.

The key factor in all of this chapter's discussion is time. Will the "soon" I just spoke of be soon enough to prevent a large number of American children of Muslim parents from leaving Islam and the community from fractionalizing? Perhaps not, but nevertheless, I do believe that Islam will survive and flourish in America even though there may initially be some set backs. I must admit that I am speaking now, as my Middle-Eastern friends often say, from the heart, or perhaps I should say, from my experience of conversion through reading the Qur'an, for this revelation has so captivated and compelled me that I cannot believe that it will not do the same for countless other Americans.

And God, the Merciful, the Wise, the Self-Sufficient, knows best.